The Wilde Century

BETWEEN MEN ~ BETWEEN WOMEN
Lesbian and Gay Studies

Lillian Faderman and Larry Gross, Editors

The Wilde Century

Effeminacy, Oscar Wilde and the Queer Moment

Alan Sinfield

COLUMBIA UNIVERSITY PRESS
NEW YORK

BETWEEN MEN ~ BETWEEN WOMEN
Lesbian and Gay Studies

Lillian Faderman and Larry Gross, editors

Columbia University Press
New York   Chichester, West Sussex

Copyright © 1994 Alan Sinfield

Library of Congress Cataloging-in-Publication Data available on request.
LC Card Number 94–15865
ISBN: 0–231–10166–X
ISBN: 0–231–10167–8

First published in the U.K. by Cassell, London
Printed and bound in Great Britain

c 10 9 8 7 6 5 4 3 2 1
c 10 9 8 7 6 5 4 3 2 1

Contents

Preface

I WAS working towards a book on theatre and homosexuality; it seemed obvious that it should begin with Oscar Wilde. After all, he is the most notorious/celebrated queer/playwright. Yet the place of homosexuality in his plays is by no means plain. Many commentators assume that queerness, like murder, *will out*, so there must be a gay scenario lurking somewhere in the depths of *The Importance of Being Earnest*. But it doesn't really work. It might be nice to think of Algernon and Jack as a gay couple, but most of their dialogue is bickering about property and women; or of Bunburying as cruising for rough trade, but it is an upper-class young heiress that we see Algernon visiting, and they want to marry. Lady Bracknell has been played as a man in drag – well, why not? And why not Lady Macbeth? – except that one would not want to fall into the notion that any effective woman must really be some kind of man. As David Savran remarks, trying to 'translate' texts by writers whom we now regard as sexually dissident, back into a supposed lesbian or gay original, produces 'an unintelligible clutter whose only coherence becomes the ill-concealed homosexuality of its author'.[1] And that is not very interesting.

All that said, Wilde's principal male characters do look and sound like the mid-twentieth-century stereotype of the queer man (I am using 'queer' to evoke this historical figure). They are effete, camp, leisured or aspiring to be, aesthetic, amoral, witty, insouciant, charming, spiteful, dandified. If these characters are not offered as homosexual (and generally they are pursuing women characters), the whole ambiance reeks, none the less, of queerness. Or, rather, it does for us. And so does Wilde himself. Wow! what a fabulous camp queen! – we would say if he came into the room today. For fifteen years, though – until the trials provoked by the strange recklessness of Lord Alfred Douglas and the strange vindictiveness of Lord Queensberry – Wilde was regarded by society, the press and the public as rather wicked, but by no means as a pariah. And well-informed people were surprised, I will show, when his queer practices came to light.

The question, then, is: how did he get away with it? – going around looking and talking the way he did, and putting such characters on the stage. And the answer must be: they didn't see queerness in the way we have come to see it. Our interpretation is retroactive; in fact, Wilde and his writings look queer because our stereotypical notion of male homosexuality derives from Wilde, and our ideas about him.

The key to the matter, I argue, is 'effeminacy' (a misogynist but powerful term): Wilde was perceived as effeminate, to be sure; but not, thereby, as queer. In the mid twentieth century, effeminacy and queerness became virtually synonymous, along with the rest of the Wildean manner. But how was effeminacy regarded before the trials? I knew that in Shakespeare and Marlowe it meant giving too much attention to women, so I went back to that, and then worked forward, exploring the scope of effeminacy, same-sex passion (a term used to avoid anachronism), and relations between the two. The dominant modern idea of the male homosexual unravelled before me as I advanced: each time he seemed to be emerging, more complex evidence disturbed the picture.

So this book begins with an elaboration of the problem, and the theoretical issues it engages. Then it jumps back to early-modern times, and proceeds briskly forward through rakes and fops, molly-houses, the eighteenth-century cult of sensibility, the Victorian cult of manliness (heterosexual and homosexual), dandies, aesthetes, decadents, sexologists. Chapter 5 shows, first, how same-sex passion was being represented, in Wilde's time, as quintessentially masculine; then how the trials reoriented it. Chapter 6 explores how an effeminate, Wildean model of the queer man became established in the twentieth century, and the various consequences for gay men. In the course of these chapters, I discuss writings by Wilde and a good many others that offer to shed symptomatic light on the issue.

The villain of the piece is the masculine/feminine binary structure as it circulates in our cultures, by which I mean the supposition that masculinity and femininity are the essential, normative properties of men and women respectively. This is scarcely valid in respect of heterosexuals – they don't in fact fall tidily into masculine and feminine attributes, all the time or in every respect; so it is perverse that lesbians and gay men should be interpreted as some kind of contorted variation upon it. Chapter 7, therefore, is a demonstration of how that binary is transmitted through its most influential modern conduit, Sigmund Freud. Finally I review some of the pressing issues in the current situations of lesbians and gay men, reassessing them in the light of my inquiry. As is generally the case, my project of historical reconstruction has substantial implications for how we handle ourselves today. Our present selves are formed out of continuity and difference: because Wilde and others were as they were, we are as we are.

With love and thanks to David Alderson, John Banks, Rachel Bowlby, Joseph Bristow, Peter Burton, Jonathan Dollimore, John Fletcher, Gowan Hewlett, Russell Jackson, Stephen Maddison, George Rousseau, Lynne Segal, Mark Sinfield, Cedric Watts, students on the Sexual Dissidence MA at Sussex, and others who have put up with me going on about it all.

Note

1. David Savran, *Communists, Cowboys, and Queers* (Minneapolis: Minnesota University Press, 1992), p. 115.

Chapter one

Queer Thinking

OSCAR WILDE appeared in three trials in 1895. In the first, he sued Lord Queensberry for libel, but dropped the case when Queensberry was discovered to have embarrassing evidence about Wilde's activities. In the second, Wilde was prosecuted by the state for gross indecency, but this proved inconclusive. At the third trial he was found guilty of gross indecency with another male person. In the middle of the second trial, Frank Harris, editor of the *Fortnightly Review* and man-about-town, was talking with Wilde about strategy. Wilde exclaimed: 'You talk with passion and conviction, as if I were innocent.' 'But you are innocent,' cried Harris in amazement, 'aren't you?' 'No,' said Wilde. 'I thought you knew that all along.' 'No,' Harris replied. 'I did not know. I did not believe the accusation. I did not believe it for a moment.'[1] This was despite the fact that young men were testifying, with circumstantial detail, that they had had sexual relations with Wilde – Harris thought they had been paid to perjure themselves. Even Queensberry, Harris deduces (p. 231), did not initially believe the same-sex allegations: he was surprised by the evidence that was offered to him.

Now, Harris is not altogether reliable, and the conversation perhaps didn't go quite the way he says in retrospect. Nevertheless, there is no reason to suppose he would wish to appear naive or ill-informed, and his story would be pointless if it were not adequately plausible; it is accepted by H. Montgomery Hyde and Richard Ellmann.[2] What it shows is that homosexuality was *not* manifest from Wilde's style. To be sure, Wilde's 'effeminate', dandy manner and interests had excited comment and hostility, but they had not led either his friends or strangers to regard him as obviously, even probably, queer. His appearance on first meeting, according to Harris, was not prepossessing: 'fleshly indulgence and laziness, I said to myself, were written all over him. ... He shook hands in a limp way I disliked; his hands were flabby, greasy; his skin looked bilious and dirty' (pp. 91–2; fortunately, all this was entirely outweighed by his pleasant personality). But Wilde's manner did not strike Harris as queer.

Wilde had adopted the manners and appearance of an effeminate aesthete in 1877; since 1882 he had presented himself as an effeminate dandy. Yet it was in late 1894, only a few months before the trials, according to Holbrook Jackson, that 'serious rumours about [Wilde's] private life and habits became more persistent in both London and Paris'. And still not everyone believed them. W. B. Yeats, who knew Wilde well, thought he was unjustly accused when the trials began.[3]

Popular opinion seems to have been no more knowing. In the second trial the jury could not reach a verdict on any of the principal charges. A sheet ballad printed at the time is titled and has as its refrain: 'Oh! Oscar Wilde, we never thought that you was built that way'.[4] The whole point is surprise at what is being revealed:

> Now wonders they will never cease, and as each day we
> read,
> The papers, why we of't say, well, 'I am surprised' indeed,
> For people who we think are 18 carat turn out brass,
> And what we thought a Lion's roar's the braying of an ass.

The surprise could be sarcastic, but there are no pointers towards that; on the contrary, the verse depends on the reader having thought, hitherto, that Wilde was 18-carat. There is here a wariness about notables in general (they often turn out to be wrong 'uns) but nothing specific to Wilde; no suggestion, at all, on grounds that we might expect today – dandyism, effeminacy and aestheticism – that we should have guessed all along. It is not my case that no one would have credited that Wilde was homosexual; but that those features of his manner which would signal it to us, then did not.

For us, it is hard to regard Wilde as other than the apogee of gay experience and expression, because that is the position we have accorded him in our cultures. For us, he is always-already queer –

as that stereotype has prevailed in the twentieth century (for the sake of clarity, I write 'queer' for that historical phase – not contradicting, thereby, its recent revival among activists – and 'gay' for post-Stonewall kinds of consciousness). But Wilde's typicality is after-the-effect – after, I believe, the trials helped to produce a major shift in perceptions of the scope of same-sex passion. At that point, the entire, vaguely disconcerting nexus of effeminacy, leisure, idleness, immorality, luxury, insouciance, decadence and aestheticism, which Wilde was perceived, variously, as instantiating, was transformed into a brilliantly precise image. The effect was comparable to that produced for lesbianism by Radclyffe Hall's *Well of Loneliness* (1928). The parts were there already, and were being combined, diversely, by various people. But, at this point, a distinctive possibility cohered, far more clearly, and for far more people, than hitherto. The principal twentieth-century stereotype entered our cultures: not just the homosexual, as the lawyers and medics would have it, but the queer.

Many commentators have attributed this kind of significance to Wilde.[5] Recently Ed Cohen has shown how newspaper reports of the trials avoided specifying Wilde's alleged crimes – they were regarded as too horrible to be named. The *Evening Standard* reported that Queensberry had written ' "Oscar Wilde posing as _____" ': the last word, 'somdomite' (Queensberry's mistake for 'sodomite'), was replaced by a blank. 'Oscar Wilde posing' stood for the whole idea. In other newspapers the entire phrasing of the libel was eliminated, leaving Wilde's person as the offence.[6] Not only did this love not dare to speak its name, it hardly *had* a name. 'The love he bore to Dan,' Sir Henry Hall Caine wrote, 'was a brotherly passion for which language has yet no name.'[7] At that very moment, of course, several names were being coined, but 'an unspeakable of the Oscar Wilde sort', as E. M. Forster's *Maurice* presents himself, became the commonest name. Thus could the unspeakable find voice. Cohen shows how this usage occurred between the wars; I remember it at school in the 1950s – along with 'Monty', which derived from the latest incarnation of the scandalous Wilde figure, Lord Montagu of Beaulieu.[8]

Wilde and his dandy characters were perceived as 'effeminate' – that was widely said – but not as queer. They *passed*, we might now say, not by playing down what we call camp behaviour, but by manifesting it exuberantly. When T. W. Higginson reviewed the *Poems* (1882) he called his article 'Unmanly manhood', but his objection was not that Wilde's writing presented the same 'offences' as Walt Whitman's homoerotic poetry. Rather, it appealed excessively to women. Ambrose Bierce made a similar complaint: Wilde's *Poems* are making him suspiciously attractive to women: by 'emitting meaningless murmurs in the blaze of women's eyes' he has become a 'dunghill he-hen'.[9] Such remarks led me to explore the historical relations between homosexuality and 'effeminacy' – the quote marks indicate that I regard this as a cultural construct, not an essential property, either of gay men or in its reference to a supposed femininity of women. In all the current preoccupation with concepts of manliness and masculinity, effeminacy is rarely addressed head-on; yet it defines, crucially, the generally acceptable limits of gender and sexual expression.

Until the Wilde trials, effeminacy and homosexuality did not correlate in the way they have done subsequently; unravelling this takes me back through the centuries before Wilde, forward into twentieth-century queer and gay culture, and on beyond that, into the potential for our sexualities in the future. In subsequent chapters I consider further complexities in Wilde's writing and career. In this chapter I try to show how we may understand and make use of references to same-sex passion in earlier times, even while recognizing their elusiveness. I review the debate about whether homosexuality is better regarded as an essential property of lesbian and gay individuals, or as a social construct, looking both at the historical moment when 'homosexual' was coined and at the political implications of constructionism. Finally I return to Wilde, finding in 'The portrait of Mr W. H.' an echo of these arguments.

Reading silences

When a part of our worldview threatens disruption by manifestly failing to cohere with the rest, then we reorganize and retell its story, trying to get it into shape – back into the old shape if we are conservative-minded, or into a new shape if we are more adventurous. That is how cultures elaborate themselves. The stories that address the unresolved issues, the ones where the conditions of plausibility are in dispute, require most assiduous and continuous reworking; I call them faultline stories.[10] This is spectacularly true of Wilde's person and writings; he is a cultural token around which contest and change occurred, and still occur.

In our cultures, the discourses through which sexuality circulates are of course among the most fraught and conflicted, and often the most obliquely apprehended. Silences, Michel Foucault has taught us, are significant:

> Silence itself — the things one declines to say, or is forbidden to name, the discretion that is required between different speakers — is less the absolute limit of discourse, the other side from which it is separated by a strict boundary, than an element that functions alongside the things said, with them and in relation to them within over-all strategies.[11]

It might seem that this point has been well taken among commentators on Wilde, for any silence is likely now to be read as a deafening roar about homosexuality. But that is too simple. Foucault continues:

> There is no binary division to be made between what one says and what one does not say; we must try to determine the different ways of not saying such things, how those who can and those who cannot speak of them are distributed, which type of discourse is authorised, or which form of discretion is required in either case. There is not one but many silences, and they are an integral part of the strategies that underlie and permeate discourses.

The danger is that, instead of unravelling the intricate silences, we assimilate them too rapidly to the model that prevails in our own cultures.

Richard Ellmann accepts that Wilde's first same-sex encounter was, as Wilde said, initiated by Robbie Ross in 1886; Montgomery Hyde, Richard Gilman and Peter Ackroyd are of the same opinion; Frank Harris points out that all the offences alleged in the trials derive from 1892 or thereabouts — after the first meeting with Douglas.[12] Despite his explicit acknowledgement, Ellmann implies, throughout his biography, that Wilde's male relationships were always, from the start, somehow already homosexual. Again, on the basis of certain close relationships and some loose associations, Brian Reade concludes that Wilde was 'seriously initiated in homosexual practices' while a student at Oxford in 1875–7, ten years before the episode with Ross.[13] But, bearing in mind the mobility of sexualities in our cultures and the pressures against same-sex practices, it is a mistake to read anyone as 'really homosexual' from the start. There is no reason to suppose that Wilde's discovery of same-sex passion was less problematic than for very many people today. Consider, again, the wide acceptance of a supposed photograph of Wilde, bewigged and bejewelled, in costume as Salomé. John Stokes points out that this is almost certainly not Wilde, and when you look again it is not very much like him.[14] It is part of the modern stereotype of the gay man that he should want to dress as a woman, especially a fatally gorgeous one. Our cultures observe the Wilde they expect and want to see.

The trial in 1871 of Stella and Fanny, also known as Ernest Boulton and Frederick Park, gained immense press attention. The two lads, it emerged, had from childhood liked to play female parts in semi-professional theatricals, and now were inclined to go about in female attire. They were arrested coming from the Strand Theatre, and appeared – still cross-dressed though perhaps somewhat dishevelled after a night in the cells – at Bow Street court. As a result of letters from admirers found at their lodgings, they and six associates were charged with conspiracy to commit a felony. One of the accused was Lord Arthur Clinton MP, but he died before the trial. The defence case was that it had all been mere frivolity. The drag was for theatricals and was worn publicly for a joke; the boys' admirers were just silly. Defence Counsel said he 'was not going to attempt to justify the execrable taste, the indelicacy of penning such letters, but he asked them [the jury] to view them in the light of notes addressed to an effeminate lad; a dainty and pleasing boy'. This (to us) surprisingly naive, and yet strangely provocative, version of events proved persuasive. The Lord Chief Justice evidently did not have the horrible crime of sodomy in his sights when, in his summing up, he said there was no evidence of felony or conspiracy; the letters might be 'no more than the romantic expression of personal admiration and affection. No doubt such feelings and attachments had existed and might exist without any evil'.[15] The jury acquitted after just fifty-three minutes; *The Times* declared that the prosecution should never have been brought.

Why were Fanny and Stella and their friends not demonized, victimized, punished? That is what we have been used to. Two explanations have been advanced. Jeffrey Weeks attributes it to 'concepts of homosexuality', as late as 1871, being 'extremely undeveloped'. 'Neither the police nor the court were familiar with the patterns of male homosexuality. The opening remarks of the Attorney General hinted that it was their transvestism, their soliciting men as *women* which was the core of their crime.' The police doctors had not encountered cases of sodomy, and were unaware of recent French work; indeed, the Attorney General thought it fortunate that there was 'very little learning or knowledge upon this subject in this country'.[16] It is not clear, even, how some of Stella and Fanny's associates perceived the liaison, for sometimes the lads passed successfully as women, and took up with men who apparently believed them to be women.

Neil Bartlett agrees that the trial focuses a single question: 'Were Fanny and Stella visible?'[17] Unlike Weeks, Bartlett believes that they were – all too visible. He makes two points: first, that they made 'determined efforts to use their frocks to create public space for themselves in London, in the separate but overlapping worlds of the actress, the prostitute and the demi-mondaine. ... They were well aware that they were playing precise games with their appearance, and that an exact understanding of the rules was a prerequisite of survival' (pp. 138–9). So concepts of homosexuality were well enough developed in certain quarters. This is surely right. However, it does not follow that the court was able to recognize this behaviour. Indeed, the strategic skills of Fanny and Stella were designed, partly, to prevent that – to enable them to make the contacts they wished without attracting unhelpful attention. The condition for their subculture may have been that it was, in many quarters, unrecognizable.

Bartlett's second argument is that the court was wilfully blind; it needed to disbelieve in the existence of such a milieu: 'Only by silencing, not punishing, the sodomites, could the court breathe a sigh of relief. When Boulton and Park were dismissed, declared improbable if not impossible, the existence of a homosexual culture in London was effectively denied' (p. 142). The opinion of *The Times* lends support to the idea that a guilty verdict would have been embarrassing; it 'would have been felt at home, and received abroad, as a reflection on our national morals'.[18] But for this strategy of disbelief to work, there has to be a genuine indeterminacy – same-sex passion has to be implausible in some degree, whatever the thinking that produced the acquittal.

The interpretations of Weeks and Bartlett could both be correct. Some people involved in bringing the prosecution may have been aware of a same-sex subculture and reluctant to press the case strongly, whilst members of the jury might have been unaware and uncomprehending. Bartlett's question remains: who understood the letters that were presented in evidence; and how, and why, and on what terms (p. 139)? The answer, probably, is that some people heard same-sex passion loud and clear, whereas others could not conceive of it. It is through that indeterminacy that indirections and evasions – those of the court, and of Fanny and Stella – could flourish.

The interpretative challenge is to recover the moment of indeterminacy. For it is not that our idea of 'the homosexual' was hiding beneath other phrases, or lurking unspecified in the silence, like a statue under a sheet, fully formed but waiting to be unveiled; it was in the process of becoming constituted. The concept was *emerging* around and through instances like Fanny and Stella, and Wilde. To presume the eventual outcome in the blind or hesitant approximations out of which it was partly fashioned is to miss, precisely, the points of most interest.

The half-heard character of homosexuality in discreet discourse has been theorized, in terms afforded by D. A. Miller, as an *open secret*. 'In some sense,' Miller observes, the secret is always open: its function 'is not to conceal knowledge, so much as to conceal the knowledge of the knowledge'.[19] It helps to constitute the public/private boundary – the binary structure that seems to demarcate our subjectivities from a public realm, while actually producing those subjectivities – and thus facilitates the policing of that boundary. The idea of a private space might seem to free an autonomous zone for self-expression, but the effect, rather, is a specific policing of the border between the two. As David Evans puts it, 'by concentrating on public manifestations of sexual deviance in the buffer zone between moral and immoral communities, this policing has effectively penetrated all "private" territories with immanent self-regulating material forms of power/knowledge'.[20]

The secret keeps a topic like homosexuality in the private sphere, but under surveillance, allowing it to hover on the edge of public visibility. If it gets fully into the open, it attains public status; yet it must not disappear altogether, for then it would be beyond control and would no longer effect a general surveillance of aberrant desire. For, as Jonathan Dollimore has argued, 'the negation of homosexuality has been in direct proportion to its actual centrality, its cultural marginality in direct proportion to its cultural significance'.[21] The open secret constitutes homosexuality as the 'unthinkable' alternative – so awful that it can be envisaged only as private, yet always obscurely present as a public penalty for deviance.

The potential for disturbance on the public/private boundary is apparent in the wording of the 1885 Labouchère amendment which criminalized male homosexual acts in Britain: it is titled 'Outrages on public decency', but begins: 'Any male person who, in public *or private*, commits ...'.[22] Such a muddle collapses, repeatedly through the twentieth century, from both sides: the state pursues homosexuals into their privacy, and homosexuals achieve reluctant or determined public visibility. The Wolfenden Report was commissioned in 1954 to re-handle and re-secure the private/public boundary; this was the effect also of the British law reform of 1967. The UK Thatcherite Section 28 legislation of 1988, forbidding municipalities to spend public money in ways that may 'promote homosexuality', is one more attempt to control public visibility in the face of the adjustments to the private/public boundary that gay activists have forced.

Such instability affects crucially the kinds of textual and cultural analysis that can usefully be undertaken. It will not be sufficient to anticipate a single, coherent interpretation; we must expect texts to reveal faultlines, and must consider the disparate reading conditions in which diverse decodings will be possible. As Pierre Macherey proposes, the point at which the text falls silent is the point at which its ideological project may be disclosed. What may there be discerned is both necessary and necessarily absent; it manifests breaking points of the text, moments at which its ideological project is under special strain.[23] Such gaps in ideological coherence are in principle bound to occur. No text, literary or otherwise, can contain within its ideological project all of the potential significance that it must release in pursuance of that project. The complexity of the social formation combines with the multi-accentuality of language to produce an inevitable excess of meaning, as implications that arise coherently enough at one point cannot altogether be accommodated at another.

The whole tendency of ideology is to efface contradiction. But it is a condition of representation that any such project will incorporate the ground of its own ultimate failure. The customary notions of sexualities in our cultures are contradictory and indeterminate. When such a key concept is structurally unstable, it produces endless textual work. The awkward issue has continually to be revisited, reworked, rediscovered, reaffirmed. And because closure is tantalizingly elusive, texts are often to be found pushing representation to a breaking point where contradiction comes to the surface. Some commentators will then seek to help the text into coherence – in literary analysis, supplying for characters feasible thoughts and motives to smooth over the difficulty. This has been the virtual *raison d'être* of traditional literary criticism. Other commentators may take the opportunity to address the ideological scope of the text – how its closures provoke collusion or questioning.

Within this mode of analysis, it is relatively unimportant to decide how far a text presents positive images of lesbians and gay men – how far it manifests a good political tendency. Textual potentiality is far more fluid than that. Even a text which aspires to contain a subordinate perspective must first bring it into visibility; even to misrepresent, one must present. And once that has happened, there can be no guarantee that the subordinate will stay safely in its prescribed place. Readers do not have to respect closures – we do not have, for instance, to accept that the independent women characters in Shakespearean comedies find their proper destinies in the marriage deals at the ends of those plays. We can insist on our sense that the middle of such a text arouses expectations that exceed the closure. Lesbians and gay men have been necessarily adroit at reading against the grain, building their culture in the margins of the dominant. Representation is always involved in contest. When, in any instance, sexual dissidence gains ground, or loses ground, that is not in the nature of things; it is because of their relative strengths in that situation. And this means that, politically, there is a great deal to play for.

Constructionism

My argument about the emergence of a queer identity around Wilde is constructionist: it holds that sexualities (heterosexual and homosexual) are not essential, but constructed within an array of prevailing social possibilities. For this reason, I try to avoid using present-day concepts anachronistically. 'Same-sex passion' is the best term I have been able to find for the period up to 1900 ('passion' is intended to include both an emotional and a physical charge, while avoiding the fraught term 'desire').

Sexual identity depends not on a deep-set self-hood (though it may feel otherwise), but on one's particular situation within the framework of understanding that makes certain, diverse, possibilities available; which makes some ideas plausible and others not. This is the ideological network that we use to explain our worlds. Ideology makes sense for us – of us – because it is already proceeding when we arrive in the world; we come to consciousness in its terms. As the world shapes itself around and through us, certain interpretations of experience strike us as plausible: they fit with what we have experienced already, and are confirmed by others around us. So we complete what Colin Sumner calls a 'circle of social reality': 'understanding produces its own social reality at the same time as social reality produces its own understanding'.[24] This is apparent when we observe how people in other cultures than our own make good sense of the world in ways that seem strange to us: their outlook is supported by their social context. For them, those frameworks of perception, maps of meaning, work.

There will also be new breaks, when the combination of circumstances enables or forces people to develop new structures. Characteristically, this will be done through a process we may call *bricolage* – Lévi-Strauss's term for the way ideological systems are 'extended and amplified to deal with new situations by "putting together", often in an illogical or incoherent way, what were, previously, the fragments of more ordered or stable meaning-systems'.[25] New constructs are 'improvised' or 'made-up' as *ad hoc* responses; we catch that process at work when the *Evening Standard* invites the reader to fill in the blank in the sentence ' "Oscar Wilde posing as ___" '. The dominant twentieth-century queer identity, I will argue, has been constructed in this kind of process – mainly out of elements that came together at the Wilde trials: effeminacy, leisure, idleness, immorality, luxury, insouciance, decadence and aestheticism.

The constructionist argument is generally indebted to the work of Michel Foucault, who argues that the big shift in homosexual identity occurs when the person who engages in same-sex activity gets perceived as a personality type. So far from repressing sex, Foucault brilliantly observes, the Victorians went on about it all the time; it became a principal mode of social regulation. In the process of this discursive proliferation, the 'homosexual became a personage, a past, a case history, and a childhood, in addition to being a type of life, a life form, and a morphology, with an indiscreet anatomy and possibly a mysterious physiology. ... The sodomite had been a temporary aberration; the homosexual was now a species'.[26] The difference is like that between nicking things from Woolworths, which any child might do, and being labelled 'a thief': with the latter, thievishness seems to pervade the whole personality. Previously, for instance in Shakespeare's time, same-sex passion was not specialized as the kind of thing only a certain kind of person might do; it was something anyone might fall into – since we are all 'fallen'. Hostility to same-sex practices, Alan Bray shows, derived hardly from a concept of homosexuality as such; rather, from 'a more general notion: debauchery; and debauchery was a temptation to which all, in principle at least, were subject'.[27]

Hence the answer to the question that seems suddenly to have hit the agenda: 'Was Shakespeare gay?' He couldn't have been, because lesbian and gay identities are modern developments: the early-modern organization of sex and gender boundaries, simply, was different from ours. However, by the same token, he couldn't have been straight either, so present-day heterosexism has no stronger claim upon him than homosexuality. In practice, his plays are pervaded with erotic interactions that strike chords for lesbians and gays today. Friendships are conducted with a passion that would now be considered suspicious; language of sexual flirtation is used in circumstances where we would find it embarrassing; and all the women's parts may, legitimately, be played by young men. It is not that Shakespeare was a sexual radical, marvellously anticipating progressive modern ideas; the ordinary currency of his theatre and society is sexy for us. And this potential may be exploited in gender-bending productions, as it was in Cheek by Jowl's *As You Like It* in 1991.

There are problems with the historical provenance of Foucault's argument, and they affect its political implications. It is understandable that he should wish to correct a naive 1960s exuberance about the liberatory consequences of everyone doing their own thing, but he falls into a somewhat paranoid slant, whereby the development of homosexuality may appear as a device through which the state gained greater control over subjectivities. There are also problems of method. Foucault finds history falling into epochs, characterized by distinct modes of thought; change occurs through a sequence of large-scale epistemological shifts. This makes his case vulnerable to almost any scrap of empirical evidence showing ideas occurring at the 'wrong' time. While accepting his broad thesis about the development of homosexual identity, as a shift from incidental behaviour to a personality type, I believe the change to have been gradual and highly uneven – as such changes generally are. A same-sex coterie may well have flourished at the court of Queen Elizabeth, around the Earl of Southampton, and may have involved a same-sex identity recognizably continuous with that experienced by some men today. At the same moment, people in other circumstances in Western Europe may have had no concept of same-sex passion. There were subcultures in Victorian times for the sexologists to observe, George Chauncey, Jr has pointed out: 'they were investigating a subculture rather than creating one'; male homosexuality was not, as Simon Shepherd puts it, a 'virgin birth'.[28]

Also, Foucault places too much emphasis on medical and legal discourses, and on their supposed collusion in consolidating state power. It would be better to regard those discourses as two among many, and as responding to and channelling social change rather than determining it. Frank Mort has shown that, in England at least, nineteenth-century changes in the regulation of sexuality derived from diverse interventions in civil society. In large part, the impetus came from outrage at the oppression of poor women through prostitution and other forms of sexual exploitation.[29] Same-sex practices came into focus as a by-product of broadly progressive campaigns, and doctors and lawyers were relatively ignorant of and uninterested in them. The Labouchère amendment, criminalizing homosexual acts in private, was tacked on to the

Criminal Law Amendment Act (1885), which was aimed ostensibly at procurers of prostitution; and the penalty of flogging on second conviction for soliciting men was introduced through the Vagrancy Law Amendment Act (1898), which mainly targeted men who accosted women.

This mode of interpretation perceives homosexuality within a complex elaboration of socio-sexual discourses, finding homosexual men caught up in the problems of heterosexuality (as they so often are), rather than as a primary focus of inexplicably sudden hostile attention. The crunch issue in Victorian England, Judith Walkowitz has argued, was not homosexuality but widespread sexual oppression by middle-class men, in the main of working-class women. This was shifted away from its logical focus and (in a manner familiar to lesbians and gay men) on to the victims. So, despite the initial reformist goals, the legislation that eventuated gave police far greater summary jurisdiction over poor working women and children. New penalizing of homosexual men occurred, opportunistically – almost casually – within this wider pattern. Such displacement of responsibility onto sexual dissidents consolidated the pattern: social ills could be attributed to a scarcely specified category of shadowy deviants, whose victims were characteristically perceived as young people. As Jacqueline Rose has observed, 'The child prostitute became the emblem for a social conscience which saw in the repairing of her moral and sexual innocence a corrective to fundamental problems of social inequality'.[30]

We need to envisage the stigmatization of homosexuality as occurring within a field of diverse interacting discourses. In many of these, it is a relatively incidental factor; in others, it may even be represented positively. There was a positive contribution from homosexual men. As Frederic Silverstolpe has pointed out, the term 'homosexual' was coined not by a doctor but by the Hungarian writer Karoly Maria Benkert. The appeal to medical knowledge was generated among activists such as Magnus Hirschfeld, Karl Heinrich Ulrichs and John Addington Symonds as a strategic move, designed to justify claims for homosexual rights.[31] Manifest, diverse and purposeful political activity appeared within several same-sex circles in Victorian England. Some of this was courageous and innovative; some was equivocal and half-submerged (for instance, members of the literary establishment published editions and studies of Greek and other suitable precursors; Wilde's tutor in Dublin hesitantly defended ancient Greek homosexuality in print – but removed the passage from a second edition).[32] To be sure, much of the publishing was in expensive, limited editions; as I have said, we have to consider who knows about a concept. Nevertheless, much of this writing (some of which I consider later on) still seems bold; as with feminism, the late nineteenth century made advances that we have had painfully to recover in recent times. In a flurry of writing and networking, more various than at any time until the 1970s, 'homosexual' identity was being explored.

With this kind of sophistication, I believe the constructionist argument stands up historically. Homosexual and heterosexual identities were in the making, crucially, in the nineteenth century; in later chapters I say more about how same-sex passion was regarded previously. The broader problem with constructionism is that it may appear to destroy the scope for political intervention. The key question is: if we come to consciousness within a language that is continuous with the power structures that sustain the social order, how can we conceive, let alone organize, resistance? If deviant identities are produced by the dominant ideology in ways that police sexualities, containing dissidence, how is a radical lesbian or gay identity to arise?

Foucault has often been taken as the theorist who has maintained that the outcome of dissidence will be the exploitation and incorporation of the subordinate. This is because he writes: 'Where there is power, there is resistance, and yet, or rather consequently, this resistance is never in a position of exteriority in relation to power'.[33] So dissidence may seem always fatally implicated with that which it aspires to oppose. Even attempts to challenge the system help to maintain it; in fact, those attempts are distinctively complicit, in so far as they help the dominant to assert and police the boundaries of the deviant and the permissible. It begins to seem that any move we make has been anticipated by the power system – you only dig yourself in deeper. Dissidence plays into the hands of containment.

D. A. Miller draws upon this sense of Foucault. *The Novel and the Police*, the title of Miller's book, suggests straightforward state intervention, but he finds that social order is achieved mainly through ideological self-policing – through 'various technologies of the self and its sexuality, which administer the subject's own contribution to the intensive and continuous "pastoral" care that liberal society proposes to take of each and every one of its charges'. Policing, Miller says, moves 'out of the streets, as it were, into the closet – I mean, into the private and domestic sphere on which the very identity of the liberal subject depends'.[34] Identifying privacy and self-policing with the gay closet is richly suggestive – as in Eve Sedgwick's deployment of the idea in *Epistemology of the Closet*. However, in so far as such self-policing is being identified as the principal mode through which surveillance is exercised in societies like ours – as a general effect inherent in the whole modern concept of subjectivity, registering 'the subject's accommodation to a totalizing system that has obliterated the difference he would make';[35] in so far as the open secret is doing all that, merging it with homosexual oppression may obscure distinctions in the historical opportunities for lesbians and gay men.

To be sure, there is good reason for students of sexualities to dwell upon self-policing and entrapment: a great difficulty in lesbian and gay subcultures is self-oppression – how we get to internalize demeaning images of ourselves. None the less, we must seek to track the open secret to specific subcultural formations in determinate historical conditions. Homosexuality is not an open secret at all times, nor is it open and secret in the same ways to different groups at any one time. To suppose otherwise would be to see lesbians and gay men as trapped eternally by their sexuality as such (this might be a psychoanalytic perspective), and that must discourage political action. In the rallying cry, Silence = Death, we assert that secrecy about the concerns of gay men makes their early and painful deaths more likely; openness makes a difference.

This approach is not in fact at odds with Foucault's. Though there is not, in his view, much scope for a grand revolutionary gesture, there is, he says, 'a plurality of resistances ... spread over time and space at varying densities, at times mobilizing groups or individuals in a definitive way'. He *denies* that these must be 'only a reaction or rebound, forming with respect to the basic domination an underside that is in the end always passive, doomed to perpetual defeat'.[36] In fact, a dissident text may derive its leverage, its purchase, precisely from its partial implication with the dominant; it may embarrass the dominant by appropriating its concepts and imagery. Foucault takes the emergence of the concept of homosexuality as an instance of what he terms 'a "reverse" discourse'. Legal,

medical and sexological discourses on homosexuality made possible new forms of control, he says, but, at the same time, they also
allowed a voice to sexual dissidents. 'Homosexuality began to
speak in its own behalf, to demand that its legitimacy or "natural-
ity" be acknowledged, often in the same vocabulary, using the same
categories by which it was medically disqualified' (p. 101).
Deviancy returns from abjection by deploying just those terms
which relegated it in the first place.

Cultural materialism has been particularly concerned to
theorize the scope for dissident perceptions and action. Foucault's
argument about the inter-involvement of power and resistance is
not complacent, in my view, because it understands that conflict
and contradiction stem from the very strategies through which the
social order attempts to sustain itself. As Raymond Williams has
observed, ideology has to be seen as a process, and one that is
always precarious: 'social orders and cultural orders must be seen
as being actively made: actively and continuously, or they may
quite quickly break down'.[37] Despite their power, dominant ideological formations are always, in practice, under pressure, as they
strive to substantiate their claim to superior plausibility in the face
of diverse disturbances. The maps of meaning are always proving
inadequate, failing to contain both inherent instabilities and the
pressures and strains that arise from new historical conditions. The
social order *cannot but produce* faultlines through which its own
criteria of plausibility fall into contest and disarray.

Looking for Mr W. H.

Constructionism means that it is hard to be gay until you
have some kind of slot, however ambiguously defined, in the current framework of ideas. This may be observed in *Teleny* (1893), to
the writing of which Wilde may have contributed. The novel
exhibits a same-sex subculture around the dandy aristocrat
Briancourt, and an outdoor cruising ground, but the middle-class
Des Grieux has initially no idea of such things. He is taken by
surprise when he falls in love. 'I afterwards came to the conclusion
that I had felt the first faint stimulus of love already long before, but
as it had always been with my own sex, I was unconscious that this
was love'; so little was same-sex passion anticipated.[38] Des Grieux

argues for the naturalness of his passion: 'I know that I was born a sodomite, the fault is my constitution's, not mine own,' he declares (p. 70); the 'fault' is in his 'nature', his 'blood' (p. 130). Despite this conviction, he does not see himself as a queer in the twentieth-century sense. He is able passionately to desire the maid (despite initial indifference), and says he 'would even have gone so far as to marry her, rather than become a sodomite' (pp. 87, 89). The phrasing there is significant: though he says it is his nature, he has still to *become* a sodomite by indulging his preference. Same-sex passion is natural to Des Grieux, but not essential; it is what you do that counts, not what you are. Indeed, although the novel breaks ground in its handling of same-sex love and eroticism, it anticipates a reader interested equally in cross-sex activity, and the dénouement is the discovery of Teleny's infidelity – with Des Grieux's mother! Same-sex passion is situated, in *Teleny*, partly in an emerging – though far from available – queer subculture, partly as one component in a general dissoluteness.

As *Teleny* and the story of Fanny and Stella suggest, there was a queer subculture, and Wilde, because of his class position (I will argue), was better placed to discover it than many men. We will observe the same pattern in E. M. Forster's *Maurice*. But there is no reason to suppose that Wilde either envisaged, or would have wanted, a distinctively queer identity. Dorian Gray, his narrator says,

> used to wonder at the shallow psychology of those who conceive the Ego in man as a thing simple, permanent, reliable, and of one essence. To him, man was a being with myriad lives and myriad sensations, a complex multiform creature that bore within itself strange legacies of thought and passion, and whose very flesh was tainted with the monstrous maladies of the dead.[39]

This sense of fluidity and constructedness informs 'The portrait of Mr W. H.' In this novella, Wilde's narrator is shown by his friend Erskine a portrait purporting to represent Willie Hughes, a boy actor in Shakespeare's theatre and the supposed addressee of the Sonnets. He was 'about seventeen years of age, and was of quite extraordinary personal beauty, though evidently somewhat effeminate. Indeed, had it not been for the dress and the closely cropped hair, one would have said that the face, with its dreamy wistful eyes and its delicate scarlet lips, was the face of a girl'.[40] The portrait had been shown to Erskine by his friend Cyril Graham, to whom it had appealed, evidently, as a precursor of Graham himself. For he too was marvellous at performing Shakespearian girl parts, and was 'wonderfully handsome', though some saw 'mere prettiness'; he was 'effeminate, I suppose, in some things, though he was a capital rider and a capital fencer' (pp. 1152–3). However, the portrait of Willie Hughes is a forgery – Graham has concocted him. The characters strive to establish the existence of Willie Hughes, but it cannot be done. The idea of a queer identity is ill-founded, the story seems to say.

'Mr W. H.' aroused suspicions about Wilde's sexuality in some quarters.[41] Nevertheless, Wilde was not being dishonest in this court exchange: 'I believe you have written an article to show that Shakespeare's sonnets were suggestive of unnatural vice? – On the contrary, I have written an article to show that they are not.'[42] What 'Mr W. H.' suggests is Wilde's interest in discovering a homosexual identity, but also his scepticism about how that might be achieved. The story depends upon the fact that the existence of Willie Hughes cannot be demonstrated. Indeed, the quest proves fatal: disappointed by his failure to persuade his friend of his theory, Graham commits suicide. The idea is sufficient, however, to get the narrator obsessed with the Hughes thesis. But when he has worked it up to the point where it becomes persuasive (though the existence of Hughes still cannot be proved), the narrator loses interest: 'Willie Hughes suddenly became to me a mere myth, an idle dream, the boyish fancy of a young man who, like most ardent spirits, was more anxious to convince others than to be himself convinced' (p. 1196). 'Mr W. H.' enacts not the discreet presentation of an existing queer identity, but the elusiveness of the quest for such an identity.

This elusiveness has two facets. Not only is the boy actor not there; the very project of using him to establish a historical fix on sexuality is ill-judged. There is 'no permanence in personality,' 'Mr W. H.' asserts, and we are 'at the mercy of such impressions as Art or Life chose to give us' (pp. 1196–7). There is something of importance to gay men in Shakespeare, Wilde suggests, but it is not to be claimed at the expense of the fluidity of sexuality, in both personal and cultural terms.

'Mr W. H.' was published in 1889, but Wilde enlarged it in

1893, approximately doubling its length.[43] The additions are mainly the narrator discovering further incidental evidence for the Hughes thesis – more quotations from the sonnets, historical investigations into boy actors, an 'explanation' of the Dark Lady. All this tends to make the thesis seem more persuasive; also, Renaissance Neo-Platonism and friendship are invoked, and Michelangelo's 'worship of intellectual beauty' (p. 1175); and 'I am that I am' is quoted from the Sonnets, implying Shakespeare's 'noble scorn' in matters of sexual orthodoxy (p. 1169). Wilde is shifting the story towards a justification of same-sex passion. Between 1888 and 1893 he became increasingly fascinated with homosexual subculture, and perhaps more inclined to think, with his narrator, that he might be 'deciphering the story of a life that had once been mine, unrolling the record of a romance that, without my knowing it, had coloured the very texture of my nature, had dyed it with strange and subtle dyes' (p. 1194). If the Victorian male same-sex lover could discover himself through a study of Shakespeare, he might lay claim to the further nobility of deriving from 'something within us that knew nothing of sequence or extension, and yet, like the philosopher of the Ideal City, was the spectator of all time and of all existence' (p. 1195). Nevertheless, the text still insists, there is no evidence that Willie Hughes ever existed. And Wilde was still affirming – in the elaboration of the collapse of the narrator's faith – that there is 'no permanence in personality' and we are 'at the mercy of such impressions as Art or Life chose to give us' (pp. 1196–7). He was still more engaged with the idea that we invest history with our own fantasies: 'No man dies for what he knows to be true,' he concludes in the enlarged version; 'Men die for what they want to be true, for what some terror in their hearts tells them is not true' (p. 1201).

Lawrence Danson rejects the thought that 'Mr W. H.' may be teasing or evasive; he believes Wilde was trying 'not to be trapped in another man's system' – not to confine his sexuality within the boundaries that seemed available in his culture. So 'the deferral of meaning was a necessary act of resistance'.[44] This might be a strategy for our time; it might involve claiming same-sex eroticism without accepting the terms and conditions, social and psychological, of being 'gay'. But Wilde, whatever his wishes, could not simply discover a queer precursor in Willie Hughes because 'Mr W. H.', the plays, the trials, and the whole package that we call

'Oscar Wilde', were key sites upon which a modern queer identity has been constituted. They did not produce male homosexuality, but they helped to produce it in a particular cultural mode. Wilde could not foresee this, but he may still help us to understand it. As Neil Bartlett puts it, in *Who Was That Man?*, Wilde 'proposed that our present is continually being written by our history; that the individual voice can hardly be separated from the historic text which it repeats and adapts'.[45] 'Mr W. H.' shows that we construct, in culture, the identities that we want – though not in conditions of our own choosing.

Notes

1. Frank Harris, *Oscar Wilde* (New York: Frank Harris, 1918), p. 286.
2. Montgomery Hyde, *The Trials of Oscar Wilde* (London: William Hodge, 1948), p. 81 (in a note, Hyde gives reasons for crediting this story); Richard Ellmann, *Oscar Wilde* (London: Hamish Hamilton, 1987), p. 440.
3. Jackson is quoted in Karl Beckson, ed., *Oscar Wilde: The Critical Heritage* (London: Routledge, 1970), p. 331; W. B. Yeats, *Autobiographies* (London: Macmillan, 1961), p. 285. Yeats added: 'I was certain that, guilty or not guilty, he would prove himself a man.'
4. Hyde, *Trials*, pp. 265–6; see H. Montgomery Hyde, *The Other Love* (London: Mayflower, 1972), p. 31. The ballad is printed by John Stokes, *In the Nineties* (Hemel Hempstead: Harvester, 1989), p. 4.
5. See Ellen Moers, *The Dandy* (London: Secker, 1960), p. 304; Brian Reade, *Sexual Heretics* (London: Routledge, 1970), pp. 53–4; Martin Green, *Children of the Sun* (London: Constable, 1977), pp. 23–40; Jeffrey Weeks, *Coming Out* (London: Quartet Books, 1977), p. 21; Eve Kosofsky Sedgwick, *Between Men* (New York: Columbia University Press, 1985), pp. 94, 216–17; Regenia Gagnier, *Idylls of the Marketplace* (Aldershot: Scolar Press, 1987), p. 139; Claude J. Summers, *Gay Fictions* (New York: Continuum, 1990), p. 60 and ch. 3; J. E. Rivers, *Proust and the Art of Love* (New York: Columbia University Press, 1980), pp. 112–41; Michael Hurley, 'Homosexualities: fiction, reading and moral training', in Terry Threadgold and Anne Cranny-Francis, eds, *Feminine, Masculine and Representation* (Sydney: Allen & Unwin, 1990), p. 164.
6. Ed Cohen, *Talk on the Wilde Side* (New York: Routledge, 1993), pp. 145–8.
7. Sir Henry Hall Caine, *The Deemster* (1887), quoted in Reade, *Sexual Heretics*, p. 208.

8. E. M. Forster, *Maurice* (Penguin: Harmondsworth, 1972), p. 136; Cohen, *Talk*, p. 100. On the Montagu trial, see Peter Wildeblood, *Against the Law* (London: Weidenfeld & Nicolson, 1955).

9. Beckson, ed., *Oscar Wilde*, pp. 50–4. I discuss Higginson's article further in chapter 4.

10. See Alan Sinfield, *Faultlines*: *Cultural Materialism and the Politics of Dissident Reading* (Berkeley: California University Press and Oxford: Oxford University Press, 1992).

11. Michel Foucault, *The History of Sexuality*, vol. 1, *An Introduction*, trans. Robert Hurley (New York: Vintage Books, 1978), p. 27.

12. Ellmann, *Oscar Wilde*, p. 261; Hyde, *Trials*, pp. 368–71; Richard Gilman, *Decadence* (London: Secker & Warburg, 1979), p. 135; Peter Ackroyd, *The Last Testament of Oscar Wilde* (London: Sphere, 1988), pp. 68, 101–3; Harris, *Oscar Wilde*, p. 152.

13. Reade, *Sexual Heretics*, pp. 24–5.

14. John Stokes, letter in *London Review of Books*, 27 February 1992, p. 4; the photo has often been printed, e.g. in Ellmann, *Oscar Wilde*, facing p. 371.

15. William Roughead, *Bad Companions* (Edinburgh: W. Green & Son, 1930), pp. 178, 180–2. See also Hyde, *The Other Love*, pp. 112–15.

16. Jeffrey Weeks, *Sex, Politics and Society*, 2nd edn (London: Longman, 1989), p. 101.

17. Neil Bartlett, *Who Was That Man?* (London: Serpent's Tail, 1988), p. 135.

18. Roughead, *Bad Companions*, p. 183.

19. David A. Miller, *The Novel and the Police* (Berkeley: California University Press, 1988), pp. 205–6. See Alan Sinfield, *Cultural Politics – Queer Reading* (Philadelphia: Pennsylvania University Press and London: Routledge, 1994), ch. 2.

20. David T. Evans, *Sexual Citizenship* (London: Routledge, 1993), p. 64.

21. Jonathan Dollimore, 'Homophobia and sexual difference', in *Sexual Difference*, ed. Robert Young (special issue of *Oxford Literary Review*, 8 (1–2), 1986), 5–12, p. 5; see also Jonathan Dollimore, 'Masculinity and homophobia', in Helen Taylor, ed., *Literature Teaching Politics 1985* (Bristol: Bristol Polytechnic and Helen Taylor, 1985), pp. 58–63. And see Suzanne Pharr, *Homophobia: A Weapon of Sexism* (Inverness, CA: Chardon Press, 1988), pp. 13–23. Guy Hocquenghem observes: 'Every effort to isolate, explain, reduce the contaminated homosexual simply helps to place him at the centre of waking dreams'; Hocquenghem, *Homosexual Desire*, trans. Daniella Dangoor (London: Allison & Busby, 1978), p. 38.

22. Hyde, *The Other Love*, pp. 153–5 (my italics). For parallel observations in respect of US law, see Robert C. Caserio, 'Supreme Court discourse vs. homosexual fiction', *South Atlantic Quarterly*, 88 (1989), 267–99.

23. See Pierre Macherey, *A Theory of Literary Production*, trans. Geoffrey Wall (London: Routledge, 1978).

24. Colin Sumner, *Reading Ideologies* (London, New York and San Francisco: Academic Press, 1979), p. 288.

25. Stuart Hall, 'Deviance, politics, and the media', in Paul Rock and Mary McIntosh, eds, *Deviance and Social Control* (London: Tavistock, 1974), p. 293. See John Clarke, 'Style', in Stuart Hall, John Clarke, Tony Jefferson and Brian Roberts, eds, *Resistance through Rituals* (London: Hutchinson, 1976), pp. 177–8; Terry Hawkes, *Structuralism and Semiotics* (London: Methuen, 1977), pp. 51–2.

26. Foucault, *History*, vol. 1, p. 43. Sociological contributions to the debate are collected in Edward Stein, *Forms of Desire: Sexual Orientation and the Social Constructionist Controversy* (New York: Garland, 1990).

27. Alan Bray, *Homosexuality in Renaissance England* (London: Gay Men's Press, 1982), p. 16. See Bruce R. Smith, *Homosexual Desire in Shakespeare's England* (Chicago University Press, 1991); Jonathan Goldberg, *Sodometries* (Stanford University Press, 1992).

28. George Chauncey, Jr, 'From sexual inversion to homosexuality: medicine and the changing conceptualization of female deviance', *Salmagundi*, 58–9 (1982–3), 114–46, pp. 142–3; Simon Shepherd, 'What's so funny about ladies' tailors? A survey of some male (homo)sexual types in the Renaissance', *Textual Practice*, 6 (1992), 17–30, p. 18.

29. See Frank Mort, *Dangerous Sexualities* (London: Routledge, 1987); Judith Walkowitz, *Prostitution and Victorian Society* (Cambridge University Press, 1980); Edward Bristow, *Vice and Vigilance* (Dublin: Gill & Macmillan, 1977); John Marshall, 'Pansies, perverts and macho men: changing conceptions of male homosexuality', in Kenneth Plummer, ed., *The Making of the Modern Homosexual* (London: Hutchinson, 1981), pp. 139–40.

30. Walkowitz, *Prostitution and Victorian Society*, pp. 246–51; Jacqueline Rose, *The Case of Peter Pan* (London: Macmillan, 1984), p. 99.

31. Frederic Silverstolpe, 'Benkert was not a doctor: on the non-medical origins of the homosexual category in the nineteenth century', in *Homosexuality, Which Homosexuality?*, Conference Papers: International Scientific Conference on Lesbian and Gay Studies, Free University of Amsterdam, December 1987 (Amsterdam: Free University and Schorer Foundation, 1987).

32. Alison Hennegan, 'Personalities and principles: aspects of literature and life in *fin-de-siècle* England', in Mikuláš Teich and Roy Porter, eds, *Fin de Siècle and Its Legacy* (Cambridge University Press, 1990), pp. 206–7; Ellmann, *Oscar Wilde*, pp. 27–8. See Reade, *Sexual Heretics*, pp. 40–6 and Introduction; Timothy d'Arch Smith, *Love in Earnest* (London: Routledge, 1970); Bartlett, *Who Was That Man?*, ch. 5.

33. Foucault, *History*, vol. 1, pp. 95–6.
34. Miller, *The Novel and the Police*, pp. viii–ix. See Sinfield, *Cultural Politics – Queer Reading*, chs 2, 3.
35. Miller, *The Novel and the Police*, p. 207; see Eve Kosofsky Sedgwick, *Epistemology of the Closet* (Hemel Hempstead: Harvester Wheatsheaf, 1991), pp. 67–75.
36. Foucault, *History*, vol. 1, pp. 95–6. See Jonathan Dollimore and Alan Sinfield, 'Culture and textuality: debating cultural materialism', *Textual Practice*, 4(1) (spring, 1990), 91–100, p. 95; and Jonathan Dollimore, 'Sexuality, subjectivity and transgression: the Jacobean connection', *Renaissance Drama*, new series, 17 (1986), 53–82.
37. Raymond Williams, *Culture* (Glasgow: Fontana, 1981), p. 201.
38. Oscar Wilde and others, *Teleny*, ed. John McRae (London: Gay Men's Press, 1986), p. 57.
39. Oscar Wilde, *The Picture of Dorian Gray*, ed. Isobel Murray (Oxford University Press, 1981), p. 143.
40. *Complete Works of Oscar Wilde*, intr. Vyvyan Holland (London and Glasgow: Collins, 1966), pp. 1150–1.
41. See Ellmann, *Oscar Wilde*, p. 282; Gagnier, *Idylls*, p. 20; Hyde, *Other Love*, p. 163; William A. Cohen, 'Willie and Wilde: reading *The Portrait of Mr W. H.*', *South Atlantic Quarterly*, 88 (1989), 219–45, pp. 233–4; Lawrence Danson, 'Oscar Wilde, W. H., and the unspoken name of love', *English Literary History*, 58 (1991), 979–1000.
42. Hyde, *Trials*, p. 130. Wilde added: 'I objected to such a perversion being put upon Shakespeare'. On 'Mr W. H.' as a critique of over-rapid assimilation of Shakespeare and others to a nineteenth-century idea of same-sex passion, see Simon Shepherd, 'Shakespeare's private drawer: Shakespeare and homosexuality', in Graham Holderness, ed., *The Shakespeare Myth* (Manchester University Press, 1988), pp. 106–7; Chris White, 'The organization of pleasure: British homosexual and lesbian discourse 1869–1914', unpub. dissertation (University of Nottingham, 1992), pp. 114–17.
43. The enlarged, 1893, version of 'Mr W. H.' was first published in 1958; it is printed in Holland, ed., *Complete Works* (from which I have been citing); the 1889 edition is reprinted in *The Works of Oscar Wilde*, ed. G. F. Maine (London and Glasgow: Collins, 1948).
44. Danson, 'Oscar Wilde', p. 997.
45. Bartlett, *Who Was That Man?*, p. 209.

Chapter two

Uses of Effeminacy

A POEM in Norman Gale's collection *More Cricket Songs* (1905) is titled: 'The female boy':

> What in the world is the use of a creature
> All flabbily bent on avoiding the Pitch,
> Who wanders about, with a sob in each feature
> Devising a headache, inventing a stitch?
> There surely would be a quick end to my joy
> If possessed of that monster – a feminine boy.[1]

It seems obvious to us, today, that the misogyny in this hearty little verse does not betoken an effortless heterosexuality. In fact, the opposite: looking at the writer's language, we might suspect that his joy – not flabby or bent – might indeed reach a 'quick end' if he dared, monstrously perhaps, to 'possess' such a boy. These innuendoes, surely, were inaudible to the writer; otherwise he would have suppressed them, for fear of what they might disclose about his own anxieties. From this I deduce that the 'feminine boy' was not understood, here, as related to same-sex passion. He is despicable simply because he is girlish. In this chapter I assess some instances and theories of effeminacy in the centuries before Wilde.

Ganymedes and warriors

Much of the unease with Wilde's appearance and behaviour, before the trials, centred upon 'effeminacy'.[2] As I said in the previous chapter, I regard 'masculinity', 'femininity' and 'effeminacy' as ideological constructs, bearing no essential relation to the attributes of men and women. Effeminacy is founded in misogyny. Certain manners and behaviours are stigmatized by associating them with 'the feminine' – which is perceived as weak, ineffectual and unsuited for the world of affairs. The terms were set by Aristotle who, in his discussion of continence and incontinence, opposes endurance and softness. 'Now the man who is defective in respect of resistance to the things which most men both resist and resist successfully is soft and effeminate; for effeminacy too is a kind of softness; such a man trails his cloak to avoid the pain of lifting it.'[3] The connotations in the *Oxford English Dictionary* are: 'Womanish, unmanly, enervated, feeble; self-indulgent, voluptuous; unbecomingly delicate or over-refined' (*OED*). The root idea is a male falling away from the purposeful reasonableness that is supposed to constitute manliness, into the laxity and weakness conventionally attributed to women. It is a way of stigmatizing deviation from proper manly and womanly stereotypes. The effeminate male is (1) 'wrong' and (2) inferior (female). The 'masculine' woman, conversely, is (1) 'wrong' and (2) impertinent (aspiring to manliness). The function of effeminacy, as a concept, is to police sexual categories, keeping them pure. The effects of such policing extend vastly beyond lesbians and gay men. As various recent commentators have shown, the whole order of sexuality and gender is pinioned by the fears and excitements that gather around the allegedly inappropriate distribution of gender categories.[4]

In the middle part of the twentieth century, effeminacy was widely believed to correlate with homosexuality. At the core of his account of the appearance of the homosexual, Foucault writes of 'a certain way of inverting the masculine and the feminine in oneself. Homosexuality appeared as one of the forms of sexuality when it was transposed from the practice of sodomy onto a kind of interior androgyny, a hermaphroditism of the soul.'[5] This is the dominant modern notion: it lurks behind the female soul in the male body – the formulation of sexologists at the turn of the century; it informs, in Freud, the Oedipal failure to identify with the 'right' parent. In 1967 the decriminalization of many male homosexual practices was advocated in the UK parliament as 'the question of how we can, if it is possible, reduce the number of faulty males in the community. How can we diminish the number of those who grow up to have men's bodies but feminine souls?'[6] The underlying notion is at work, today still, both in popular belief and in some radical ideas about the transgressive impact of gender-bending.

Up to the time of the Wilde trials – far later than is widely supposed – it is unsafe to interpret effeminacy as defining of, or as a signal of, same-sex passion. Mostly, it meant being emotional and spending too much time with women. Often it involved excessive cross-sexual attachment. To be manly was of course to go with women, but in a way that did not forfeit mastery. This was the principal meaning in Shakespeare's time. In *Samson Agonistes* Samson's explanation of his subjection to Dalila is: 'foul effeminacy held me yoked / Her bondslave'. Shakespeare's Romeo says he is effeminate – not in respect of his love for Mercutio, but when he is distressed at his failure to prevent the death of Mercutio. Juliet's beauty 'hath made me effeminate', he says. It is love for a woman that produces the problem for masculinity; had Romeo been swayed more strongly by his love for Mercutio, that would have been manly.[7]

An element of the feminine might be proper for the hero. Marlowe's Tamburlaine, at the height of his achievement, finds himself moved by Zenocrate's sympathy for her father, the Soldan, and attributes this to her heavenly beauty. This rapture, he says, is problematic:

> But how unseemly is it for my sex,
> My discipline of arms and chivalry,
> My nature, and the terror of my name,
> To harbour thoughts effeminate and faint!

However, such effeminacy is all right, for beauty contributes to warrior culture:

> Save only that in beauty's just applause,
> With whose instinct the soul of man is touch'd,
> And every warrior that is rapt with love
> Of fame, of valour, and of victory,
> Must needs have beauty beat on his conceits.[8]

In fact, Tamburlaine's appropriation of the feminine occurs immediately after he has killed the Virgins of Damascus and during the slaughter of the remainder of the people, so he is scarcely succumbing to thoughts effeminate and faint; moreover, he needs the Soldan's approval to legitimate his relationship with Zenocrate. Effeminacy is risky; in *Antony and Cleopatra* it marks an area of anxiety. The Romans are dubious about Antony's devotion to Cleopatra, though Caesar's condemnation is evidently self-interested:

> This is the news: he fishes, drinks, and wastes
> The lamps of night in revel; is not more manlike
> Than Cleopatra; nor the queen of Ptolemy
> More womanly than he: hardly gave audience, or
> Vouchsaf'd to think he had partners.[9]

But while Antony is dominating an empire none of their suspicions really sticks; to the contrary, his devil-may-care attitude signals his stature. He can dress up in Cleopatra's clothes and she can wear his sword, and there is no threat to his masculinity. A real man can do whatever he chooses; after all, Hercules with whom Antony is identified, dressed up as a woman when it suited him. The cautious Caesar gets called 'boy'.[10] But it is an ambitious project, fit only for heroes. When Antony allows Cleopatra to determine the conduct of the war, and begins to lose, these feminizing practices seem to indicate his weakness and dependency.

In Shakespeare's *Troilus and Cressida*, similarly, unmanly behaviour is attending to the feminine at the expense of heroic responsibility. Achilles is warned about effeminacy in respect of his devotion to a woman, Hector's sister Polyxena:

> A woman impudent and mannish grown
> Is not more loath'd than an effeminate man
> In time of action.[11]

This is Patroclus speaking; 'Sweet, rouse yourself', he says to Achilles (line 221). Thersites calls Patroclus 'boy' and accuses him of being Achilles' 'Male varlet', 'his masculine whore' (V.i.13–16). However, the same-sex relationship between Achilles and Patroclus is not the problem – not the ground of effeminacy – because it does not compete with warrior values. Patroclus has 'little stomach to the war' (III.iii.219), but he is urging Achilles to fight.

Coriolanus is not apparently effeminate when he expresses

affection for his comrade Cominius, though he compares his
embrace to his honeymoon night:

> Oh! let me clip ye
> In arms as sound as when I woo'd; in heart
> As merry as when our nuptial day was done,
> And tapers burn'd to bedward.[12]

This is not a psychological disturbance peculiar to Coriolanus; in
warrior culture they all do it. 'Flower of warriors', Cominius calls
Coriolanus in response (line 32). Aufidius' greeting to Coriolanus is
in the same vein:

> Know thou first,
> I lov'd the maid I married; never man
> Sigh'd truer breath; but that I see thee here,
> Thou noble thing, more dances my rapt heart
> Than when I first my wedded mistress saw
> Bestride my threshold. (IV.v.114–19)

Coriolanus usurps the place of the maid Aufidius married, but he
does not become feminine. It is submitting to the citizens that risks
that:

> Away my disposition, and possess me
> Some harlot's spirit! My throat of war be turn'd,
> Which quired with my drum, into a pipe
> Small as a eunuch, or the virgin voice
> That babies lull asleep! (III.ii.111–15)

And when Coriolanus submits to his mother and loses military
authority, submission makes him feminine – 'at his nurse's tears /
He whin'd and roar'd away your victory' (V.vi.97–8), Aufidius
complains. To be womanly is all right so long as you are indubita-
bly a man at the time. Achilles is not effeminate when he says he has

> a woman's longing,
> An appetite that I am sick withal,
> To see great Hector in his weeds of peace. (III.iii.236–8)

Nor is the Duke of York when, at the point of death at Agincourt in *Henry V*,

> over Suffolk's neck
> He threw his wounded arm, and kiss'd his lips;
> And so espous'd to death, with blood he seal'd
> A testament of noble-ending love.[13]

These assumptions appear also in Marlowe's *Dido Queen of Carthage*, which opens with Jupiter playing with Ganymede. Venus complains:

> Ay, this is it: you can sit toying there,
> And playing with that female wanton boy,
> Whiles my Aeneas wanders on the sea
> And rests a prey to every billow's pride.[14]

The problem is the imperial business, not the boy. Jupiter agrees to sort out Aeneas' mission and exits – with Ganymede. Aeneas, too, is effeminate when he neglects imperial responsibilities, but this time the distraction is a woman. His comrade Achates exhorts:

> Banish that ticing dame from forth your mouth,
> And follow your foreseeing stars in all;
> This is no life for men-at-arms to live,
> Where dalliance doth consume a soldier's strength,
> And wanton motions of alluring eyes
> Effeminate our minds inur'd to war. (IV.iii.31–6)

The scope of effeminacy in early modern England, simply, was different from ours; they used a different organization of sex and gender boundaries.

This is, in principle, the Foucauldian argument that I considered in Chapter 1. As Alan Bray shows, the seventeenth century did not have our concept of 'the homosexual'. The commonest legal and medical terms for same-sex practices were sodomy and buggery, but these were (by our notions) ill-defined. The sodomite was not a same-sex personality type; he was generally disreputable – indolent, extravagant and debauched. And he was not distinctively effeminate – transvestism was not a sign of same-sex passion, but 'a vice in its own right'. Very likely, he was 'a young man-about-town, with his mistress on one arm and his "catamite" on the other'.[15]

However, as I have said, it is not necessary to assume an even development, whereby one model characterizes an epoch and then is superseded by another. There may have been in early modern Europe, especially in aristocratic circles, coteries where something like our concept of the same-sex-oriented individual developed, though the concept was still neither coherent nor generally known. Perhaps, despite the law against sodomy and its occasional use, it didn't matter very much (as Bray shows, the law was used mainly in response to manifest scandal and as part of a general vilification of an individual). Simon Shepherd argues that there were 'homosexual types', such as the fop and the royal favourite. However, even such figures might be notorious for accepting male and female partners indiscriminately, rather than being distinctively homosexual, and the men Shepherd evidences as reputed most unmanly – ladies' tailors – were not generally linked with same-sex passion. They were perceived as indulging women and sharing their interests, and as 'heterosexually lecherous'.[16] The roles of same-sex passion were, perhaps above all, ambivalent.

Bruce Smith disputes Bray's assumption that literary evidence is unimportant (Bray now concurs on this). Smith argues that we should recognize various kinds of discourse: moral, legal, medical, and poetic. Each of them contributes, within its own discursive arrangements, to the circulation of stories, such as I have proposed as establishing the boundaries of the plausible. Although same-sex practices were heavily penalized in law, they were validated in literature and the visual arts.[17] This was principally because of the huge prestige of ancient Greek and Roman texts. The intellectual and rhetorical sophistication of classical writings was hard to equal, but they planted in the midst of a mainly Christian culture powerful images of forbidden ideas (it was the same in respect of religion itself).[18] Smith isolates six 'cultural scenarios' for same-sex relations, founded in classical sources: heroic friendship, men and boys (mainly in pastoral and educational contexts), playful androgyny (mainly in romances and festivals), transvestism (mainly in satirical contexts), master–servant relations, and an emergent homosexual subjectivity (in Shakespeare's Sonnets). Within such a network of possibilities, individuals might negotiate quite diverse sexual alignments.

Very often, Smith observes, 'Behavior that we would label homosexual, and hence a rejection of maleness, was for them an *aspect* of maleness' (p. 75); this seems right for Coriolanus and Aufidius, Suffolk and York. Effeminacy appears at two points in these scenarios, in both cases as a ground of stigma. Very often it is an aspect of general dissoluteness (as Bray argues). On that basis, Jupiter's dallying with Ganymede is comparable to Antony's with Cleopatra. Also, effeminacy correlates with boyishness, and attaches to the subordinate partner – hence to Patroclus and Ganymede, dependants on the ultimate masculine power of Jupiter and Achilles. The term 'Ganymede' was applied 'not to sodomites in general, but only to the younger, passive partner who serves another man's pleasure', Smith shows (p. 186). Women and boys were both regarded as objects of male passion, were both socially inferior, and hence occupied a similar structural position. A comparable assumption was made in ancient Greece, David Halperin points out, and recent studies have discovered it today in Turkey, Thailand and Latin America.[19] Being a man means taking the 'active' or inserter role in sexual practice; any receptor is regarded as passive, inferior, some kind of woman. Caesar is accused of being a boy by Antony; and Coriolanus, finally, by Aufidius: 'Thou boy of tears', Aufidius accuses (V.vi.101). The change that produces this taunt is not that Coriolanus has become a homosexual, but that he has submitted to his mother. This shifts his relations with men out of the heroic friendship model and into the Ganymede model. In *Twelfth Night*, Valerie Traub observes, the desire of the sea captain Antonio for the boy Sebastian is characterized by a 'rhetoric of penetration', unlike the mode of the men enamoured of women;[20] Antonio seeks continually to position Sebastian as his effeminate-boy dependant. Orsino does the same with Viola. Both prove problematic, as gender and affections refuse to fall into line.

In a further essay, Bray shows that the signals of male friendship – meaning the whole relation of kinship and patronage – overlapped with those of sodomy. He writes of 'the unwelcome difficulty the Elizabethans had in drawing a dividing line between those gestures of closeness among men that they desired so much and those they feared'. Jonathan Goldberg regards the very 'impossibility' of sodomy in early modern societies not as closing down the topic but as having afforded scope for innumerable deviant sexual acts. It was an ever-present prospect around the edges of male bonding. The goal, Goldberg says, is not to track down gay writers or characters, but 'to see what the category [sodomy] enabled and disenabled, and to negotiate the complex terrains, the mutual implications of prohibition and production'.[21] With this in mind, we may now identify a faultline in early modern ideas of effeminacy, one that has provoked much critical confusion. The boy-lover may be regarded as masculine – in so far as real men (Tamburlaine, Jupiter, Achilles, Antony, Orsino) may love whom they want, heroically confusing gender categories, so long as s/he is a social inferior. Simultaneously and contradictorily, the boy-lover, like any excessive lover, may be perceived as feminine – in so far as he is dissolute and irresponsible. To discuss these alternatives as if we might decide which represents the truth of same-sex desire in that society, or which is the truth of a character in a play, is a mistake. None of the instances considered is merely private or personal, they all involve affairs of state. And they all involve cross-sex relations as well. It was a necessarily confused terrain, one well-suited for the contestation of male power.

Fops and cuckolds

In the second half of the seventeenth century, Bray and Randolph Trumbach have shown, the aggressively manly rake, though reproved by the churches and in violation of the law, would feel able to indulge himself with a woman or a young man; he lost no status so long as he was the inserter rather than the recipient.[22] Instances occur, relatively unselfconsciously, in plays of the time. *The Princess of Cleve* by Nathaniel Lee (1682–83) opens with Duke Nemours speaking affectionately with his boy, Bellamore, 'Now by this damask cheek I love thee,' he says; he calls him 'My bosom Dear', and later on 'Thou Dear Soft Rogue, my Spouse, my Hephestion, my Ganymed'.[23] Speaking of the love that he might have for a friend, Nemours expresses this too in sexual terms: 'Guide him the perfect temper of your selves', he prays to the Fates,

> With ev'ry manly Grace and shining Vertue;
> Add yet the bloom of Beauty to his Youth,
> That I may make a Mistress of him too.   (IV.i.279–82)

Nemours is not effeminate, though; 'The soldiers love him, and he bears the Palm / Already from the Marshalls of the Field' (III.ii.24–5). The main action is his courting of diverse women, married and unmarried, and there is no awkwardness between his two kinds of love.

In William Wycherley's *The Country Wife* (1675), Horner has it put about that he has been maimed sexually in the wars, in order to gain access to the women of the town; their husbands thrust them into his company, thinking they will be safe there. No one suggests that the supposedly emasculated Horner should now be involved in same-sex practices; rather, that he has joined the women: 'Come, come, man, you must e'en fall to visiting our wives, eating at our tables, drinking tea with our virtuous relations after dinner, dealing cards to 'em, reading plays and gazettes to 'em, picking fleas out of their shocks for 'em, collecting receipts, new songs, women, pages and footmen for 'em.'[24] The man who is not a man is a kind of woman, but not a homosexual. How much attention a man should give to women, at the expense of male bonding, is an explicit question between Horner and his friends. Male fellowship is rational; consorting with women, effeminate:

> HORNER: Well, a pox on love and wenching; women serve but to keep a man from better company. Though I can't enjoy them, I shall you the more: good fellowship and friendship are lasting, rational and manly pleasures.
> HARCOURT: For all that, give me some of those pleasures you call effeminate too: they help to relish one another.
> HORNER: They disturb each other.
> HARCOURT: No, mistresses are like books: if you pore upon them too much they doze you, and make you unfit for company; but if used discreetly, you are the fitter for conversation by 'em. (I.i.219–29)

Horner's line is related, of course, to the pretence that he cannot enjoy women; it provokes Harcourt into making a case for indulging an element of the 'effeminate' – for associating with women. Eventually, Harcourt marries the handsome and intelligent woman he loves, and Horner ends with his strategy sufficiently secure to retain Mrs Pinchwife as his mistress.

The opposite to manly behaviour is represented in *The*

Country Wife by the man who cannot either gain, or hold, a woman. Failure to hold her produces the cuckold; failing to gain her produces the beau or fop. Beaux are despised not for same-sex passion, but for chasing women excessively and ineffectually. They are 'shadows of men', 'half-men' – not boys, but 'your old boys, old *beaux garçons*, who, like superannuated stallions, are suffered to run, feed, and whinny with the mares as long as they live, though they can do nothing else' (I.i.210–18). They are allowed to hang around women because they will do no real damage.

Fops and cuckolds are fair game to Nemours in *The Princess of Cleve*. In Sir John Vanbrugh's play *The Relapse* (1696), Lord Foppington is a beau, a cross-sex philanderer. He is set against the real men: 'What a difference there is between a man like [Worthy] and that nauseous fop, Sir Novelty [Lord Foppington].'[25] The fop does not get far with the women – because the ladies are so clever at handling him, and because he chases so many, like a puppy in a warren (II.472). Berinthia draws up a table of differences between men and fops or beaux:

> These have brains; the beau has not.
> These are in love with their mistress, the beau with himself.
> They take care of her reputation; he's industrious to
>   destroy it.
> They are decent; he's a fop.
> They are sound; he's rotten.
> They are men; he's an ass.   (II.506–11)

Both men and fops pursue women, but fops do it badly. As in *The Country Wife*, the latter are said to be shadows of men (II.501). The male anxiety that structures these plays is of falling into the wrong category; being insufficiently impressive to women.[26]

There are interesting same-sex moments in both plays. Pinchwife has returned from the country with an attractive young wife, who takes readily to the opportunities of town life. Not having heard of Horner's supposed disability, and wanting to keep her away from Horner, Pinchwife dresses his wife as a boy, her own brother. Horner sees through the disguise, and seizes the chance to proposition Mrs Pinchwife in front of her husband: 'Who is he? I never saw anything so pretty in all my life' (III.ii.411–12). Horner gives the 'dear, sweet little gentleman' several kisses, on the pretext that 'he' will pass it on to Mrs Pinchwife; and the other gallants kiss 'him' as well. 'What do you kiss me for? — I am no woman,' she protests — cleverly pretending to maintain the disguise while fishing for a compliment (III.ii.481, 491). The episode is of course 'all right' because these men are actually kissing a woman. Even so, the pretext has to be adequate; if kissing a boy were totally outrageous, Horner would not be able to cover his approach to Mrs Pinchwife in this manner, and Pinchwife would be able to intervene and end the exchange (as, of course, he wishes desperately to do). The plausibility of the scene depends on the assumption that appreciating and kissing a pretty boy is within the conventional bounds of social behaviour — both for the reluctant eunuch the characters believe Horner to be, and for the manly chap the audience knows him to be. As Trumbach has argued, despite religious and legal embargoes, it was acceptable in late-seventeenth-century England for adult males to have sexual relations with women and with male adolescents — neither of whom threatened their status as adult male. The real man might go in for sodomy as much as adultery, whereas the fop wouldn't dare.[27] As *The Country Wife* suggests, same-sex passion was not the threat.

In *The Relapse*, Coupler, a pander, indicates clear same-sex preference, and is recognized as doing so by Young Fashion. Coupler approaches the latter entirely explicitly: 'Ha, you young lascivious rogue, you! Let me put my hand in your bosom, sirrah.' 'Stand off, old Sodom,' Fashion rejoins (I.iii.181–3), but they are evidently on friendly terms. Coupler expresses affectionate disappointment, and offers to set up Young Fashion with a pretty heiress. 'Show me but that, and my soul is thine,' Fashion exclaims. 'Pox o'thy soul, give me thy warm body,' Coupler bargains. 'Out with it then, dear dad, and take possession as soon as thou wilt' (I.iii.202–7). The deal is done, and Coupler claims a kiss: 'Ah, you young hot lusty thief, let me muzzle you. — (*kissing*) Sirrah, let me muzzle you.' Fashion, in aside, expresses distaste: 'Psha, the old lecher!' They kiss again (I.iii.264–6). This is hard for a modern reader to decode. Moreover, Young Fashion was acted initially by a woman. Curt A. Zimansky comments: 'Despite the convention of the "breeches part" — women playing men's parts — this is unusual casting: a role usually did not become a breeches part until the play was established. Coupler's homosexual gestures must have lost some effect with Fashion played by a woman.'[28] Perhaps.

But three things are clear. First, Coupler is not presented as extraordinary, or as merely disgusting. Second, no connection, submerged or otherwise, is posited between Coupler and Foppington; as in *The Country Wife*, the fop is unmanly because of the way he addresses women. The text offers no encouragement, to the initial audiences of these plays, to read the fop as 'really homosexual' (as many – despite and because of his cross-sex philandering – might do today). Third, the boy object of same-sex attentions is feminine in his role, but not necessarily in his constitution. In *The Princess of Cleve* the boy Bellamore not only helps Nemours to court ladies, he is delegated by him to take his place in bed when he finds he is engaged to two simultaneously. Effeminacy is despised, but is not a special characteristic of the sodomite.

Same-sex passion is handled with relative equanimity in these plays because it was not, I think, a great problem in the contemporaneous organization of gender and sexuality. It was not where the key questions were posed; not where the faultline ran. As the pretty-boy scene in *The Relapse* indicates, kissing boys matters only if in fact they are someone's wife. Problems, in these plays, arise within same-sex manliness: they centre upon an effeminate failure to dominate women (foppishness), and its opposite, an excess of manly competitiveness that leads to adultery. Both disturb the hierarchies of family, inheritance, alliance and property.[29] In this context, boys are relatively unimportant.

Mollies and aristocrats

Around 1700, Trumbach argues, the pattern changed. The convention that a man might, more or less evenly, approach a woman or a boy became largely obsolete. 'The sodomite became an individual interested exclusively in his own gender and inveterately effeminate and passive', and the manly libertine had to restrict himself to women as sexual partners. So, 'in the public mind, effeminacy in dress began to be associated with sodomy between males'. And it is from the early eighteenth century, therefore, that we should date 'the model of the gay minority, with its subcultures and its roles'.[30] In broadly similar vein, G. S. Rousseau argues that, towards the end of the seventeenth century, there was a change 'from the old-style bisexual sodomite who held a male on one arm and female on the other while kissing both, to the new-style sodomite who was exclusively homocentric and male oriented'.[31] At this point, it is argued, homosexuality as we know it comes into being; and the key move is the relocation of effeminacy.

In my view, though there was such a shift, the situation remained far more confused, and for far longer. Trumbach makes his case mainly from the early-eighteenth-century 'molly-houses' (named from the Latin for 'soft'). The mollies, it is reported, set up clubs, cross-dressed and took women's names; they were said to 'rather fancy themselves women, imitating all the little vanities that custom has reconciled to the female sex, affecting to speak, walk, tattle, curtsy, cry, scold, and to mimic all manner of effeminacy'.[32] They were subjected to assault, and to arrest for the offences of sodomy and attempted sodomy. Trumbach's argument that this amounted to the development of a same-sex subculture is surely correct. Bray makes a similar case, while allowing that earlier models continued alongside: 'There was now a continuing culture to be fixed on and an extension of the area in which homosexuality could be expressed and therefore recognised; clothes, gestures, language, particular buildings and particular public places.' It was 'a subculture, a miniature society within a society, in its own right'. Rictor Norton concurs, in his full re-presentation of this material.[33] And this subculture continues, recognizably, through the nineteenth century (for instance in the persons of Fanny and Stella in 1870 and Quentin Crisp in 1940), to the present day.

Despite this continuity, it is not safe to conclude that the mollies signal a decisive stage in western ideas of sexuality; that same-sex passion became at this point identified with effeminacy. We should not suppose that the molly-house model was the only one in circulation, or that it was widely known about. It is entirely likely that an elaborate social structure should entertain diverse sexual schema. After all, as has been repeatedly attested, twentieth-century queer subculture was not apparent to innumerable men who were, in effect, looking for it. Nor should we regard these changes as affording, from our point of view today, either a loss or a gain. In one aspect, the freebooting aristocratic sexual culture seems attractive: you just did as you pleased – if you were sufficiently privileged. In another aspect, the mollies are a crucial stage towards modern gay awareness; yet, I will show, the framework within which they lived was very unlike the ones we know. It is not unreasonable to celebrate these people as our precursors, experiencing love and fun, frustration and prejudice, and offering instances from which we can learn. But, above all, the differences between them and us indicate the scope for historical change – change which we may influence through political action.

There are difficulties with the molly-house evidence. Most of it is from popular trial stories and hostile accounts, Cohen points out; Jeffrey Weeks observes that male prostitutes were by no means always effeminate, let alone transvestite; in *Teleny* (1893), in which Wilde may have had a hand, a cruising ground evidences both effeminate men and 'a strong and sturdy fellow, either a butcher or a smith by trade'.[34] Norton believes many instances of transvestism derive from balls and ceremonies. In his transcriptions effeminacy is often attributed, but with a range of connotations such as we have already observed – general dissoluteness, effeteness, softness, preciousness, excess. As Norton says, it seems not to signify the modern idea that homosexuals suffer a psychic confusion of gender categories. He observes no butch/femme role-playing; the mollies were trying to identify as mollies, not as women; the main impression is of 'vigorous and lusty bonhomie' rather than softness. In a rare instance of self-ascription, effeminacy means emotional excess: 'I could write much on this subject [of friendship]', the Reverend John Church wrote to his would-be boyfriend in 1809, 'but I dare not trust you with what I could say[,] as much as I esteem you – You would consider it as unmanly and quite effeminate.'[35] How rash it might be to assimilate these men to modern patterns is suggested by reports, dating from 1709 and 1813, that mollies mimicked not just marriage but childbearing – with a midwife, nurse, and doll to represent the child.[36] It is *very* hard to imagine 'childbearing' scenes in twentieth-century queer or gay culture: there are breaks as well as continuities in the transmission of the molly-house model.

Above all, we need to bear in mind class: the mollies seem to have been lower- to middle-class (servants and tradesmen – see 'Occupations' in Norton's index), and their practices should not be elided with behaviours attributed to the upper classes. The pamphlet *Plain Reasons for the Growth of Sodomy in England* (1749) addresses the social transgressions of 'fine gentlemen' – their 'unnatural vices' and 'unmanly' behaviour – blaming girlish education, together with foppish clothes, continental manners, tea-drinking and opera (whereas men 'used to go from a good comedy warmed with the fire of love; and from a good tragedy fired with the spirit of glory; they [now] sit indolently and supinely at an opera'). Such a young gentleman, scarcely capable of reproducing at all, 'leaves a race as effeminate as himself'. As Norton and Cohen remark, this image has precious little to do with mollies.[37]

Aristocratic practices seem to have remained closer to the early-modern pattern, whereby the privileged man might address both boys and women. The two correspondents in *Love Letters between a Certain Late Nobleman and the Famous Mr Wilson* (1723), the apparent record of a scandalous association, seem prepared to go with women and men as the opportunity arises. As David Greenberg points out, Wilson responds initially to what he believes to be an approach from a lady, and dresses as a woman only for purposes of disguise. His gender identity is conventionally masculine throughout.[38] Lord Hervey, Pope's Sporus, appears to have responded sexually to both men and women. That is how he is represented in Pope's 'Epistle to Arbuthnot':

> Now high, now low, now master up, now miss,
> And he himself one vile Antithesis.
> Amphibious thing! that acting either part,
> The trifling head, or the corrupted heart,
> Fop at the toilet, flatterer at the board,
> Now trips a Lady, and now struts a Lord.[39]

Hervey's effeminacy includes same-sex passion, but as part of an alternation; effeminacy and sodomy are not presented here in a distinctive relation. (Pope, who was actually rather successful at the toilet and the board, quickly asserts, of himself, 'That, if he pleased, he pleased by manly ways' (line 337).) Hervey was stigmatized for passivity in relation to his lover, Stephen Fox, but the behaviour of Fox does seem to have accorded with the model of the 'masculine', 'bisexual' rake.[40]

The change is that during the eighteenth century effeminacy came to function as a general signal of aristocracy. Sedgwick writes of 'the feminization of the aristocracy as a whole', whereby 'the abstract image of the entire class, came to be seen as etherial, decorative, and otiose in relation to the vigorous and productive values of the middle class'.[41] The impact of this is indicated in

41: Uses of Effeminacy

Michael Rey's study of police records of men accused of same-sex practices in Paris from around 1800:

> to people of the lower class, a noble – powdered, pomaded, refined – was both elegant and effeminate; but that bothered no one as long as the mode of attire remained faithful to the specific superior social condition which its wearer represented. If someone lower on the social scale assumed this costume ... not only did he betray his social condition, but in addition, his effeminacy, by losing its accepted association with elegance and the upper class, became an indication of the wearer's real effeminacy.[42]

I don't agree that what was revealed was 'real effeminacy': rather, it was another cultural mode. However, this does not spoil the relevance of Rey's observation to my argument. The aristocrat was expected to be effeminate, so same-sex passion was not foregrounded by his manner; with lower-class young men, it was otherwise. At the same time, still, the dissolute aristocrat might indulge in any kind of debauchery. The point is that effeminacy overlapped unevenly with same-sex passion. By no means did it constitute its essence; indeed, it had no essence.

As Trumbach suggests, these two models of effeminacy must have interacted in unstable ways.[43] On the one hand, lower-class mollies enjoyed affecting a stylish, aristocratic manner, but at the risk of being thought insolent; on the other, same-sex passion and the upper classes were stigmatized as characteristic of each other. The latter move is made in Tobias Smollett's *Roderick Random* (1748), where Captain Whiffle comes on board ship from a barge as if he were Cleopatra in Shakespeare's play, elaborately attired and perfumed, and followed by his personal surgeon, 'a young man gaily dressed, of a very delicate complexion, with a kind of languid smile on his face, which seemed to have been rendered habitual by a long course of affectation' (the delicate complexion, it turns out, owes more to art than nature). Whiffle's demand that his officers improve their appearance provokes hostility: 'These singular regulations did not prepossess the ship's company in his favour; but on the contrary, gave scandal an opportunity to be very busy with his character, and accusing him of maintaining a correspondence with the surgeon not fit to be named.'[44] Even in such a case, observe, effeminacy does not, *of itself*, signal same-sex passion – the captain has to offer a further affront in order to arouse such an accusation; and, still, the narrator does not altogether confirm it. Same-sex passion figures as a plausible part of an effete aristocratic demeanour.

In Smollett's *Peregrine Pickle* (1751), Pickle seeks out an Italian count and a German baron 'whom he knew to be egregious coxcombs' suitable for subjecting to practical jokes. They get drunk and are discovered in same-sex embraces; the Italian sings 'with infinite grace and expression', but neither of them is otherwise remarked as effeminate. Pickle and his friend Pallet, having a 'just detestation for all such abominable practices', arrange a punishment.[45] The next episode may point us towards some of the anxieties that the instability of effeminacy, as a concept, was provoking. Pickle and Pallet wish to attend a masquerade: because Pallet is a stranger to the town and might get lost, he is persuaded to dress as a woman – on the altogether unconvincing pretext that this will oblige Pickle to attend him 'with more care, as he could not with decency detach himself from the lady whom he should introduce: besides, such a supposed connexion would hinder the ladies of pleasure from accosting, and employing their seducing arts upon a person already engaged' (p. 243). The upshot of this strange project, unsurprisingly, is that Pallet is accosted by a nobleman who takes him for a woman. In this incident, no one is given to same-sex passion; cross-dressing is a convenience and then a mistake. There are legitimate reasons for cross-dressing, the episode seems designed to say; it may be all good clean fun, and conducted by the very men who in the previous episode punish 'abominable practices'.

A cross-sex grid

In so far as there was an enhanced focusing upon effeminacy in relation to same-sex passion around the mollies in the eighteenth century, this did not produce a workable model. In the account of the Vere Street coterie of 1810, two of the most sought after partners were 'an athletic bargeman' and 'a Herculean coal-heaver'. And yet the bargeman and coal-heaver were known, respectively, as Fanny Murray and Lucy Cooper.[46] This will surprise no one familiar with present-day derivatives of the molly-house subculture. It illustrates, precisely, the structural confusion in the idea that same-sex passion is characterized by effeminacy. The Vere Street observer actually expected, he says, same-sex practitioners to be effeminate: 'It is generally received opinion, and a very natural one, that the prevalency of this passion has for its object effeminate delicate beings only.' Fanny Murray and Lucy Cooper perplexed him by indicating otherwise.

What we are seeing here is (1) the determined perception of same-sex practices through a grid of cross-sexual gender roles and (2) the failure of that grid to cope satisfactorily with the complexity of what was happening.

At Harrow School in the 1850s, J. A. Symonds records, 'Every boy of good looks had a female name, and was recognised either as a public prostitute or as some bigger fellow's "bitch".'[47] But if these younger boys were marked as feminine, what were the 'bigger fellows'? And what were the men who appreciated the effeminate mollies? This is the central confusion. If there are two partners in a same-sex liaison, and one is reckoned to be effeminate, what is the other supposed to be? Perceived through the cross-sexual grid, there are two, incompatible answers to this question. (1) They are both sodomites, but one partner is presumptively masculine; this spoils the idea of effeminacy as the defining characteristic of same-sex passion. (2) One partner is 'passive', effeminate and transvestite, and hence the 'real' sodomite; this leaves the other partner as an unspecifiable absence.

Both these potential answers suggest that the notion scholars have attributed to the seventeenth century – that a man might address any subordinate creature – was still offering a relative protection from stigma. The man who took the 'manly' role was either exonerated (to a degree) from the charge of effeminacy, or rendered conveniently invisible.

Overwhelmingly, I suggest, the 'masculine' partner became difficult to conceive, within this model – because the model is designed to explain cross-sex passion and therefore defines men in terms of their propensity to love women. This confusion made it difficult to get any clear fix on the topic. The effeminacy model, therefore, was inhibiting, not producing, what we regard as gay identity. As John Marshall has said, while sexual preference is perceived within the assumption that men are defined by a propen-

sity to be sexually attracted to women, and vice versa, 'any devi-
ations or ambiguities are likely to be regarded as gender anomalies'
– assimilated to the cross-sex grid. Biological males experiencing
same-sex passion might think of themselves as possessing a 'feminine temperament', and men 'with a strong sense of their male
gender identity' might quite easily 'enter same sex sexual relations
without challenging their heterosexual sense of self'. Between the
two, there would be little call for 'a homosexual concept' as such.[48]
Furthermore, it would be difficult to get any clear fix on current
same-sex practice.

'They would get up, dance and make curtsies, and mimic the
voices of women ... Then they would hug, and play, and toy, and
go out by couples into another room on the same floor, to be
married, as they called it.'[49] In this account of the mollies, marriage
implies masculine as well as feminine roles. Did both partners in the
'marriage' mimic women? Perhaps they did, for role-play may be
endlessly inventive. My point is that the framework of interpretation makes it hard for this account to give any specificity to the
'husbands'. Another witness observes mollies 'hugging, kissing, and
tickling each other as if they were a mixture of wanton males and
females, and assuming effeminate voices and airs'.[50] Again, a masculine role is mooted, only to be submerged in the general proposition that everyone present must be effeminate. Norton observes
that the terms of endearment were 'special Sweetheart', 'Husband'
and 'Spouse' and 'there is no recorded use of the term "wife"'. In
molly marriages, he believes, both partners had feminine names and
both were husbands.[51] Trumbach comes upon evidence of this
confusion, though without developing its implications: 'When a
homosexual scandal broke, a man might ask, as Lord Pembroke did
of William Beckford, "what was the exact business, how, when,
and by whom, and with whom discovered? Who passive and who
active ...?" But when an author set out to titillate the public, he
portrayed only misogyny and effeminate passivity.'[52]

The change in the eighteenth century, I believe, was towards
a situation where the masculine/feminine binary structure was
much more clear-cut and much more important; it became both
more necessary and more significant to apply it. This argument is
compatible with the work of Ian Maclean and Thomas Laqueur,
which shows that in a major strand of early modern thought, deriving from Aristotle and Galen, women and men were not reckoned

to be essentially different biologically. Rather, women were taken
to be incomplete versions of men. The danger for the male, on this
thesis, was the disastrous slide back into the female; that is what
was meant by effeminacy. And same-sex passion, so long as it
maintained social hierarchies, was relatively unimportant, might
even be heroic, and at any rate avoided dangerous intimacy with
women.[53] This would explain aspects of the way same-sex passion
was regarded in Shakespeare's time. What changes, then, from
around 1700, is that male and female become polar opposites,
rather than a matter, almost, of degree. This makes sliding between
them inconceivable; each person is essentially one or the other. This
perhaps correlates with Henry Abelove's deduction, from figures of
population growth, that during the eighteenth century vaginal
intercourse gained a more distinct privilege among the range of
sexual practices, with other activities defined, newly, as foreplay.[54]
So masculine and feminine became more fixed in relation to each
other. And hence the determined application of a cross-sex grid to
same-sex practices, despite the evident failure of such a grid to
describe such practices.

Men arrested in Vere Street in 1810 were assaulted with
exceptional violence on the way to the pillory, and particular rage
was aroused by James Cook, 'a big strong fellow': 'his apparently
manly attitude called forth increased wrath, and only the passing of
the wagon prevented his being lynched'. After the pillory, despite
his bleeding and fainting condition, he was still lying on the seat of
the wagon, rather than in the dung on the floor, so 'a coachman
stood up in his vehicle and gave Cook five or six blows with his
whip'.[55] Cook's failure to behave in a cowardly way – to appear
effeminate – was distinctively provoking. The masculine molly
drew attention to the prevailing ideological confusion; such a contradiction in terms was intolerable.

However, and this is crucial, although there was a tendency
to perceive same-sex passion as effeminate, effeminacy still did not
necessarily signal same-sex passion. Masculine and feminine
became more settled categories, but it was not settled which
persons and practices, and in what terms, were to be identified
through that binary structure. Still among sexologists in the late
nineteenth century, George Chauncey, Jr has shown, 'the fact of
active or passive sexual aim' was 'seen as paradigmatic for one's
complete gender role' and 'was at least as important as sexual

object in the social classification of sexuality'.[56] That is to say, a woman would be classified as an invert because of her 'masculine' behaviour – if her sexual object was another woman, that was a confirmatory corollary. Social behaviour was defining, and sexual practice was secondary. Only gradually did homosexual and heterosexual become the distinction that must precede and inform all others, and even then the change was negotiated by making it important to decide whether a homosexual was 'active' or 'passive'. So, up until the time of Wilde, effeminacy and same-sex passion might be aligned, but not exclusively, or even particularly; and the masculine/feminine boundary could be deployed for diverse significations.

These histories help us to see the extent to which sexuality is constructed within culture. This means that we cannot assume that the available images of same-sex passion correspond to the desires, to the fantasies, of individuals. Hence, perhaps, the effeminacy of many male prostitutes in the face of the knowledge that likely clients do not desire effeminacy: certain codes and signals may be deployed as signals of availability, rather than because they are sexually arousing in themselves. (Of course, availability may itself be arousing.) As Norton remarks, 'First and foremost, effeminacy is a form of self-advertisement.'[57] In fact, it may be specially characteristic of gay subculture that 'there is no necessary connection between sexual activities and social roles. ... In other words, if one partner gets fucked, he is not necessarily expected to make the breakfast next morning or act effeminately'. This may well, Gregg Blachford suggests, offer a challenge to normative assumptions in the dominant culture.[58] However, it also indicates that subordinated groups do not entirely control their own representations. It would be rash to suppose that the imagery through which lesbians and gay men make themselves apparent, even to each other, reflects their aspirations. 'It never occurred to any of us to try to be more loveable,' Quentin Crisp remarks.[59] Their manner was not designed to attract men; it was the only one they could envisage, and they developed and reinforced it subculturally. On the other hand, again, social codes and signals feed back into psychic realities; we should expect a complex interaction between representation and desire.

In the final chapter, I discuss the scope for masculine and feminine styles in gay culture today. I do not suppose that we can simply jump out of these powerful organizing structures. Men should be what-is-called-feminine, and women what-is-called-masculine, and vice versa, if they want. The aim is to challenge the rules, not to increase them. Socialized into patriarchal society, we are all trying to make the best of a bad job anyway. As Jonathan Dollimore has remarked, 'the association between homosexuality and femininity is not necessarily insulting to either'.[60] What is untenable and intolerable is the expectation that sexualities must be comprised within and defined through some version of a masculine/feminine binary structure.

Notes

1. Quoted in J. A. Mangan, *Athleticism in the Victorian and Edwardian Public School* (Cambridge University Press, 1981), p. 189.

2. See Richard Ellmann, *Oscar Wilde* (London: Hamish Hamilton, 1987), pp. 57, 220; Holbrook Jackson, in Karl Beckson, ed., *Oscar Wilde: the Critical Heritage* (London: Routledge, 1970), pp. 329–30.

3. *The Nicomachean Ethics of Aristotle*, VII.7, trans. Sir David Ross (London: Oxford University Press), p. 177.

4. Harold Beaver, 'Homosexual signs (in memory of Roland Barthes)', *Critical Inquiry*, 8 (1981), 99–119; Eve Kosofsky Sedgwick, *Between Men* (New York: Columbia University Press, 1985), pp. 83–90 *et passim*; Jonathan Dollimore, *Sexual Dissidence* (Oxford: Clarendon, 1991); Marjorie Garber, *Vested Interests* (London: Routledge, 1992), especially pp. 137–41.

5. Michel Foucault, *The History of Sexuality*, vol. 1, *An Introduction*, trans. Robert Hurley (New York: Vintage Books, 1978), p. 43.

6. See Alan Sinfield, *Literature, Politics and Culture in Postwar Britain* (Oxford: Blackwell and Berkeley: California University Press, 1989), p. 64.

7. *Samson Agonistes*, lines 410–11, in John Milton, *Poetical Works*, ed. Douglas Bush (Oxford University Press, 1969); William Shakespeare, *Romeo and Juliet*, ed. Brian Gibbons, New Arden edn (London and New York: Methuen, 1980), III.i.116.

8. *The Plays of Christopher Marlowe*, ed. Roma Gill (Oxford University Press, 1971), *Tamburlaine*, 1: V.i.174–82.

9. Shakespeare, *Antony and Cleopatra*, ed. M. R. Ridley, New Arden edn (London: Methuen, 1962), I.iv.4–8. See Janet Adelman, *Suffocating Mothers* (New York: Routledge, 1992), pp. 184–92.

10. *Antony and Cleopatra*, II.v.22–3, III.xiii.17, IV.i.1.

11. Shakespeare, *Troilus and Cressida*, ed. Kenneth Palmer, New Arden edn (London and New York: Methuen, 1982), III.iii.216–18.

12. Shakespeare, *Coriolanus*, ed. Philip Brockbank, New Arden edn (London: Methuen, 1976), I.vi.29–32. See Bruce R. Smith, *Homosexual Desire in Shakespeare's England* (Chicago University Press, 1991), ch. 2.

13. Shakespeare, *Henry V*, ed. John H. Walter, New Arden edn (London: Methuen, 1954), IV.vi.24–7. See Alan Sinfield, *Faultlines* (Berkeley: California University Press and Oxford: Oxford University Press, 1992), pp. 127–36.

14. *Dido Queen of Carthage*, I.i.50–3, in Gill, ed., *Plays of Christopher Marlowe*. See Gregory Woods, 'Body, costume, and desire in Christopher Marlowe', in Claude J. Summers, ed., *Homosexuality in Renaissance and Enlightenment England* (New York: Harrington Park, 1992); Jonathan Goldberg, *Sodometries* (Stanford University Press, 1992), pp. 126–37.

15. Alan Bray, *Homosexuality in Renaissance England* (London: Gay Men's Press, 1982), pp. 34, 88, 130–1. See Ed Cohen, *Talk on the Wilde Side* (New York: Routledge, 1993), p. 211.

16. Shepherd, 'What's so funny about ladies' tailors?', *Textual Practice*, 6 (1992), 17–30, p. 21.

17. Smith, *Homosexual Desire in Shakespeare's England*, pp. 13–14, 74–6.

18. See Sinfield, *Faultlines*, pp. 187–92, 215–18.

19. David Halperin, *One Hundred Years of Homosexuality* (New York: Routledge, 1990), p. 25; Huseyin Tapinc, 'Masculinity, femininity and Turkish male homosexuality', in Ken Plummer, ed., *Modern Homosexualities* (London: Routledge, 1992); Stephen O. Murray, 'The "underdevelopment" of modern/gay homosexuality in Mesoamerica', in Plummer, ed., *Modern Homosexualities*.

20. Valerie Traub, *Desire and Anxiety* (New York: Routledge, 1992), pp. 130–8. See Sinfield, *Faultlines*, pp. 66–73.

21. Alan Bray, 'Homosexuality and the signs of male friendship in Elizabethan England', *History Workshop*, 29 (1990), 1–19, p. 14; Goldberg, *Sodometries*, p. 20.

22. Bray, *Homosexuality in Renaissance England*, ch. 4; Randolph Trumbach, 'Sodomitical subcultures, sodomitical roles, and the gender revolution of the eighteenth century: the recent historiography', in Robert Purks Maccubin, ed., *'Tis Nature's Fault* (Cambridge University Press, 1987); and Trumbach, 'Gender and the homosexual role in modern western culture: the 18th and 19th centuries compared', in Dennis Altman, Carole Vance, Martha Vicinus, Jeffrey Weeks and others, *Homosexuality, Which Homosexuality?* (London: Gay Men's Press, 1989).

23. *The Princess of Cleve*, I.i.17–18, 32–3, II.iii.1–2, in Thomas B. Stroup and Arthur L. Cooke, eds, *The Works of Nathaniel Lee* (New Brunswick, NJ: The Scarecrow Press, 1955), vol. 2.

24. William Wycherley, *The Country Wife*, ed. David Cook and John Swannell (London: Methuen, 1975), II.i.520–5.

25. Sir John Vanbrugh, *The Relapse*, ed. Curt A. Zimansky (London: Arnold, 1970), II.523–4.

26. This argument is not incompatible with Sedgwick's, that the ultimate goal of the men is to impress other men; see Sedgwick, *Between Men*, ch. 3. Fops could be associated with sodomitical tendencies, especially in satire; see Shepherd, 'What's so funny about ladies' tailors?', pp. 22–3; Smith, *Homosexual Desire in Shakespeare's England*, ch. 5.

27. Trumbach, 'Gender and the homosexual role', pp. 152, 156. See also Raymond B. Waddington, 'The bisexual portrait of Francis I: Fontainebleau, Castiglione, and the tone of courtly mythology', in Jean R. Brink, Maryanne C. Horowitz and Allison P. Coudert, *Playing with Gender* (Urbana and Chicago: Illinois University Press, 1991), pp. 118–21.

28. Vanbrugh, *The Relapse*, ed. Zimansky, p. 8.

29. See Stephen Orgel, 'Nobody's perfect: or why did the English stage take boys for women?', *South Atlantic Quarterly*, 88 (1989), 7–29; Stephen Orgel, 'The subtexts of *The Roaring Girl*', in Susan Zimmerman, ed., *Erotic Politics: Desire on the Renaissance Stage* (New York: Routledge, 1992); Valerie Traub, 'The (in)significance of "lesbian" desire in early modern England', in Zimmerman, ed., *Erotic Politics*.

30. Trumbach, 'Sodomitical subcultures', p. 118; Trumbach, 'Gender and the homosexual role', p. 150.

31. G. S. Rousseau, *Perilous Enlightenment* (Manchester University Press, 1991), p. 142. Rousseau suggests that six categories of homosexual emerged, pp. 9–13.

32. Bray, *Homosexuality in Renaissance England*, p. 86.

33. Bray, *Homosexuality in Renaissance England*, pp. 92, 104; Rictor Norton, *Mother Clap's Molly House* (London: Gay Men's Press, 1992).

34. Cohen, *Talk*, pp. 245–6; Jeffrey Weeks, *Against Nature* (London: Rivers Oram Press, 1991), pp. 56–60, 64; Oscar Wilde and others, *Teleny*, ed. John McRae (London: Gay Men's Press, 1986), pp. 105–6. Trumbach remarks that many frequenters of molly-houses cannot have been either effeminate or exclusively homosexual in behaviour: Randolph Trumbach, 'London's sodomites: homosexual behavior and western culture in the eighteenth century', *Journal of Social History*, 11 (1977–78), 1–33, p. 18.

35. Norton, *Mother Clap*, p. 203; see also pp. 67, 93, 96–105, 124–7, 131, 184, 188.

36. Ivan Bloch, *Sexual Life in England* (London: Corgi, 1965), pp. 329, 333–4.

37. Norton, *Mother Clap*, pp. 126–7; Cohen, *Talk*, pp. 113–14 (the quotations are from these sources).

38. David Greenberg, 'The socio-sexual milieu of the *Love-Letters*', in Michael S. Kimmel, ed., *Love Letters between a Certain Late*

Nobleman and the Famous Mr Wilson (New York and London: Harrington Park Press, 1990), pp. 96–7.

39. 'Epistle to Arbuthnot', lines 324–9, in Alexander Pope, *Selected Poetry and Prose*, ed. W. K. Wimsatt, Jr (New York: Holt, Rhinehart & Winston, 1961). Horace Walpole was regarded similarly: 'by nature maleish, by disposition female, so halting between the two, that it would very much puzzle a common observer to assign to him his true sex'; quoted by Rousseau, *Perilous Enlightenment*, p. 173.

40. Randolph Trumbach, 'Sodomy transformed: aristocratic libertinage, public reputation and the gender revolution of the 18th century' in Kimmel, ed., *Love Letters*, pp. 117–18; Norton, *Mother Clap*, ch. 9.

41. Sedgwick, *Between Men*, pp. 93.

42. Michael Rey, 'Parisian homosexuals create a lifestyle, 1700–1850: the Police archives', in R. P. Maccubbin, ed., *'Tis Nature's Fault* (Cambridge University Press, 1988), p. 189. Cf. David Kuchta, 'The semiotics of masculinity in Renaissance England', in James Grantham Turner, ed., *Sexuality and Gender in Early Modern Europe* (Cambridge University Press, 1993), pp. 238–41.

43. Trumbach, 'Sodomy transformed', in Kimmel, *Love Letters*, p. 117.

44. Tobias Smollett, *Roderick Random* (London: Dent, 1927), pp. 196, 199, 200. Later in the novel, Earl Strutwell accosts the narrator, argues at length for the admissibility of same-sex passion, and is subsequently said to be notorious for it; effeminacy is not indicated (pp. 305–9). See Rousseau, *Perilous Enlightenment*, pp. 18–24.

45. Tobias Smollett, *The Adventures of Peregrine Pickle*, ed. James L. Clifford (Oxford University Press, 1964), pp. 233–4, 241–3.

46. *The Phoenix of Sodom, or the Vere Street Coterie*, quoted by H. Montgomery Hyde, *The Other Love* (London: Mayflower, 1972), p. 96. See Louis Crompton, *Byron and Greek Love* (London: Faber, 1985), pp. 163–9; Norton, *Mother Clap*, pp. 93, 127 and ch. 12.

47. Jeffrey Richards, ' "Passing the love of women": manly love and Victorian society', in J. A. Mangan and James Walvin, ed., *Manliness and Morality* (Manchester University Press, 1987), p. 113; see also Bartlett, *Who Was That Man?* (London: Serpent's Tail, 1988), p. 126.

48. John Marshall, 'Pansies, perverts and macho men', in Kenneth Plummer, ed., *The Making of the Modern Homosexual* (London: Hutchinson, 1981), pp. 135–6 *et passim*; see George Chauncey, Jr, 'From sexual inversion to homosexuality', *Salmagundi*, 58–9 (1982–3), 114–46, pp. 125–6. A similar predicament has been noted in John Cleland's novel: Kevin Kopelson, 'Seeing sodomy: *Fanny Hill*'s blinding vision', in Summers, ed., *Homosexuality in Renaissance and Enlightenment England*.

49. Bray, *Homosexuality in Renaissance England*, p. 81; Norton, *Mother Clap*, pp. 100–2.

50. Bray, *Homosexuality in Renaissance England*, p. 87.

51. Norton, *Mother Clap*, p. 101.

52. Trumbach, 'London's sodomites', p. 12. Cf. Terry Castle, *Masquerade and Civilization* (London: Methuen, 1986), pp. 45–50.

53. See Ian Maclean, *The Renaissance Notion of Women* (Cambridge University Press, 1980); Thomas Laqueur, 'Orgasm, generation, and the politics of reproductive biology', *Representations*, **14** (1986), 1–41; and Laqueur, *Making Sex* (Cambridge, MA: Harvard University Press, 1990), pp. 123–5.

54. Henry Abelove, 'Some speculations on the history of "sexual intercourse" during the "long eighteenth century" in England', in Andrew Parker, Mary Russo, Doris Sommer and Patricia Yaeger, eds, *Nationalisms and Sexualities* (New York and London: Routledge, 1992).

55. Bloch, *Sexual Life*, pp. 340–1, 341–2.

56. Chauncey, 'From sexual inversion to homosexuality', p. 123.

57. Norton, *Mother Clap*, p. 104.

58. Gregg Blachford, 'Male dominance and the gay world', in Kenneth Plummer, ed., *The Making of the Modern Homosexual* (London: Hutchinson, 1981), p. 199.

59. Quentin Crisp, *The Naked Civil Servant* (1968; New York: Plume, 1983), p. 23.

60. Dollimore, *Sexual Dissidence*, p. 263.

Chapter three

Manly Sentiments

Men and feeling

CHAPTER 2 traced effeminacy through from early-modern Europe into the nineteenth century, mainly in its peculiarly sexual deployments. The masculine/feminine binary structure has, of course, been deployed in far wider cultural structures. By the time of Wilde, the link between the (supposed) feminine and emotional sensitivity, which figures in Shakespeare and still pertains today, had long been the ground of substantial cultural contest. Broadly speaking, in the eighteenth century the cultivation of true feelings, by men as well as women, was proposed as the basis of civilization; in the nineteenth century, there was a new insistence that men be manly – together with a demand that women be domestic. Each of these movements was fraught with the anxieties that cluster, so persistently, around gender constructs in our cultures. In this chapter I trace some of this through some symptomatic texts, in order to map the context within which Wilde and queerness were to occur.

While effeminacy figured leisure-class uselessness (as I have shown), it also embodied aspirations towards refinement, sensitivity and taste. J. G. A. Pocock has demonstrated the emergence, at the end of the seventeenth century, of 'a new ruling elite (or "monied interest") of stockholders and officeholders'. This group required a new justifying mythology: the idea of the ancient virtue of the farmer–soldier was largely superseded by an ideological nexus comprising commerce, leisure and cultivation. The advance of civilization, it was reckoned, required that men compromise with what were regarded as feminine qualities. This was rendered attractive and plausible by a consumer boom, such that 'goods that had been deemed rich men's luxuries in 1540 were being made in so many different qualities and at such varying prices that they came within the reach of everyman'.[1] Fine living and fine feeling seemed to belong together.

'Sentiment' was the watchword: it meant both judgement and feeling, and hence constituted perhaps the most ambitious claim to combine what were regarded as masculine and feminine properties until the 'new man' of today. These aspirations were simultaneously ethical and material. Principles and manners overlapped, as they still do, in concepts like 'decent', 'decorous' and 'civilized'; and, above all, in 'sensibility'. If manliness produced wealth, femininity might show how to consume it elegantly, and how to be a finer human being and more effective citizen.

However, the man of feeling was an insecure construct, always liable to tilt into affectation, self-indulgence and licentiousness. The third Earl of Shaftesbury, in his *Characteristics of Men, Manners, Opinions, Times* (1714), announced the goal of softening the manners of the landed gentleman, but not to the point of inducing 'so much softness or effeminacy as unfits him to bear poverty, crosses or adversity'. Bernard Mandeville, David Hume and Adam Smith strove to discount this threat of weakness, in order to celebrate the advance of reform, prosperity, consumption and comfort.[2]

So uncertain was the sentimental project that commentators had, and still have, trouble discerning when sentiment is being advocated and when it is being satirized. Henry MacKenzie's novel *The Man of Feeling* (1771) has been read innocently, for instance by Brian Vickers, as recommending the spontaneous display of sympathetic benevolent emotion as an ultimate good; John K. Sheriff argues that it is a demonstration of the dangers of unrestrained sensibility in a man.[3] In this writing, feeling is hard to distinguish from mockery of feeling; sentiment tips over into absurd excess. 'I burst into a flood of tears,' the reader is told in Laurence Sterne's *Sentimental Journey* (1768), 'but I am as weak as a woman; and I beg the world not to smile, but pity me.'[4] Both responses are acknowledged as attending upon the womanly man – to smile and to pity. Further, Sterne indulges in what was at once perceived as a disconcerting stream of sexual innuendo. In the case of his *Tristram Shandy* (1759–67), contest around whether the book should be admired or disdained for its indecent travesties, or admired or disdained for its delicate sentiments, began immediately upon publication.[5]

For imagining the feminine as a source of pure feeling did not, of course, produce feminism. As John Mullan observes in respect of novels such as *Pamela* and *Clarissa*, Samuel Richardson 'mythologizes femininity – and, like many male writers before and since, he isolates virginity as its essential representation'. Mullan adds: 'A feminine body is the private place in which the novel finds a responsive confirmation of masculine virtue.' Male sentiment required of women, Margaret Anne Doody remarks, a specially narrow casting as 'extra feminine – all blushes, tears and imbecility – in order to assure the male that he is really being masculine, even if he uses a handkerchief'.[6] In *A Sentimental Journey* the narrator's compulsive flirting with women is not offered in the manner of the devil-may-care rake, nor of the foolish fop. The man of feeling is not seeking anything so clumsy as satisfaction. Sterne's narrator cultivates what he regards as an exquisite teasing: he is the connoisseur of 'a sort of pleasing half guilty blush, where the blood is more in fault than the man – 'tis sent impetuous from the heart, and virtue flies after it – not to call it back, but to make the sensation of it more delicious to the nerves' (p. 169). This process relies upon the greater femininity of the woman, who is expected to collaborate – it is the nakedness of women's hearts that attracts him, the narrator says (p. 155). Masculine philandering colonizes and exploits feminine sentiment – yet at the cost of appearing ridiculous or indecent. This unstable formation could not become the dominant recipe for manliness, but some of it fed into the seductive/disreputable upper-class dandy.

Richard Brinsley Sheridan was keen to mark the boundary between proper feeling and unmanly affectation. In *The Rivals* (1775) he endorses true love in young Absolute while mocking foolish feeling in Faulkland. In *The School for Scandal* (1777) excessive sentiment is hypocritical. Joseph Surface is much given to the expression of fine feelings, for which he is widely admired: 'Joseph is indeed a model for the young men of the age. He is a man of sentiment, and acts up to the sentiments he professes.' But he is involved in intricate scheming with three women, one of whom he means to marry and two of whom he uses; his unmasking is the mainspring of the action. His philandering is typed as feminine because it involves cultivating the company of the women who operate a half-playful surveillance over the scandalous behaviour of others. 'I know there are a set of malicious, prating, prudent gossips, both male and female,' says Sir Oliver Teazle (whose insecurity over his wife obliges him neither to forsake nor to endorse the scandalmongers).[7] 'Gossip' means 'a person, mostly a woman, of light and trifling character, esp. one who delights in idle talk; a newsmonger, a tattler' (*OED*). In 'gossips, both male and female', Sir Oliver marks Joseph as effeminate.

The contrast to Joseph is his brother Charles. He has manifestly rakish characteristics, including, to the delight of the scandalmongers, dissipation of his fortune in manly roistering. None the less, Charles is not altogether a rake. He proves to have his share of genuine, spontaneous sentiment: he will not sell the portrait of his uncle, and gives money to a distant relative ruined by a series of undeserved misfortunes. These manly commitments please his wealthy uncle, so Charles gets the money, the social approbation, and the nice young lady to marry. Joseph is disinherited and exposed as a selfish humbug, putting an end to his adulterous games. He will marry Lady Sneerwell, the chief scandalmonger; the marriage of the Teazles is restored as well. This is conservative, of course: acceptable sentiment correlates with family, inheritance, male bonding, apparent monogamy and traditional male privilege. A production of *The School for Scandal* against the grain would have somehow to validate Joseph's figurative cross-dressing. There is a germ for this in the text: the scandalmongers' malicious wit is the most amusing part of the play and they are lightly treated at the end, so manly feeling is not altogether superior. This is the territory Jane Austen was to work, and that Wilde was to transform by validating the frivolous and knowing stance of the dandified, feminine woman.[8]

Jean-Jacques Rousseau and Mary Wollstonecraft would probably have agreed that all Sheridan's characters are intolerably trivial. Rousseau reoriented the debate by privileging nature as the ground of true feeling, as against urbane, civilized social intercourse, and hence opposed the cult of sensibility; he complained in *Emile* (1762) that 'the exaggeration of feminine delicacy leads to effeminacy in men'.[9] Wollstonecraft also was suspicious of femininity: she wanted to persuade women that 'the soft phrases, susceptibility of heart, delicacy of sentiment, and refinement of taste, are almost synonymous with epithets of weakness'.[10]

Rousseau's idea of education, in *Emile*, is to socialize men and women into conventional gender roles: 'The man should be strong and active; the woman should be weak and passive' – 'You must follow nature's guidance if you would walk aright. The native characters of sex should be respected as nature's handiwork' (pp. 322, 326). For Rousseau, nature is female, but on terms that leave women without power. 'It is men who make Rousseau's journey from corrupted Reason to Nature. It is they who enact the full drama of Reason's transformation so that it reflects and enhances true human nature,' Genevieve Lloyd observes.[11] Actually, Rousseau allows us to see that gender roles are cultural: all the way through, he is manipulating his boy and girl pupils into the behaviour which he claims is natural to them (and which therefore should not require manipulation). Keep your girls busy, he says, for 'idleness and insubordination are two very dangerous faults, and very hard to cure when once established'. Girls 'must be trained to bear the yoke from the first, so that they may not feel it, to master their own caprices and to submit themselves to the will of others' (p. 332). Women are not womanly, it appears, unless you train them to it. And there is the threat, always, that they will get out of hand and, through their sexuality, overwhelm masculine authority. As throughout *Emile*, 'Nature' works only when Rousseau fixes it.

In *A Vindication of the Rights of Woman* (1792), Wollstonecraft opposed bitterly Rousseau's ideas on how women should be educated. She despised conventional femininity – 'that weak elegancy of mind, exquisite sensibility, and sweet docility of manners, supposed to be the sexual characteristics of the weaker vessel' (p. 82). She wanted women to achieve their full humanity, which men were denying them. Wollstonecraft mocks the idea of distinctive masculine virtues. Why the outcry against 'masculine women'? 'If by this appellation men mean to inveigh against their [i.e. women's] ardour in hunting, shooting, and gambling, I shall most cordially join in the cry; but if it be against the imitation of manly virtues, or, more properly speaking, the attainment of those talents and virtues, the exercise of which ennobles the human character', that is another matter (p. 80). What have been called 'manly virtues' are human qualities, the development of which has been withheld from women. However – perhaps for tactical reasons – Wollstonecraft presents a fuller education as a way of fitting women properly 'to fulfil the peculiar duties which Nature has assigned them' – namely those of wife and mother: if women were 'led to respect themselves, if political and moral subjects were opened to them', then this would 'make them properly attentive to their domestic duties' (p. 288). In this aspect Wollstonecraft was 'developing a class sexuality for a radical, reformed bourgeoisie,' Cora Kaplan says, with 'a puritan sexual ethic' for men and women alike.[12]

The initial reception of the *Vindication* was generally favourable, though at the price of Wollstonecraft being termed 'our fair authoress'; however, when she was revealed to have lived scandalously, she was vilified as an amazon. Her book was favoured when it was regarded as delivering women more effectively to bourgeois marriage, feared when the revelations about her life pointed up its more subversive potential.[13]

The dispute between Rousseau and Wollstonecraft shows how by the end of the eighteenth century, with the stakes enhanced by the French Revolution, masculinity and femininity were circulating as the ground for both radical change and extreme reaction. Briefly, reliance on nature, human nature, reason, the passions, masculinity, femininity, even the people, might be either conservative or revolutionary, depending on the context. These supposed entities were both the ground of decorum and the threat to it.

'Misplaced affection' and 'nobler sentiments'

There is no question, of course, of surveying in this book the relations of the Enlightenment, the novel, Romanticism and effeminacy (I discuss the emergence of the idea of literature in the next chapter). But we may begin to see the odds, as they had developed by the mid nineteenth century, when Tennyson published *In Memoriam* (1850), a long, passionate poem about his deceased friend, Arthur Hallam. Provocatively, we might think, the poet goes out of his way to draw cross-sex analogues. He is like a maiden waiting for her fiancé, a poor girl whose heart is set on a social superior, a wife (sections 6, 60, 97); Arthur is compared to an absent fiancée, a deceased wife, a bride leaving her parents' house (sections 8, 13, 40). The effect is to assert male tenderness as part of the fullness of the friend's humanity. These analogues lead towards section 109, where the poet celebrates Arthur's sociability, discrimination, intellect, morals and political wisdom, and credits him also with nurturing skills – with

> manhood fused with female grace
>   In such a sort, the child would twine
>   A trustful hand, unasked, in thine,
> And find his comfort in thy face.[14]

'Female grace' is partly upper-class sensibility, reclaimed for a confident middle class as the proper mode of the gentleman; and partly – as it is elaborated in the action of the child – the woman's nurturing power. Arthur has it all. Section 111 invokes his 'gentleness' and 'noble manners, as the flower / And native growth of noble mind':

> And thus he bore without abuse
>   The grand old name of gentleman,
>   Defamed by every charlatan,
> And soiled with all ignoble use.   (111)

The more the economy depended on brutal entrepreneurs, the more it seemed that the middle classes should evince the sensitivity and responsibility that they imagined had characterized the ancient gentleman.

What is striking is that Tennyson believed he could write in such a manner without fear of a damaging same-sex implication being drawn. This shows the extent to which an element of feminine feeling might still be legitimate. However, two factors complicate the outcome. First, the poetic models available to Tennyson carried sexual resonances. Both his general approach and specific poems suggest the Latin elegy and the Greek pastoral, and these had often accommodated same-sex passion. This embarrassment in classical sources had been registered by Arthur Hallam himself. He derived the idea of intense friendship as an inspiration to virtue from Plato, but felt he had to justify 'that frequent commendation of a more lively sentiment than has existed in other times between man and man, the misunderstanding of which has repelled several from the deep tenderness and splendid imagination of the Phaedrus and the Symposium'.[15] Shakespeare's Sonnets, another evident forerunner of Tennyson's poem, were also regarded with suspicion. Arthur Hallam's father was sensitive on the topic. 'It is impossible not to wish that Shakespeare had never written them', he complained in 1869. 'There is a weakness and folly in all excessive and mis-placed affection, which is not redeemed by the touches of nobler sentiments.'[16]

Second, *In Memoriam* was seventeen years in the writing. By the time it was published, in 1850, the topic was becoming distinctly touchy. *The Times*'s reviewer complained about the tone of 'amatory tenderness': 'Very sweet and plaintive these verses are, but who would not give them a feminine application?' Charles Kingsley, conversely, worked hard to assimilate *In Memoriam* to his idea of Christian manliness:

> Blessed, thrice blessed, to find that hero-worship is not yet passed away; that the heart of man still beats young and fresh; that the old tales of David and Jonathan, Damon and Pythias, Socrates and Alcibiades, Shakespeare and his nameless friend, of 'love passing the love of woman', ennobled by its own humility, deeper than death, and mightier than the grave, can still blossom out if it be but in one heart here and there to show men still how sooner or later 'he that loveth knoweth God, for God is Love!'[17]

Kingsley takes risks here: the Greeks were dangerous ground, and it sounds almost as if the love between Shakespeare and his friend is unnameable. As in the poem, the sweep through to divine love is evidently ambitious; perhaps 'sooner or later' is put in to allow that the process might not be quite secure.

The impact of *In Memoriam*, arguably, derived from its anxious/innocent treatment of same-sex love. By invoking contemporary cross-sex paradigms and ancient same-sex models, Tennyson allowed his poems to risk a (mis)interpretation which he perhaps half courted. For my present purpose, the point is how the culture was poised at the moment where friendship and feminine qualities might become an embarrassment. Later on, Tennyson was at some pains to disavow excessive intimacy with Arthur. In 1889, after the Cleveland Street scandal and the Labouchère Amendment, he wrote a nasty little squib, qualifying his earlier flirtations with gender-bending:

> While man and woman still are incomplete,
> I prize that soul where man and woman meet,
> Which types all Nature's male and female plan,
> But, friend, man-woman is not woman-man.

The theory still holds, it seems, but it has to be distinguished from unacceptable effeminacy. 'Friend' in the last line is patronizing in so far as it addresses the person Tennyson is reproving, but sad if we recall its frequent use in *In Memoriam*.

The Victorians were preoccupied with the proper limits of middle-class manliness. The mid-century shift in the status of feminine sentiment is signalled in two best-selling school stories published in 1857–58. In Frederic W. Farrar's novel *Eric or Little by Little*, manly aspirations are troublesome because they lead Eric into rebellious ways – cheeking the masters, smoking and getting drunk: 'He was full of misdirected impulses, and had a great notion of being manly, which he thought consisted in a fearless disregard of all school rules, and the performance of the wildest tricks.'[18] Eventually he runs away to sea, where life with the manly sailors is violent, degrading and physically punishing. He returns home to die, and his saintly submission is celebrated: 'All was gentleness, love and dependence, in the once bright, impetuous, self-willed boy.' This makes him 'unspeakably winning, and irresistibly attractive' (p. 310). There are wrong kinds of manliness, then, kinds that override proper deference, sensitivity, and Christian submission. However, two other young troublemakers join the army and 'there are not two finer or manlier officers in the whole service' (p. 316). Manliness is not altogether wrong.

At the same time, passionate attachments among boys of the same age are endorsed in *Eric*. The reader's approval is expected when 'stooping down [Eric] kissed fondly the pale white forehead of his friend' who has fainted after being injured (pp. 139–40). When young Eric is 'taken up' by an older boy, however, there is some danger. Even so, the anxiety is not explicitly sexual. A master sees them standing together, intimately but 'very harmlessly', the narrator says, and experiences 'an especial dislike of seeing the two boys together, because he fancied that the younger had grown more than usually conceited and neglectful since he had been under the fifth-form patronage' (p. 103). Insubordination is the acknowledged issue, not sex. Even so, the master's 'especial dislike' leaves an opening; sex may be lurking. For the overwhelming danger, in *Eric*, is failing to repudiate indecent words and rude stories in the dormitory at night. This leads to masturbation: 'Before that evening was over, Eric Williams was "a god, knowing good and evil"', and at risk of 'that burning marle of passion where [other boys] found nothing but shame and ruin, polluted affections, and an early grave' (p. 91). Masturbation is not linked explicitly with intense friendship, but the potential seems to lurk, again, when Eric 'takes up' a younger boy. At one point this lad is 'quietly sitting on Eric's knee by the study fire', but this open physical intimacy – unthinkable in what we now think of as the mainstream English public school ethos – is reported without comment. However, there is a problem: the boys go on to smoke and break bounds to buy beer (p. 178). Physical intimacy is not presented as a problem, but problems seem to occur in its proximity.

Eric aroused disquiet. The *Saturday Review* complained that the boys, 'to the infinite indignation of all English readers, occasionally kiss each other (principally, however, when they are *in articulo mortis*) exchanging moreover such endearments as "dear fellow" and the like'.[19] The objection here is to mawkishness rather than sexuality, though. It is the feminine that falls under suspicion; same-sex issues are absent or, at most, implicit. Both manliness and intimacy figure in Thomas Hughes's *Tom Brown's Schooldays* (1857). Here friendship is a great boon, and no tinge of indecency is allowed to hover around it. The rebellious-masculine and religious-feminine tendencies are initially separate, located in Tom and Arthur respectively. But Arthur's mild influence is gradually absorbed into and contained within Tom's manliness. Tom subsumes both sets of virtues and Arthur proves too feeble/etherial to live. So the problem of effeminacy is magicked away; only Tom, the boy with no more than a proper degree of femininity, survives into manhood. There are specifically effeminate boys – 'miserable, little, pretty, white-handed, curly-headed boys, petted and pampered by some of the big fellows, who wrote their verses for them, taught them to drink and use bad language, and did all they could to spoil them for everything in this world and the next'.[20] But such boys are not allowed to enter the issue of friendship. While manliness wrecks Eric and is retrieved only secondarily in other boys who lack his spiritual potential, Tom Brown incorporates in himself all that a decent chap could require of both manliness and gentleness: a lot of the former, and a decent ration of the latter. In each case, a sexual component in male friendship is disavowed via an acknowledgement that it may appear elsewhere in the system; but *Tom Brown* is the more cautious version, indicating a strengthening anxiety about intense male friendship. In this, it was the more modern of the two books – more modern, indeed, than the period it purported to describe. Coleridge, in his *Aids to Reflection in the Formation of a Manly Character*, David Newsome points out, opposes manliness to childishness; it is maturity. By the time of Tom Brown, it was opposed to effeminacy.[21] Even so, the distinction is not complete. Manly friendship continues as a positive value – but in danger, always, of collapsing into disreputable sensuality.

The men and the boys

The anxieties that attended the publication of *In Memoriam*, *Eric* and *Tom Brown's Schooldays* reflected and contributed to a cult of 'manliness', which swept through the public (private) school system, especially in the form of compulsory, organized sport. By the 1880s, athletic manliness dominated ideas about character-training suitable for boys of all classes; the emotional repression stereotypically associated with the ex-public-school Englishman dates from this point.[22] However, as Sedgwick shows in *Between Men*, male bonding in modern western societies is effected by policing itself against same-sex passion. Effeminacy is not banished by manliness; it is its necessary corollary, present continually as the danger that manliness has to dispel.

We should not expect to unearth any single cause for the Victorian demand for manliness. The key was the assumption that women belonged at home while men should go out into the world. As Joel Pfister observes, 'recent histories of family life, privatization, the body, and gender have established that a middle-class personal life as it consolidated in the mid-nineteenth century made certain assumptions about "family", "private", "public", "masculine", "feminine" and psychological "depth".'[23] The category of psychological space — interiority, sensitivity, privacy — has depended on a strengthened masculine/feminine binary structure. The Industrial Revolution promoted such ideas by moving paid work outside the home, and aspirations towards progress and empire required the notion that men were specially equipped to go out into the world and control it. With Darwinism dominant intellectually, it seemed axiomatic that the superiority of the British race was expressed in its manly men.[24]

The project, all round, was to produce a sense of the place people should be in and a pressure to keep them there: manliness made for deference to the system. It seemed a useful ground on which to incorporate lower-class youth who, it was feared, were physically unfit for imperial rule and given to political disaffection. Such worries were well founded, since many of these people were overworked, undernourished and living in insanitary dwellings.[25] An ideology of manliness was more convenient than attending to the material conditions. Promotional literature for the Boys' Brigade stressed:

> All a boy's aspirations are towards *manliness*, however mistaken his ideas may sometimes be as to what that manliness means. Our boys are full of earnest desire to be brave, true *men*; and if we want to make them brave, true *Christian* men, we must direct this desire into the right channel.... We must show them the *manliness* of Christianity.

'Earnest' here is presumably not a coded allusion to 'uraniste', as some have claimed in relation to *The Importance of Being Earnest*.[26] Pressure to be manly helped to discipline the elite as well as the workers — generally speaking, it was not much fun being an empire-builder without modern medicines.

As we have seen, the more precarious the actuality, the more assertive the ideology; manliness was always fragile. 'Its existence', William Acton wrote in 1857, 'seems necessary to give a man that consciousness of his dignity, of his character as head and ruler, and of his importance, which is absolutely essential to the well being of the family, and through it, of society itself.'[27] With so much hanging upon it, manliness was continually at issue. And it was not, actually, well-adapted to the prevailing social arrangements. At each end of the class spectrum, gender roles were not clear-cut. The lower-class woman probably did work outside her own home, in manufacture or service, while the upper-class woman had so little to do that it was hard to see why she should be located anywhere in particular. She was 'idle, an object to display her husband's wealth, totally dependent economically and politically, a part of his property'.[28] Both cases made it more necessary to assert a domestic role for women. At the same time, manly work was not so clear cut either. The labourer was certainly worth his hire, but his conditions of (un)employment made it hard for him to assert manly dignity; many middle- and upper-class men performed no useful function at all. Loss of self-determination in work may have stimulated male fantasies of control in the family.

Above all, the pretensions and opportunities with which manliness was invested helped to provoke the programme for female emancipation; this led, in turn, to more insistent assertions of masculinity. The idea of women owning property, for instance, produced this kind of argument in a Parliamentary Select Committee in 1867–68: 'the authority of husbands would be diminished by the fact that they did not possess *absolutely* both their own property and the property of their wives'.[29] Authority and property overlap and reinforce each other to the point where the authority of the husband over his wife amounts to a demand that she be his property. In the United States, Joe L. Dubbert finds, 'many men began to feel that too many women were taking too seriously their duties as mothers in pledging to protect America's moral integrity when they criticized sports, agitated for prohibition, became socially and culturally sophisticated, and even became politically informed'.[30] These anxieties, of course, are still with us.

The middle-class public school system was the main site where manliness was supposed to be established. That system did have other priorities. It was convenient for parents, including mothers, who had society tasks to fulfil. Above all, perhaps, it seemed to resolve the dilemma over who was to be recognized as a gentleman, at a time when traditional patterns of deference were in question and new kinds of wealth were being created in the business and industrial sector.[31] But, distinctively, it was to keep men masculine – away from the excessive influence of women – that parents put their male children into public schools. That is why the cruelty, violence and viciousness was tolerated by fathers who, in many cases, had ample reason to know of what was likely to happen to their sons. Parents believed that the capacity to endure physical and psychological hardship with a stiff upper lip was the best thing one could bestow upon a boy-child. The parting of boys from the women who were generally dominant in their childhood, and subjecting of them to systematic brutalization, were not the incidental price of 'a good education'; *they were the point.* Thus boys might develop a man-to-man loyalty, and an insensitivity, suitable for the prevailing pattern of cross-sex relations, and for service to Britain's imperial destiny, or in the law, administration, the army or business.[32]

Yet the very institutions that were supposed to protect men from effeminacy were the ones where same-sex practices flourished.[33] After all, Greek and Roman texts were at the core of the public school curriculum, and they were the place where one might find some treatment of same-sex passion. 'Isn't it really rather dangerous to let boys read Plato,' A. C. Benson wondered, 'if one is desirous that they should accept conventional moralities?' – Benson had read a lot of Plato and knew what he was talking about. Lytton Strachey discovered the *Symposium* at sixteen 'with a rush of mingled pleasure and pain ... of surprise, relief, and fear to know that what I feel now was felt 2,000 years ago in glorious Greece'. Symonds declared that it was a mistake teaching the classics in school.[34] By 1894, Jerome K. Jerome was writing: 'That young men are here and there cursed with these unnatural cravings, no one acquainted with our public school life can deny. It is for such to wrestle with the devil within them; and many a long and agonised struggle is fought, unseen and unknown, within the heart of a young man.' Cyril Connolly found the same contradictory pattern, centred upon Plato, in the early twentieth century.[35]

'If all persons guilty of Oscar Wilde's offences were to be clapped in gaol, there would be a very surprising exodus from Eton and Harrow, Rugby and Winchester, to Pentonville and Holloway,' W. F. Stead remarked in 1895, in response to the Wilde trials; 'But meanwhile public school boys are allowed to indulge with impunity in practices which, when they leave school, would consign them to hard labour.'[36] Commentators generally agree that same-sex practices thrived in public schools. I go further: public schools were crucial in the development of homosexual identity because, despite the official taboo, they contributed, in many instances, an unofficial but powerful cultural framework within which same-sex passion might be positively valued. The poetry of boy-love, towards the end of the nineteenth century, presents the virtues of same-sex passion as elaborated and eroticized versions of the standard public school virtues – service, physical vigour, hero-worship and personal loyalty. The school ethos was seized for just those purposes which it was supposed to be repudiating. The boy-love writer often aspired to join his lad in 'natural' schoolboy activities. 'Philebus' (John Leslie Barford) wrote in *Young Things* (1921):

> Is it unnat'ral that I should joy
>   To join you in the heart of natural things?
> To run and swim and ride with you, my boy?
>   To feel the thrill that sweating effort brings?
> To watch with envious love your limbs' display?[37]

William Johnson Cory (dismissed from Eton in 1872 because of over-intense relations with boys) was unashamedly jingoistic, liked watching soldiers, and composed the 'Eton Boating Song'. He wrote:

> I cheer the games I cannot play;
> As stands a crippled squire
> To watch his master through the fray,
> Uplifted by desire.[38]

Even a crippled squire is a man manqué; he is still capable of being 'uplifted'.

It became very urgent to appear to restrain the same-sex schoolboy subculture that was being produced. Boys were expelled when caught; there was a preoccupation with masturbation; friendships between boys came under suspicion; an eye was kept on unmarried teachers; there was less preparedness to accommodate the mild, gentle or diffident boy.[39] Jeffrey Weeks locates four modes within which same-sex practices may occur: 'the casual encounter, which rarely touches the self-concept'; 'the highly individualised, the deeply emotional, sometimes even sexual, relation between two individuals who are otherwise not regarded, or do not regard themselves, as "deviant"'; the 'situational: activity which may be regarded as legitimate in certain circumstances, for example in schools or the army and navy or prisons'; and fourth, 'a total way of life ... involvement in an identity and sub-culture ... with its own system of values and ideologies'.[40] Only the last amounts to what is generally considered 'homosexuality' today, but the first three might be important precursors for some people, and public schools were ideal for developing them. Various celebrated imperialists, including Cecil Rhodes and General Gordon, married late, were accompanied by boys, and wrote in praise of them. Lord Kitchener, whose World War I poster told British boys that their country needed them, found his own peace with an aide-de-camp.[41]

In 1917, when manliness was at a premium, Alec Waugh caused a scandal by showing in his school novel *The Loom of Youth* that sex between boys was customarily legitimated by older boys ('bloods'), whose athletic accomplishments made them prestigious role models, and taken as a norm. When Jeffries is expelled from Fernhurst school because his liaison with Fitzroy is discovered, he complains bitterly at the unfairness:

> Who made me what I am but Fernhurst? Two years ago I came here as innocent as Caruthers there; never knew anything. Fernhurst taught me everything. ... I heard men say about bloods whose lives were an open scandal, 'Oh, it's all right, they can play football'. I thought it was all right too. Fernhurst made me think it was.[42]

Of course, it is Fernhurst that must expel Jeffries when what he has learnt from it becomes too apparent. Caruthers, the initially innocent central character, finds himself behaving as Jeffries had done: 'As soon as we begin to look on a thing as ordinary and natural, we also begin to think it is right' (p. 101). That is indeed how ideology naturalizes itself. Waugh was removed from the old boys' society at his former school for saying so, and the *Spectator* ran for ten weeks, and the *Nation* for six, a correspondence in which one schoolmaster after another asserted that his school was not like that. *The Loom of Youth* ran through eight reprints in 1917–18.[43]

Idleness and immorality

Manliness was a particularly middle-class preoccupation. The newly-dominant middle class justified itself by claiming manly purity, purpose and responsibility, and identified the leisure class, correspondingly, with effeminate idleness and immorality. I discussed in the previous chapter the developing perception of the aristocracy as generally feminine; leisure-class effeminacy became the counterpart of the claim that usefulness, purity and manly vigour were middle-class virtues.

'The characteristic feature of leisure-class life is a conspicuous exemption from all useful employment,' Thorstein Veblen argued; 'abstention from labor is the conventional evidence of wealth and is therefore the conventional mark of social standing.'[44] Actually, this 'was, to a great extent, a working aristocracy', Geoffrey Best writes; its members were magistrates, directors of banks, railway, canal and dock companies. Men from aristocratic families 'filled the bulk of the higher executive as well as the bulk of the higher legislative positions'.[45] To Lord Goring's father, in Wilde's *An Ideal Husband*, there is too much at stake in the modern world for dandyism – he cannot take Goring with him to Downing Street, he remarks drily, because 'it is not the Prime Minister's day for seeing the unemployed'.[46] Even Lord Illingworth, in *A Woman of No Importance*, is going to be a diplomat. But not having to work was crucial to class ideology; it was (and remains) a key indicator in that very long revolution, not yet accomplished, whereby the old social structure of rank and degree is displaced by one of sheer wealth.[47]

Along with idleness went immorality. 'Purity' was in part a feminist cause, deriving much of its impetus from outrage at the Contagious Diseases Acts of 1864–69, which brutally shamed and punished female prostitutes for what campaigners perceived as the inevitable demands of male sexuality.[48] Middle-class males adopted purity as a way of opposing the effeminate philandering of the upper-class male. In *A Woman of No Importance*, the MP, Mr Kelvil, is making purity the topic of an address to his constituents; he complains that Lord Illingworth 'regards woman simply as a toy' whereas he, Kelvil, believes 'Woman is the intellectual help-meet of man in public as in private life. Without her we should forget the true ideals'.[49] Frank Mort observes:

> Practically, purity usually worked by forging alliances between sections of the evangelical middle-class, the petty-bourgeoisie and the respectable working-class against the

aristocracy. Attacks on the immorality and decadence of aristocratic culture were the staple diet of purity tracts and speeches. They focused popular discontent over the double-standard and the complicity of aristocratic men in child prostitution.[50]

The results were uneven. The earnest rhetoric of purity led campaigners into demands for state regulation; and, as tends to happen, whatever the initial intentions of the reformers, the new laws bore upon the victims rather than the powerful. The purity lobby scarcely touched the upper-class men with whom it had begun; it produced instead the Criminal Law Amendment Act of 1885, which increased penalties for brothel-keeping, raised the age of consent for girls to sixteen, and criminalized male homosexual acts in private.[51] It was (is) not easy to attack upper-class men.

In the face of middle-class validation of work and purity, there were two alternatives for the wealthy and those who sought to seem wealthy. One was to collaborate, appearing useful and good; the other was to repudiate manly, middle-class authority by displaying conspicuous idleness, moral scepticism and effeminacy; in other words, to be a dandy. From Beau Brummell (1788–1840) through to Wilde, the dandy represents the over-refinement and moral laxness that middle-class hegemony ascribed as one way of stigmatizing upper-class pretensions (another way was to regard them as brutal and stupid). He is the inheritor of the effeminate and hence trivial (as they came to appear) characters and preoccupations of Sterne and Sheridan. Like the rake, the dandy might debauch himself in any direction. The change is that it becomes difficult for the upper-class male to appear masculine whatever he does; so the distinction between the rake and the fop disappears. 'Profligate young lords in Victorian novels', Sedgwick observes, 'almost *all* share the traits of the Sporus-like aristocratic homosexual "type", and it is impossible to predict from their feckless, "effeminate" behavior whether their final ruin will be the work of male favorites, female favorites, the racecourse, or the bottle; waste and wastage is the presiding category of scandal.'[52]

Jack and Algernon in *The Importance of Being Earnest* are thoroughly effeminate young men, and this includes their leisured idleness, their indifference to moral conventions, their exploitation of and romantic devotion to women, and suggestions of diverse further profligacies. 'It is awfully hard work doing nothing,' Algernon complains; 'However, I don't mind hard work where there is no definite object of any kind.'[53] The women's demand that their beaux be 'earnest' is a characteristically frivolous play upon prevailing middle-class mores; a further mark of the excessive leisure-class frivolity of all the principals.

This opposition structures *An Ideal Husband*. Mabel Chiltern is teasing when she denies that Lord Goring leads an idle life; 'How can you say such a thing? Why, he rides in the Row at ten o'clock in the morning, goes to the Opera three times a week, changes his clothes at least five times a day, and dines out every night of the season. You don't call that leading an idle life, do you?' (p. 136). Goring appears not just idle, but conspicuously so; he almost, as Miss Chiltern suggests, works at it. Goring's father wants him to marry, and this amounts to an entire repudiation of the dandy programme: 'You must get a wife, sir. Look where your friend Robert Chiltern has got by probity, hard work, and a sensible marriage with a good woman' (p. 217). Goring, too, might become useful and good – Sir Robert is an idealistic and energetic government minister who, though not from an old family, has established himself by affirming, with his wife's specific support, middle-class earnestness. According to the *Times* critic, Chiltern was played by Lewis Waller 'in his manliest and most robust style'.[54] However, Chiltern's manly public-spiritedness correlates with his involvement in a financial swindle; there is a good deal to be said for the idleness and moral flexibility of Lord Goring.

The effeminacy of the dandy, I suggested earlier, derives from a class perception, and does not specially involve same-sex passion. Popular radicalism might invoke the effeminacy of upper-class men in homophobic terms, Crompton points out.[55] But this was not central – generally, Ellen Moers shows, the effeminate dandy was a cross-sex philanderer. In Edward Bulwer's *Pelham* (1828), for instance, the dandy is said repeatedly to be effeminate in respect of his philandering with women (after many flirtations and affairs, he settles to wedded bliss); he is not linked with same-sex practices. *Fraser's Magazine* was against such novels. Are they calculated, it asked, 'to brace up manly energy, and promote heroic virtue? Or rather, have they not an evident tendency to effeminate and enfeeble the mind?'[56]

Attempting to explain how Wilde's dandy characters could

have passed with his first audiences, when they seem so camp to us, was one of the initial springs of my work on effeminacy. Broadly, they are heterosexual philanderers, in the manner described by Moers. Lord Darlington in *Lady Windermere's Fan* tries to persuade Lady Windermere to run away with him. Lord Augustus, in the same play, is especially effeminate. He has been married and divorced several times, and is infatuated with Mrs Erlynne despite evidence of her unreliability. He falls too easily for female charms; he is flabby; men insult him. 'Tuppy', they call him, mocking his ram-ish proclivities. Even in *Dorian Gray*, where the plot springs from the response of Wotton, the dandy, to the attractions of Dorian, Wotton's other involvements seem to be with women. He reflects with wonderment upon Basil Hallward's infatuation with Dorian – 'He remembered something like it in history. Was it not Plato, that artist in thought, who had first analysed it?'[57] Hallward is the homosexual, if anyone in *Dorian Gray* is, but he is not a dandy; he is earnest – moral and hard-working (I return to this in the next chapter).

The history of effeminacy as I have been tracing it – as it runs through the rake, the fop, and the man of feeling – means that the Wildean dandy – so far from looking like a queer – was distinctively exonerated from such suspicions. Because of his class identification, or aspiration, he above all need not be read as identified with same-sex practices. At the same time, however, the dissolute aristocrat might indulge in any kind of debauchery; so while same-sex passion was not ruled in, neither was it ruled out. Cecil Graham, a dandy in *Lady Windermere's Fan* (1892), is open to divergent readings. He becomes very appreciative of Mrs Erlynne: she 'looked very handsome tonight', he says; he has become 'one of her admirers'.[58] Graham, here, could certainly be the heterosexual philanderer. But he appears to have no personal attachments to women, and could equally (in the manner we might associate with some gay men today) be admiring the style with which the stigmatized Mrs Erlynne is managing her re-entry into Society (rather like Judy Garland making a come-back). Asked how long he could love a woman who didn't love him, Graham replies: 'Oh, all my life!' (p. 66). This might indicate either boundless passionate devotion to women, or a preference for relations that never get anywhere. Simply, the representation labelled 'Graham' allows two readings. The critical task is not to resolve such an uncertainty, but to observe the plausible scope of the effeminate dandy. It runs from the exploitative cross-sexual seducer to the witty, off-hand romantic who makes an appropriate marriage; same-sex passion is not clearly indicated, but it is a possibility. Wilde is exploiting the indeterminacy of the dandy image; it represents less a distinct entity than a device for unsettling conventional ideas.

By far the most interesting instance is Lord Illingworth in *A Woman of No Importance*, a success on the fashionable Haymarket stage in 1893, two years before the trials. Illingworth has asked Gerald Arbuthnot, a young clerk whose mother has evidently come down in the world (the father is absent), to become his secretary. 'I took a great fancy to young Arbuthnot the moment I met him,' he says; 'It is because I like you so much that I want to have you with me,' he tells him. Such language sounds amorous to us; indeed, the relationship is like those Wilde liked to form with young men of promise (however, perhaps in a moment of self-perception, Wilde makes Gerald notably dull). But not on the London stage in 1893. It soon transpires that Gerald is Lord Illingworth's son – the outcome of Illingworth's treacherous behaviour towards Mrs Arbuthnot (as she calls herself). This seems to afford a double distraction from any idea of same-sex passion: Illingworth is a cross-sexual philanderer (we see him harassing another woman in the course of the play); and it seems only natural that he should be attached to his son. Indeed, the father–son relationship may seem to justify Illingworth in intensifying his devotion to Gerald. 'The world will know him merely as my private secretary,' he tells the hostile Mrs Arbuthnot, 'but to me he will be something very near, and very dear' (p. 66).

Even so, the situation is strange and uneasy. Illingworth expostulates, to the outraged Mrs Arbuthnot, 'If I were a perfect stranger, you would allow Gerald to go away with me, but as he is my own flesh and blood you won't. How utterly illogical you are!' (p. 69). And yet, are her fears altogether illogical? For the more explicitly heterosexual Illingworth appears, the more he is a selfish cad – having seduced and abandoned Mrs Arbuthnot; and hence the less likely, suddenly, to be drawn to his son by wholesome familial ties. Illingworth discovers 'paternal feelings he never even suspected he had', says one recent reviewer; 'The basis of this change of heart is never dramatized,' notes Kerry Powell.[59] The more Illingworth claims the devotion of a father, the more he may seem to manifest a strange excess of male-to-male attachment. To modern commentators, at least, it 'suggests one of the stereotypes of homosexual relationships: the surrogate father'.[60]

Other characters in *A Woman of No Importance* find little impropriety in the attachment, even though they are unaware that Gerald is Illingworth's son – of the factor that may form his alibi for the audience. 'It means a very brilliant future in store for you. Your dear mother will be delighted,' Lady Hunstanton enthuses (pp. 16–17); evidently she does not hear a same-sex implication. However, Lord Illingworth's amorousness is stronger in drafts of the play, and in some cancelled dialogue the knowing Mrs Allonby seems to be on to something. 'How you delight in disciples!' she teases; 'What is their charm?' Illingworth replies: 'It is always pleasant to have a slave to whisper in one's ear that, after all, one is immortal. But young Arbuthnot is not a disciple ... as yet. He is simply one of the most delightful young men I have ever met.' When Lady Hunstanton reiterates how Illingworth has 'taken such a fancy' to Gerald, Mrs Allonby comments: 'Lord Illingworth would talk about nothing else but Mr Arbuthnot, the whole of yesterday afternoon. He looks on him as his most promising disciple. I believe he intends him to be an exact replica of himself, for the use of schools' (pp. 272, 281). The deleting of such dialogue suggests that Wilde knew that it was open to disturbing interpretation.

There was a further perspective for Mrs Allonby's amusement and Mrs Arbuthnot's disquiet. Leisure-class men did have intimate secretaries, and they didn't turn out to be sons. In 1894, Lord Alfred Douglas's twenty-five-year-old brother, Francis, Viscount Drumlanrig, was found dead from a gunshot wound. Drumlanrig was assistant private secretary to Lord Rosebery, the Foreign Minister, and the Douglas family were convinced that his death was brought about by the pressures of a same-sex relationship with Rosebery.[61]

The dandy figure served Wilde's project because he had a secure cross-sex image, yet might anticipate, on occasion and in the main implicitly, an emergent same-sex identity. The point, again, is not to decide the 'reality' of the 'character' Illingworth. Wilde is exploiting the capacity of the image of the dandy to commute, without explicit commitment, between diverse sexualities. This means, for sure, there will have been those who shared aspects of

Wilde's mind-set and registered such ambiguities. But equally, there must have been very many who did not. Because of, rather than despite, the ambiguity of Illingworth's representation, the image of the queer emerged around and through the figure of Wilde.

The question has been raised, whether we should regard the dandy as a radical disturbance or an instrument of containment. Ellen Moers presents him as a pallid, synthetic imitation of the original Regency figure; Richard Dellamora associates him with 'middle-class uppityism'. Regenia Gagnier agrees that he is a remnant of Regency culture, a creation of the market and the media, but finds him thereby to be a critical force – an outsider, ill-at-ease, 'the man removed from life, a living protest against vulgarity and means–end living'.[62] Each of these judgements may be sustained, for the dandy is not to be understood simply as an actual sociocultural formation. Rather, he was an image, a cultural construct, a site upon which issues of class, culture and sexuality were contested. In Brummell's case, the dandy figured the aggressive otioseness of a court in waiting; as he became more residual, he represented a protest against middle-class hegemony but at the cost, typically, of falling into a stigmatized stereotype.

The implications for gender politics, also, are intricate. 'The feminized male,' Rita Felski acknowledges, 'deconstructs conventional oppositions between the "modern" bourgeois man and the "natural" domestic woman; he is male, yet disassociated from masculine rationality, utility, and progress; feminine yet profoundly unnatural.' The effect is double-edged, however, because a division is presumed 'between the refined and the vulgar, a division that separates the self-conscious aesthete from the common and sentimental herd' – and the latter, often, includes women.[63] This reactionary effect plainly occurs in the treatment of Sybil Vane in *Dorian Gray*. But in Wilde's plays the women are as involved in feminine power as the men, and in unsettling conventional assumptions about gender and sexuality. Mrs Cheveley, in *An Ideal Husband*, is said to have complained that Society is made up of dowdies and dandies. Lord Goring quips: 'She is quite right, too. The men are all dowdies and the women are all dandies, aren't they?' (p. 152). Goring accepts the idea of the dowdy woman, but chivalrously (he no doubt thinks) reapplies it to men: they are dull, plain and domesticated, whereas Society women – such as Mrs Cheveley herself – display dandified leisure-class frivolity. In fact neither is right. In the plays' version of Society, male and female characters, equally, may be dowdily earnest, and may display dandy attributes. Mabel Chiltern keeps pace with Lord Goring's banter; when it comes to a marriage proposal it is he who asks her to 'be serious'. Illingworth and Mrs Allonby spar on even terms (one of her aphorisms is shared with Wotton in *Dorian Gray*: 'The secret of life is never to have an emotion that is unbecoming'). Mrs Erlynne in *Lady Windermere's Fan* gets her way by playing along the male dandies. Wilde undermines earnest middle-class feminism in order to empower feminine, Society women (I discuss this elsewhere).[64]

Deciding whether Wilde's dandies are, in essence, progressive or reactionary is in my view not a feasible project. His comedies have held the stage before basically conservative, boulevard audiences for a hundred years; they afford ample scope for indulgence in deference towards the upper classes. At the same time, successful plays are usually risky; they flirt, at least, with the danger that prevailing values might not be satisfactory, or might not prevail. In the face of such a production, some audience members will retreat into conformity, while others will entertain more radical possibilities. It is a mistake to posit a unitary 'audience response'.[65] The dandy offered the opportunity and the danger that dissident strategies often admit: he disturbed certain orthodoxies at the expense of admitting other regressive implications. The really significant intrusion of the dandy, in the figure of Wilde, was his last, for it marked his transformation into the queer. 'The dandy as effeminate seducer (or, rather, seducee) could be swallowed by the writers of the 'nineties,' Moers remarks, 'but not the dandy as homosexual.'[66]

Catholics, anarchists, Jews, women

Some of the scope for negotiation and contest around effeminacy and the masculine/feminine boundary should now be apparent. As a signifier, effeminacy has been as potent as homosexuality, and perhaps the more so because so flexible and indeterminate; it could be deployed all over the sex/gender system, and carried across into diverse class concerns. As has been often documented, it has been widely attributed to imperial subjects, from Ireland to India – if you want to dominate people, it makes you feel more confident if you declare that it is in their nature to submit.

Effeminacy was used in Protestant hostility to Anglo-Catholicism. Charles Kingsley wrote in 1851:

> In ... all that school, there is an element of foppery – even in dress and manner; a fastidious, maundering, die-away effeminacy, which is mistaken for purity and refinement; and I confess myself unable to cope with it, so alluring is it to the minds of an effeminate and luxurious aristocracy; neither educated in all that should lead them to distinguish between bad and good taste, healthy and unhealthy philosophy or devotion.

There is same-sex stigma in this passage, but it is less important than misogyny and class hostility. Similarly, Anglo-Catholicism was said to appeal especially to 'women, in the artificial and luxurious atmosphere of our wealthier classes'.[67] Same-sex practices might be invoked, especially around monasticism. When the *Norfolk News* got hold of a love letter in 1864 it felt able to declare that such communities 'cannot fail to produce abominations'.[68] But this was a distinct manoeuvre within the more general stigma of effeminacy.

Anarchists also might be stigmatized as effeminate. In W. F. Barry's novel *The New Antigone* (1887) we read of a group of well-to-do anarchists: their conversation was

> high-pitched and then languorous, abounding in prose which apparently exhausted the resources of impassioned verse, yet could not express its meaning to the speaker's satisfaction. Some of the guests were gentle almost to effeminacy, and their out-of-the-way learning contrasted singularly with the mincing, tender tones in which they gave utterance to it.

The narrator finds he 'could remember only the names of women to match these *simulacra* of men'. Effeminacy here means not having a realistic grasp of the world: 'They denied, doubted, disparaged; they had nothing but refined scorn for all that makes life worth living.' And to sustain this mood 'they satirised everything that was not sensuous feeling, that did not feed delightful moments'.[69] Effeminacy correlates with a readiness to overthrow received categories, and with slighting masculine rationality (compare the way hippies were regarded in the 1960s).

Otto Weininger, who wrote *Sex and Character* and then killed himself in 1903 at the age of twenty-three, held that Judaism (by which, he says, he means a tendency of the mind more than a race, people or a religion) 'is saturated with femininity'. This was bad news for Jews, since 'the woman of the highest standard', in Weininger's view, is 'immeasurably beneath the man of lowest standard'. His case has nothing to do with same-sex passion – indeed, Weininger could not allow it to do so, since he was both Jewish and covertly homosexual.[70] Supposedly female qualities are the issue – for instance, 'The congruity between Jews and women further reveals itself in the extreme adaptability of the Jews, in their great talent for journalism, the "mobility" of their minds, their lack of deep-rooted and original ideas, in fact the mode in which, like women, because they are nothing in themselves, they can become everything' (p. 320).

Above all, of course, effeminacy was to do with women. As Linda Dowling has shown, decadence and the New Woman were often attacked in the same breath. These two disruptions to the supposedly natural disposition of masculine and feminine attributes seemed to effect a twin assault on order and decency, on 'vital bonds of state and culture'; they encouraged sex and emotionalism, and, through their alleged rejection of procreative sex, threatened the survival of the race.[71] In 1894 a controversy in *The Times* about problem plays provoked a grumpy editorial: 'The leading doctrine of the New Woman school, which contains a certain number of effeminate males, is that the thing worth living and working for is the free discussion of unsavoury subjects by men and women.'[72] Effeminacy is an aspect of a general dissolution focused upon women. Even as the second of the Wilde trials opened, a rhyme published in *Punch* displays a preoccupation with women as much as men:

'When Adam delved and Eve span'.
No one need ask which was the man.
Bicycling, footballing, scarce human,

All wonder now 'Which is the woman?'
But a new fear my bosom vexes;
Tomorrow there may be *no* sexes!
Unless, as end to all the pother,
Each one in fact becomes the other.
E'en *then* perhaps they'll start amain
A-trying to change back again!
Woman *was* woman, man *was* man,
When Adam delved and Eve span.
Now he can't dig and she won't spin,
Unless 'tis tales all slang and sin.[73]

Effeminacy preceded the category of the homosexual, over-lapped with and influenced the period of its development, and has continued in potent interaction with it. To run the two together prematurely is to miss the specificity of their relations, both in historical sequence and as they overlap. Partly as a consequence of the distinctive negotiation conducted by Victorian feminists (some of whom repudiated the feminine), but especially in the context of the normative demand for manliness, effeminacy might be attached to almost any deviant perspective. It floated free of specific gender issues, becoming available for diverse deployments. It might even be used positively, as I show in the next chapter; it afforded a ready stigma for various purposes, and opportunities for affirmative identification as well.

Notes

1. Joan Thirsk, *Economic Policy and Projects* (Oxford: Clarendon, 1978), p. 179. See J. G. A. Pocock, *Virtue, Commerce, and History* (Cambridge University Press, 1985), pp. 48–9, 114–15.
2. See G. J. Barker-Benfield, *The Culture of Sensibility* (Chicago University Press, 1992), p. 113 and ch. 3.
3. Brian Vickers, Introduction to Henry MacKenzie, *The Man of Feeling* (London: Oxford University Press, 1967); John K. Sheriff, *The Good-Natured Man* (University, Alabama: Alabama University Press, 1982), ch. 6. Sheriff's reading is accepted by Barker-Benfield, *The Culture of Sensibility*, p. 144.
4. Laurence Sterne, *A Sentimental Journey* (London: Oxford University Press, 1928), p. 35.
5. On the reception of *Tristram Shandy*, see John Mullan, *Sentiment and Sociability* (Oxford: Clarendon, 1988), pp. 147–58.

6. Mullan, *Sentiment and Sociability*, pp. 67, 89; Margaret Anne Doody, 'Vibrations', *London Review of Books*, 5 August 1993, p. 12.

7. *The Works of Richard Brinsley Sheridan* (London: Chatto & Windus, n.d.), pp. 255, 245. Wilde thought of setting *The Importance of Being Earnest* in Sheridan's time. On gossip, see also Simon Shepherd, 'What's so funny about ladies' tailors?', *Textual Practice*, 6 (1992), 17–30, p. 27.

8. See Alan Sinfield, ' "Effeminacy" and "femininity": sexual politics in Wilde's comedies', *Modern Drama*, 37 (1994).

9. Jean-Jacques Rousseau, *Emile*, trans. Barbara Foxley (London: Dent, 1911), p. 329.

10. Mary Wollstonecraft, *A Vindication of the Rights of Woman*, ed. Miriam Brody Kramnick (Penguin: Harmondsworth, 1975), p. 82.

11. Genevieve Lloyd, *The Man of Reason* (London: Methuen, 1984), p. 64.

12. Cora Kaplan, 'Wild nights: pleasure/sexuality/feminism', in Nancy Armstrong and Leonard Tennenhouse, eds, *The Ideology of Conduct* (New York: Methuen, 1987), pp. 163–4.

13. Barker-Benfield, *The Culture of Sensibility*, pp. 364–82.

14. Alfred Tennyson, *In Memoriam*, in *The Poems of Tennyson*, ed. Christopher Ricks (London: Longmans, 1969). See Alan Sinfield, *Alfred Tennyson* (Oxford: Blackwell, 1986), ch. 5.

15. Arthur Henry Hallam, *The Writings*, ed. H. Vail Motter (New York: Modern Language Association, 1943), pp. 158–9; see Richard Dellamora, *Masculine Desire* (Chapel Hill: North Carolina University Press, 1990), ch. 1. Hallam's interest in Plato is more significant than we might think, since he had been little attended to in the eighteenth and early nineteenth centuries; see Louis Crompton, *Byron and Greek Love* (London: Faber, 1985), pp. 285–92.

16. Sinfield, *Alfred Tennyson*, pp. 127–9.

17. John D. Jump, ed., *Tennyson: The Critical Heritage* (London: Routledge, 1967), p. 185; see Sinfield, *Alfred Tennyson*, pp. 143, 151.

18. Frederic W. Farrar, *Eric or Little by Little* (London: Ward Lock, n.d.), p. 77. See also Richard Jenkyns, *The Victorians and Ancient Greece* (Oxford: Blackwell, 1980), pp. 285–91.

19. H. Montgomery Hyde, *The Other Love* (London: Mayflower, 1972), p. 131.

20. Thomas Hughes, *Tom Brown's Schooldays* (London: Dakers, n.d.), p. 146. See Joseph Bristow, *Empire Boys* (London: Harper-Collins, 1991), pp. 60–4 and ch. 2; Robin Gilmour, *The Idea of the Gentleman in the Victorian Novel* (London: Allen & Unwin, 1981), ch. 3. Hughes presents his novel as a tribute to Rugby School, but actually *Eric* is closer to the ethos of Thomas Arnold: when he was headmaster (until 1842), there was a 'tendency to

emotionalism and to passionate friendship' (David Newsome, *Godliness and Good Learning* (London: John Murray, 1961), p. 83).

21. Newsome, *Godliness and Good Learning*, pp. 36–7, 83, 196–7; Alison Hennegan, 'Personalities and principles: aspects of literature and life in *fin-de-siècle* England', in Mikuláš Teich and Roy Porter, eds, *Fin de siècle and Its Legacy* (Cambridge University Press, 1990), p. 191. On the ambiguous scope of friendship, see Robert K. Martin, 'Knights errant and gothic seducers: the representation of male friendship in mid-nineteenth-century America', in Martin Duberman, Martha Vicinus and George Chauncey, Jr, eds, *Hidden from History* (New York: Penguin, 1989); Crompton, *Byron and Greek Love*, pp. 72–82, 187–93. Cf. Lillian Faderman, *Surpassing the Love of Men* (London: Junction Books, 1980).

22. Newsome, *Godliness and Good Learning*, pp. 26–7 and ch. 4; in J. A. Mangan and James Walvin, eds, *Manliness and Morality* (Manchester University Press, 1987): Jeffrey Richards, ' "Passing the love of women": manly love and Victorian society', pp. 102–4; John Springhall, 'Building character in the British boy: the attempt to extend Christian manliness to working-class adolescents, 1880–1914', pp. 62–8. In fiction: Jeffrey Richards, *Visions of Yesterday* (London: Routledge, 1973), chs 3–5, then taking the topic on into film; Bristow, *Empire Boys*.

23. Joel Pfister, *The Production of Personal Life* (Stanford University Press, 1991), p. 2.

24. J. A. Mangan, 'Social Darwinism and upper-class education in late Victorian and Edwardian England', in Mangan and Walvin, eds, *Manliness and Morality*, p. 142.

25. Walvin, 'Social Darwinism', pp. 251–8; Bristow, *Empire Boys*, p. 182.

26. Quoted by John Springhall, 'Building character in the British boy: the attempt to extend Christian manliness to working-class adolescents, 1880–1914', in Mangan and Walvin, *Manliness and Morality*, pp. 55–6. On 'uraniste' see Sinfield, ' "Effeminacy" and "femininity" '.

27. Jeffrey Weeks, *Sex, Politics and Society*, 2nd edn (London: Longman, 1989), p. 39; and see Ellen Moers, *The Dandy* (London: Secker, 1960), pp. 308–14. Hence, Weeks suggests, the penchant for sexual relationships based on class exploitation: here the man had a status advantage.

28. Margaret Coulson, 'The struggle for femininity', in Gay Left Collective, eds, *Homosexuality: Power and Politics* (London: Allison & Busby, 1980), p. 23.

29. Rachel Harrison and Frank Mort, 'Patriarchal aspects of nineteenth-century state formation: property relations, marriage and divorce, and sexuality', in Philip Corrigan, ed., *Capitalism, State Formation and Marxist Theory* (London: Quartet, 1980), p. 88.

See George Chauncey, Jr, 'From sexual inversion to homosexuality', *Salmagundi*, 58–9 (1982–3), 114–46, pp. 139–42.

30. Joe L. Dubbert, 'Progressivism and the masculinity crisis', *Psychoanalytic Review*, 61 (1974), 443–55, p. 447.

31. Gilmour, *The Idea of the Gentleman*, p. 182; Geoffrey Best, *Mid-Victorian Britain 1851–75* (London: Fontana/Collins, 1979), pp. 276–8.

32. J. R. de S. Honey, *Tom Brown's Universe* (London: Milington, 1977), pp. 203–29; Bristow, *Empire Boys*, pp. 82–9; Christine Heward, *Making a Man of Him* (London: Routledge, 1988); Dellamora, *Masculine Desire*, pp. 195–6. And T. C. Worsley's *Barbarians and Philistines* (London: Robert Hale, 1940) is still powerful.

33. See Edouard Roditi, 'Fiction as allegory: *The Picture of Dorian Gray*', in Richard Ellmann, ed., *Oscar Wilde*, Twentieth Century Views (Englewood Cliffs, NJ: Prentice-Hall, 1986), p. 59 (cited hereafter as Ellmann, *Wilde*, Views); Dellamora, *Masculine Desire*, p. 196.

34. Norman Vance, *The Sinews of the Spirit* (Cambridge University Press, 1985), p. 188; Michael Holroyd, *Lytton Strachey* (London: Book Club Associates, 1973), pp. 101–2; for Symonds's view, see H. Montgomery Hyde, *The Other Love* (London: Mayflower, 1972), pp. 118, 137–8. See also Jenkyns, *The Victorians and Ancient Greece*, pp. 280–92; Crompton, *Byron and Greek Love*, pp. 85–98; Eve Kosofsky Sedgwick, *Between Men* (New York: Columbia University Press, 1985), pp. 176–7.

35. Timothy d'Arch Smith, *Love in Earnest* (London: Routledge, 1970), p. 58; Cyril Connolly, *Enemies of Promise* (1938; London: Deutsch, 1973), pp. 217–19.

36. Quoted in H. Montgomery Hyde, *The Trials of Oscar Wilde* (London: William Hodge, 1948), p. 359, Ivan Bloch, *Sexual Life in England* (London: Corgi, 1965), p. 347.

37. Smith, *Love in Earnest*, p. 176.

38. Newsome, *Godliness and Good Learning*, pp. 85–8; see Smith, *Love in Earnest*, pp. 4–11.

39. Honey, *Tom Brown's Universe*, pp. 167–96, 339; Richards, ' "Passing the love of women" ', pp. 111–13; Springhall, 'Building character', pp. 62–3.

40. Jeffrey Weeks, *Coming Out* (London: Quartet, 1977), pp. 33–5.

41. Hyde, *Other Love*, pp. 126, 175, 182; Richards, ' "Passing the love" ', pp. 107–13.

42. Alec Waugh, *The Loom of Youth* (London: Grant Richards, 1917), p. 60. See David Alderson, 'Male homosexuality and Englishness 1895–1918', unpublished dissertation, University of Sussex, 1991.

43. Alec Waugh, *The Early Years of Alec Waugh* (New York: Farrar, Strauss, 1963), pp. 119, 117.

44. Thorstein Veblen, *The Theory of the Leisure Class* (New York: Mentor, 1953), p. 44.
45. Best, *Mid-Victorian Britain*, pp. 275, 263; see C. Wright Mills, introduction to Veblen, *Theory*, p. xv.
46. Oscar Wilde, *Two Society Comedies: A Woman of No Importance, An Ideal Husband*, eds Ian Small and Russell Jackson (London: Benn, 1984), p. 249.
47. Gilmour, *Idea of the Gentleman*, p. 8; Dellamora, *Masculine Desire*, pp. 197–9.
48. Philippa Levine, *Victorian Feminism 1850–1900* (London: Hutchinson, 1987), pp. 132–3; and see Edward Bristow, *Vice and Vigilance* (Dublin: Gill & Macmillan, 1977).
49. Wilde, *Two Society Comedies*, p. 30.
50. Frank Mort, *Dangerous Sexualities* (London: Routledge, 1987), p. 113. Judith R. Walkowitz finds that 'The crucial conflict seems to have been between the older male libertine ethos and mid-Victorian social and medical modifications of that ideology': Judith R. Walkowitz, *Prostitution and Victorian Society* (Cambridge University Press, 1980), pp. 80–1.
51. See F. B. Smith, 'Labouchere's amendment to the Criminal Law Amendment Bill', *Historical Studies*, 17 (1976), 165–73; Mort, *Dangerous Sexualities*, pp. 126–30; Dellamora, *Masculine Desire*, pp. 199–205.
52. Sedgwick, *Between Men*, pp. 174–5.
53. Oscar Wilde, *'The Importance of Being Earnest' and Related Writings*, ed. Joseph Bristow (London: Routledge, 1992), p. 46.
54. Quoted in Wilde, *Two Society Comedies*, p. 131.
55. Crompton, *Byron and Greek Love*, pp. 307–8.
56. Moers, *Dandy*, pp. 81, 172. See Regenia Gagnier, *Idylls of the Marketplace* (Aldershot: Scolar Press, 1987), pp. 67–90; Hyde, *Other Love*, p. 139; Weeks, *Sex, Politics and Society*, pp. 110–11.
57. Oscar Wilde, *The Picture of Dorian Gray*, ed. Isobel Murray (Oxford University Press, 1981), p. 36; and see pp. 101–2.
58. Oscar Wilde, *Lady Windermere's Fan*, ed. Ian Small (London: Benn, 1980), p. 60.
59. Pat Moorman, reviewing a Royal Shakespeare Company production, *Brighton and Hove Leader*, 26 March 1992, p. 26; Kerry Powell, *Oscar Wilde and the Theatre of the 1890s* (Cambridge University Press, 1990), p. 71.
60. Wilde, *Two Society Comedies*, Introduction, p. xxv.
61. Hyde, *Other Love*, pp. 166–7; Gagnier, *Idylls*, p. 206.
62. Moers, *Dandy*, pp. 294–308; Dellamora, *Masculine Desire*, p. 198; Gagnier, *Idylls*, p. 7, and see p. 82.
63. Rita Felski, 'The counterdiscourse of the feminine in three texts by Wilde, Huysmans and Sacher-Masoch', *PMLA*, 106 (1991), 1094–1105. See Elaine Showalter, *Sexual Anarchy* (London: Bloomsbury, 1991), ch. 9.

64. *An Ideal Husband*, Wilde, *Two Society Comedies*, p. 251; *A Woman of No Importance*, Wilde, *Two Society Comedies*, p. 84; Wilde, *Picture of Dorian Gray*, p. 84. See Sinfield, ' "Effeminacy" and "femininity" '.
65. On such complications of interpretation, see Alan Sinfield, 'Private lives/public theatre: Noel Coward and the politics of homosexual representation', *Representations*, 36 (Fall 1991), 43–63.
66. Moers, *Dandy*, p. 312.
67. *Charles Kingsley: His Letters and Memories of His Life*, ed. Frances Kingsley, 2 vols, 10th edn (London: C. Kegan Paul, 1881), vol. I, p. 201; *The Rock*, 29 April 1898; quoted in David Hilliard, 'Unenglish and unmanly: Anglo-catholicism and homosexuality', *Victorian Studies*, 25 (1983), 188, 190, 181–210.
68. Hilliard, 'Unenglish and unmanly', pp. 191–4, 196, 198.
69. William Francis Barry, *The New Antigone*, 3 vols (London: Macmillan, 1887), III, 130–1.
70. Otto Weininger, *Sex and Character* (New York: AMS, 1975), pp. 306, 302. See Martha Nussbaum, 'The softness of reason', *The New Republic*, 13 and 20 July 1992, p. 27; Hans Mayer, *Outsiders* (Cambridge, MA: MIT Press, 1982), ch. 5.
71. Linda Dowling, 'The decadent and the New Woman in the 1890s', *Nineteenth-century Fiction*, 33 (1979), 434–53, p. 438.
72. Quoted in Wilde, *Two Society Comedies*, p. xx.
73. *Punch*, 27 April 1895, p. 203.

Chapter four

Aestheticism and Decadence

Sweetness and light

'HOW did the association of homosexuality with creativity arise?' J. E. Rivers asks, in his study of Proust and his context. 'It arose partly from the belief that an interest in the "finer things of life – art, music, poetry, fashion, and so on – is a feminine characteristic, and from the corresponding belief that "homosexuals" are more feminine than "heterosexuals". Both beliefs are relatively recent in Western society but were firmly established in Proust's time.'[1] In 1886, however, in *Affinities: A Romance of Today*, an Australian novel set in the period of Wilde's aesthetic phase, Rosa Praed presents a decadent 'Oscar Wilde' character as marked not by same-sex, but by cross-sex passion. It would be wrong, Michael Hurley has shown, to read this Wildean figure as 'really' homosexual; such a subject is, rather, 'an effect of the discourses which circulate in the *post-trial* figure of "Wilde"'.[2] The challenge in *Affinities* comes from the non-sexual comradeship of the women characters.

Aestheticism became a component in the image of the queer as it emerged, but it is a mistake simply to read this attitude back before the Wilde trials. Despite his own inability to see Wilde as queer at the time, Frank Harris in 1916, thirty years after the event, linked Wilde's early success to 'a small minority of passionate admirers' who 'for the most part' were 'persons usually called "sexual inverts"'. These men had been corrupted by public school and Oxbridge; they were 'epicene' and 'naturally enough ... usually distinguished by a certain artistic sympathy'.[3] Harris doesn't offer any names, and other biographies give little sense of any such group. As the self-conscious use of the term 'sexual inverts' indicates, Harris is effecting a retrospective consolidation of the queer image – and an early instance of the allegation that this or that institution is run by a 'gay mafia'.

The idea of the aesthetic as effeminate is grounded in the fact that literature, and poetry especially, has, since the time of the Romantics, been in a state of conflict around imputations that there is something intrinsically feminine in its constitution. Very many poets and novelists have been women, despite the attempts of academic English to write them out of the story, and a hint of effeminacy lurks around many male writers. In the nineteenth century this provoked a spate of disavowals. Often it was claimed that only false literature is feminine; in 1870 Alfred Austin lamented that whereas great art is 'manly', those were 'feminine, timorous, narrow, domesticated' times, and hence inclined to produce feminine poetry.[4] The issue was even more anxious in the United States, where more tends to hang upon manliness. In the mid nineteenth century the fashionable writer Nathaniel Willis observed: 'It is the women who read. It is the women who are the tribunal of any question aside from politics or business. It is the women who give or withhold a literary reputation.' Henry James, Ann Douglas points out, felt he had to insist 'to the reading public, and himself, that fiction, the traditional province of women, be accorded all the seriousness of history, the customary province of men'.[5]

This anxiety cannot easily be set aside, for it is neither incidental nor aberrant but fundamentally constitutive. The modern conception of poetry developed as the alternative ethos within the dominant nineteenth-century, middle-class ideology of utilitarianism and political economy, the market and empire. How was poetry to be defined in relation to those powerful concepts? Three approaches emerged: relegation, incorporation and marginalization. Many people were inclined, simply, to dismiss poetry as frivolous; in the perspective of making the world run efficiently, it seemed a trivial concern (this is relegation). Others demanded that it should sing the progress of trade and manufacturing (incorporation). The third idea, which generally won out, was that poetry should ascend into an autonomous, visionary realm, allegedly above the ideology of utilitarianism and political economy, the market and empire, in which exquisite personal sensations and spiritual intuitions might be expressed. I call this third idea *marginalization* because, although it asserts for poetry a transcendent (non-political) status, it is at the expense of quarantining it from the main concerns of economic and political life.[6]

The assertion of a distinctive kind of importance for literature was a project of middle-class dissidence. Since the late eighteenth century, when enclosures, the factory system and urbanization helped to provoke the Romantic movement, the middle class has thrown up a dissident fraction partly hostile to the hegemony of that class. The line runs through the Pre-Raphaelites, the decadent and aesthetic movements, Fabianism, Modernism, Bloomsbury, public-school communists, Leavisism, the New Left, feminism, the peace and green movements. Characteristically, middle-class dissidence constitutes poetry, literature, the spirit, nature, personal religion, intimate and family relations as 'the human'; it sets them over against mechanical, urban, industrial and commercial organization in the modern world.

And since manliness is celebrated as the proper inspiration, validation and necessary condition of trade and manufacturing, the protest of art takes, in counterpart, a feminine role. Consider Matthew Arnold's phraseology: sweetness and light versus philistines and barbarians. The latter two sound like the real men. The middle-class tendency to regard aristocrats (barbarians) as effeminate causes Arnold to pause; he acknowledges that they have 'gifts and graces'. But only to the superficial eye, the grace is only 'outward': more fundamentally, barbarians are associated with 'all manly exercises'. Even aristocratic women, 'the feminine half', for all their 'charming gifts', would be better for 'a shade more soul'.[7] Faced with a contradiction over which is to be feminine, poetry or the aristocracy, Arnold opts for poetry.

Literary dissidence accepts – in the main very gingerly – a touch of the feminine. Its invocation of a 'human' protest depends on a strategic deployment of the feminine: of culture against brutality, the spirit against the system, style against purpose, personal emotion against compulsion. Hence the commonplace that the great writer is androgynous. There mustn't be too much of the 'wrong' sex, though, because that undermines the credibility of the work. The trick in artistic dissidence is to appropriate sufficient of the radical aura of androgyny, without more than is necessary of the disabling stigma.

Literary culture depends, then, upon an effeminacy which it also needs to disavow. Through the nineteenth century, this provoked a spate of awkward repudiations and negotiations. Charles Kingsley, in his 'Thoughts on Shelley and Byron' (1853), declared that 'the age' is 'an effeminate one', and that this may be seen from the popular preference for Shelley over Byron. Kingsley finds in Byron 'the sturdy peer proud of his bull neck and his boxing, who kept bears and bull-dogs, drilled Greek ruffians at Missolonghi, and "had no objection to a pot of beer"'; all this went, it seems, with a strong sense of moral law. Of course, we know now that Byron had sexual relations with both women and men; the point is not what he did or didn't do but the need for literary culture to set boundaries between itself and the unacceptably effeminate. The bad opposite of Byron, in Kingsley's view, is Shelley: his nature 'is utterly womanish. Not merely his weak points, but his strong ones, are those of a woman. Tender and pitiful as a woman; and yet, when angry, shrieking, railing, hysterical as a woman. The physical distaste for meat and fermented liquors, coupled with the hankering after physical horrors, are especially feminine.'[8]

The need to discriminate acceptable kinds of artistic sensitivity may be observed in W. F. Barry's novel *The New Antigone*. The central figure, Glanville, exhibits 'a certain air of distinction, of dainty though not effeminate carefulness in his attire'.[9] Dainty carefulness is all right – artists are different from other men; but not to the point of effeminacy, the narrator at once insists. The distinction correlates with a healthy approach to life and art:

> he was free, ironical, and, as the critics said sometimes, joyously pagan. What he painted was full of life; life, running over at the brim, energetic, bold, adventurous, taking the infinite resources of existence for granted. But his pictures had in them nothing sensuous or over soft; they did not represent joy as the intoxication of a Silenus, still less did they affect the *morbidezza*, the pallid waxen tints which in their excessive refinement denote that the artist has sought beauty in decline and is enamoured of consumption. Glanville's art was healthy; one might almost have called it, to use the philosopher's jargon, optimist. (I, 148)

A contest is implied, about the values that should inform art and life, and it is gendered: energetic, bold and adventurous health is contrasted with the 'sensuous', the 'over soft', 'beauty in decline'.

While many writers tried to disavow effeminacy, or negotiated it hesitantly, a line of nineteenth-century poets purposively cultivated it. Up till the publication of *In Memoriam*, Tennyson made little effort to protect himself from such an accusation. The delicacy of expression, cultivation of exquisite sensations and evocations of feminine experience in his early poetry bespoke a critique of a brutally purposeful ideology of utilitarianism, political economy and machinery. However, even his supporter in this project, William Johnson Fox, was defensive: 'A considerable number of the poems are amatory; they are the expression not of heartless sensuality, nor of a sickly refinement, nor of fantastic devotion, but of manly love.'[10] The Pre-Raphaelites occupied the platform of feminine delicacy when Tennyson vacated it, in mid-century – to the annoyance of Robert Browning. 'I hate the effeminacy' of Rossetti and his 'school', he said; 'the men that dress up like women, – that use obsolete forms, too, and archaic accentuations to seem soft – fancy a man calling it a lilý'.[11]

In the twentieth century, Bloomsbury is the obvious example of how the feminine may be positively valued by some men. When E. M. Forster declared that public school products have 'well-developed bodies, fairly developed minds, and undeveloped hearts' he was explicitly preferring the feminine to the masculine.[12] In *Howards End* (1910), Forster distinguishes the Wilcoxes and the Schlegels. The former represent imperial and business enterprise: they produce the wealth of the country, but are sadly vulgar, clumsy and dishonest. The Schlegels represent a finer sensibility: they are artistic, not altogether English, gifted with human understanding, sincerity and even sexual spontaneity. And they are feminine. Margaret says theirs is a 'female house' – 'it was irrevocably feminine, even in father's time'; whereas the house of the Wilcoxes, the empire-builders, is 'irrevocably masculine'.[13] (Both, of course, are middle class: the Schlegels admit to living off money made by people like the Wilcoxes.) Effeminacy could be endorsed – despite the whole pressure of patriarchy – by a sufficiently confident cultural formation. Of course, it was patriarchal pressure that made effeminacy an excellent way of bucking the system.

Aestheticism and decadence

In the dissidence encoded in aesthetic effeminacy, Wilde saw his great opportunity. In his commonplace book in 1874, when he was twenty, he endorsed Keats's and Swinburne's 'effeminacy and languor and voluptuousness which are the characteristics of that "passionate humanity" which is the background of true poetry'. But this does not justify Ellmann's assumption that Wilde was in some sense always queer. Wilde's friend J. E. C. Bodley said that 'intimacy' with Walter Pater as a student at Oxford had turned Wilde into an 'extreme aesthete'; and this phrase, Ellmann adds, was 'in context almost a euphemism for homosexual'.[14] 'Almost a euphemism' invokes (without addressing) my whole argument about who hears what.

The aesthetic movement took off from the ideas of Pater. To be sure, he wrote indiscreet letters to an undergraduate who was reputed to have engaged in same-sex practices, and there are features in his work that strike us as infused with scarcely disguised homosexual feeling. But, as Richard Jenkyns says, those features will have been opaque to most of Pater's early readers, and perhaps to Pater himself.[15] Like Johann Winckelmann, as Pater presents him in an essay (1867), he 'nurtured and invigorated' his Hellenic temperament 'by friendships which kept him always in direct contact with the spirit of youth'.[16] But that doesn't make Pater 'really' homosexual. And even if he did experience same-sex desire in something like a modern mode, our quest is not for the essence of this or that individual's sexuality, but for the cultural patterns through which people may have understood their sexualities. As with *In Memoriam*, we need to bear in mind that Pater could not have published what he did if a same-sex construction was likely. His importance lies not in a possible covert or submerged homosexuality, but in his articulation of a framework that did not depend on such categories. His whole point is that Hellenic art is unaware of sex in a Freudian sense – 'still uninfected by any spiritual sickness', innocent of 'any sense of want, or corruption, or shame' (pp. 182, 221). Though always implicit, these malaises entered western culture later, starting with tragedy, and then thrived within Christianity. 'The beauty of the Greek statues was a sexless beauty; the statues of the gods had the last traces of sex.

Here there is a moral sexlessness, a kind of ineffectual wholeness of nature, yet with a true beauty and significance of its own' (pp. 220–1). In Pater's view, Hellenic art *is* the ground of same-sex passion, but also of an aesthetic, asexual serenity. So aestheticism does not, as in the later stereotype, stand in for same-sex passion; it produces it, but in a 'sexless' mode.

Pater's theory served to consolidate the structural double-think in Classics, since Winckelmann, whereby it has served as a conduit for same-sex passion while at the same time disavowing any such concern. At a key moment in Mary Renault's novel *The Charioteer* (1953), Laurie approaches and then evades revelation when he shows Andrew his copy of Plato's *Phaedrus*. 'I haven't read this one,' Andrew says. 'I thought it was the *Phaedo* for a minute, we did that at school.' The *Phaedo* was a safe text, the *Phaedrus* not. 'What's it about?' Andrew asks, allowing Laurie a second chance to reveal or conceal himself: 'Well, primarily, it's about the laws of rhetoric.'[17] There were acceptable and unacceptable Plato texts, and acceptable and unacceptable ways of addressing them. (Further uses of Plato in *The Charioteer* and Forster's *Maurice* are discussed in chapter 6.)

To be sure, the aesthete was regarded as effeminate – but not, so far as I can see, as distinctively homosexual. That was lurking in potential; for some people it was more; but excessive concern with women was still the mainspring. George du Maurier established the image of the aesthete in a series of cartoons in *Punch* in 1880–81, initially with Swinburne mainly in mind; this seems to be where Wilde got the idea. Of the four instances reprinted in illustrations by Martin Fido in his book *Oscar Wilde*, just one plays upon a same-sex anxiety. The artist Maudle, a Wilde-like figure, tells Mrs Brown how consummately lovely her son is. He wants to be an artist; 'Why should he *Be* anything?', Maudle asks; 'Why not let him remain for ever content to *Exist Beautifully?*' The caption concludes: '*Mrs Brown determines that at all events her Son shall not study Art under Maudle.*'[18] However, this hostility is qualified by the earlier specifying of Mrs Brown as a 'Philistine from the country', implying that a more sophisticated woman would not be disconcerted. Two of these cartoons encourage readers to entertain a question about the aesthete's sexual potency. In one, a limp figure declines the proposal of a swim: 'Thanks, no. I never bathe. I always see myself so dreadfully foreshortened in the Water, you know!' In another a bride and groom admire a fine china tea-pot. 'It is quite consummate, is it not?' he asks, languid yet eager. 'Oh, Algernon, let us live up to it!' she exclaims, eyeing the spout intensely. Neither of these suggests homoeroticism. A fourth cartoon represents the aesthetic poet and artist as objects of excessive admiration by Society women.

In a review of Wilde's *Poems* (1882) Thomas Wentworth Higginson, a puritanical New England minister and champion of women's suffrage, complains not that Wilde might be interested in boys, but that his effete writing has made him attractive to 'women of high social position'. Higginson expects women to be 'guardians of the public purity', but the poems contain 'offences against common decency'.[19] Higginson compares Whitman, but not straightforwardly. The latter may appear manly, but his poetry sounds 'hollow' because Whitman 'never personally followed the drum'. Similarly Wilde, at the moment when Ireland 'needs every wise head and brave heart she has ever produced', chooses 'to cross the Atlantic and pose in ladies' boudoirs or write prurient poems which their hostesses must discreetly ignore' (Sir Philip Sidney would not have acted so). But there is a contrast: 'Whitman's offences rest on a somewhat different ground and need not here be considered. Mr Wilde may talk of Greece; but there is nothing Greek about his poems.' Higginson's point is that being intense and 'Greek' about male bonding, in the mode of Whitman, is problematic – it has awkward same-sex resonances; but being feminine is unacceptable – because it means having too much to do with women. In fact, Higginson himself was proud to acknowledge a passionate friendship; hence, we may suppose, his wish to address these matters.[20] My argument is not that there is no embarrassment around aestheticism and homosexuality at this date, but that we should discern confusion rather than covertness. Ellmann's 'almost a euphemism' suggests (or *almost* suggests!) that these people really had our conceptual framework, and we just have to decode their utterances, as their initial readers are supposed to have done. Rather, they were at the point of stumbling upon our framework, and the confusion is the interesting part.

Patience or Bunthorne's Bride, which W. S. Gilbert wrote in 1881, focuses upon the sex life of the aesthete. The poet Bunthorne is passionately in love with Patience the milkmaid, and for this reason scorns the devotion of twenty love-sick maidens in 'aesthetic draperies'.[21] This produces a static situation, so to get the plot going a second aesthetic poet appears, Grosvenor, and he too turns out to be one for the ladies. Bunthorne complains: 'The damozels used to follow me wherever I went; now they all follow him!' (p. 119). So the manifest image of the aesthetic poet is that of lady-killer: he desires and is desired by women, and no one is interested in the dragoon guards. The latter retrieve the situation by abandoning their uniforms, dressing like the poets and striking aesthetic poses, though with 'stiff, constrained and angular attitudes' (p. 121). The main implication, then, is that the effeminate men do better with women than the manly men do.

Commentators have proposed one same-sex allusion in *Patience*:

> Then a sentimental passion of a vegetable fashion must excite your languid spleen,
> An attachment *à la* Plato for a bashful young potato, or a not-too-French French bean.[22]

There is no reason, I believe, to associate same-sex passion with vegetables; the lines surely say that one might love a vegetable and it would have to be in a platonic – non-sexual, non-meaty, blood-less – way; hence 'not-too-French' – not too lusty. The seriousness of the aesthete's attachments is brought into question, but the implication is narcissistic, not homoerotic; this is the Plato who prefers an ideal world. So Grosvenor admires himself in a mirror and Bunthorne says he craves admiration (p. 124). Finally, Bunthorne is left gazing affectionately at a lily, the only one without a partner: there is something self-defeating about his involvement with women. The Freudian pattern that associates narcissism and homosexuality is still some years ahead, however. More strikingly, the whole set-up is what we would call camp – and specially the supposedly manly singing and dancing dragoons. Vain and pompous in their splendid uniforms, and about their attractiveness to women, they don't seem too virile either. Aesthetic effeminacy is not limited to aesthetes.

George Bernard Shaw displays a comparable delight in overthrowing simple categories in *Candida*, written in 1894–95, on the eve of the Wilde trials. Marchbanks is the stereotype of the effeminate poet:

He is a strange, shy youth of eighteen, slight, effeminate, with a delicate childish voice, and a hunted tormented expression and shrinking manner that shew the painful sensitiveness of very swift and acute apprehensiveness in youth, before the character has grown to its full strength. ... He is so uncommon as to be almost unearthly; and to prosaic people there is something noxious in this unearthliness, just as to poetic people there is something angelic in it. His dress is anarchic.[23]

The issue in the play is Marchbanks's competition for the love of Candida; his rival is her conventionally manly husband. She chooses the husband – not because of his manly strength, though, but because he is the weaker of the two and therefore needs her more. The Shavian paradox is that the immature Marchbanks, with his excessive attachment to a woman, is the stronger man; the effeminate poet is presented as a critique of masculine purposefulness.

Richard Dellamora writes, 'In the nineteenth century, "effeminacy" as a term of personal abuse often connotes male–male desire'.[24] But that 'often' must not be extended to an assumption that effeminacy was read, customarily, as meaning same-sex passion, or vice versa. It *might* do this, for some people, and in some contexts, but it was by no means a settled correlation. Henry Labouchère (sponsor of the 1885 criminalization of male same-sex acts in private) turned against Wilde in July 1883, and wrote of him as 'the epicene youth' at Oxford and 'an effeminate phrase-maker'. This – virtually but not altogether – associates aestheticism with same-sex passion. However, that was not what Labouchère had in mind eighteen months earlier, in December 1881, when he was helping to promote Wilde's tour of the United States. He declared then, in a three-page article, that hyper-aestheticism might be just what America needs as antidote to its hyper-materialism.[25] Effeminacy was still flexible, with the potential to refute homosexuality, as well as to imply it.

Decadence, similarly, lingers trembling on the brink of homosexuality. Cesare Lombroso had claimed in *The Man of Genius* (1864, trans. 1894) that hereditary degeneration might explain diverse phenomena, and this offered a convenient way of perceiving effeminate aristocratic excess. Wilde plays on the idea in

An Ideal Husband when he has Lady Markby enquire: 'Dear Duchess, and how is the Duke? Brain still weak, I suppose? Well, that is only to be expected, is it not? His good father was just the same. There is nothing like race, is there?' (pp. 137–8). In Joris-Karl Huysmans's novel *Against Nature* (*A Rebours*, 1884), Des Esseintes, an aristocrat from an old family, gets a new house, decorates it exotically, dresses up eccentrically and shows himself off. He then becomes a recluse, using his wealth to indulge in a sequence of elaborate decor renovations and aesthetic experiences, with periods of sexual debauchery in between. Moving from excess to excess, he cultivates disdain for everyone else, transgression of respectable norms, exquisite bodily sensation, hypochondria, art, literature (culminating in Baudelaire and Mallarmé), religiosity, and physical and mental collapse. Aestheticism, it appears, derives from aristocratic decadence. Yet degeneracy achieves a certain validity in *Against Nature*, embodying a febrile, romantic, bohemian-aristocratic intensity of living. 'One hardly knew at times whether one was reading the spiritual ecstasies of some medieval saint or the morbid confessions of a modern sinner,' the narrator says in *Dorian Gray*.[26] In the last analysis, *Against Nature* prefers decadence to vulgarity; a culminating statement asserts that while the aristocracy has never had 'enough money to pay for all the dark venereal pleasures of besotted descendants of the old families', the new aristocracy of wealth is even worse, resulting in 'the suppression of all intelligence, the negation of all honesty, the destruction of all art'.[27]

Max Nordau's *Degeneration* (1893) admits no such undertow of respect for the decadent. Nordau believes that society should be an organism composed of productive cells. The word 'decadence', he alleges, 'denotes a state of society which produces too great a number of individuals unfit for the labours of common life'; they are 'enemies of all institutions which they do not understand, and to which they cannot adapt themselves'.[28] Degeneration is associated with idleness, immorality, aristocracy and aestheticism. Nordau supports this by proposing a relation between genius and insanity; he complains, in particular, that degeneracy is being perversely endorsed in contemporary literature: 'Degenerates are not always criminals, prostitutes, anarchists, and pronounced lunatics; they are often authors and artists' (p. vii). The culprits cover quite a spectrum – Wagner, Tolstoy, Ibsen, Nietzsche, Zola. Huysmans's

Des Esseintes is an obvious case – 'physically an anaemic and nervous man of weak constitution, the inheritor of all the vices and all the degeneracies of an exhausted race', Nordau says (p. 302). And Wilde has a chapter to himself: he is the chief English aesthete, a man whose ideal of life is inactivity (pp. 317–22).

The degeneracy critique did not pass unchallenged. An article in the *Spectator* in 1889 considered the charge that young men were becoming 'softs' – playing 'ladylike' games such as tennis; there had been letters about it in the *Standard*. The writer acknowledged that, owing to medical science, 'there is a child in almost every large family who, on evolution principles, ought not to be alive, and, of course, when he reaches twenty, he avoids all violent exertion'. Some of these unfortunates tend to a 'vicious laziness' like that of 'savages' and to a 'selfish voluptuousness of life'. None the less, the *Spectator*'s writer professed faith in the continuing vitality of young people, remarking that tennis, while offering opportunities for trivial flirtation, demands considerable exertion. Further, 'a large proportion of this kind of "softs" finds a useful place in the world, monopolises, or nearly monopolises, its lighter or half-intellectual work, and breeding a powerful progeny with a tendency towards thinking, benefits the race, which, be it remembered, tends of itself to revert to animalism'.[29] Like Arnold and Wilde, in their differing degrees, the author asserts culture over trade and manufacturing by validating an element of effeminacy.

In the debate over decadence, same-sex passion is still only a minor and indeterminate element. In *Against Nature*, 'the men becoming less manly' (p. 17) is a crucial factor, but it is still not clearly demarcated from dependence upon women, or from general debauchery. For one of his more adventurous exploits (there is an awful lot of interior decoration), Des Esseintes picks up a young street boy and takes him to a brothel. The madam suggests that his attachment to the boy is sexual: 'No, you're wide of the mark there,' he says, 'very wide of the mark' (p. 81). His aim is to make the boy into a murderer by leading him into tastes which he cannot afford to satisfy. Sex figures more as Des Esseintes becomes more bored. He takes up with a circus acrobat, seeing in her 'the agile, vigorous charms of a male': he goes 'to the point of imagining that he for his part was turning female' (p. 111). But the acrobat is disappointing, treating him to 'none of those rough, athletic caresses he at once desired and dreaded', so he can only resume 'the man's part he had momentarily forgotten; his feelings of femininity, of frailty, of dependence, of fear even, all disappeared' (p. 112). However, it is a special moment when he is picked up by an effeminate boy. This is not, he says, what he was seeking, but he became fascinated:

> Des Esseintes slackened his pace, taking thoughtful note of the youth's mincing walk. From this chance encounter there had sprung a mistrustful friendship that somehow lasted several months. Des Esseintes could not think of it now without a shudder; never had he submitted to more delightful or more stringent exploitation, never had he run such risks, yet never had he known such satisfaction mingled with distress. Among the memories that visited him in his solitude, the recollection of this mutual attachment dominated all the rest. (pp. 116–17)

The juxtaposition here is just that I quoted earlier from Michael Rey's article, where he shows how the effeminacy of an aristocrat is taken for granted, but not that of the lower-class hustler.[30] Des Esseintes is effeminate, but 'the youth's mincing walk' signals same-sex interests. So, generally in *Against Nature*, Des Esseintes is implicated in same-sex passion only when he elects to be. This episode appears as his ultimate debauchery, a climactic feature of decadent aestheticism. But he is by no means a queer personality, in the way that the Wilde trials were to establish.

Even Nordau, despite his determination to show the corruption of decadent aestheticism, makes almost nothing of same-sex practices. 'Vice looks to Sodom and Lesbos, to Bluebeard's castle and the servants' hall of the "divine" Marquis de Sade's *Justine*, for its embodiments,' he writes (p. 13). But there is just this *one sentence* on Sodom and Lesbos. It is a single item in one paragraph of *Degeneration*, in a list of diverse behaviours and attitudes – including zoophilia, for instance, 'excessive love for animals' (p. 315). No argument or instance involving same-sex passion is developed. Wilde is criticized, but not for this. His aesthetic attire is attacked on the utilitarian ground that the proper function of adornment is to attract the opposite sex, whereas Wilde's 'strange costume ... excites disapproval instead of approbation' (p. 318). In ignoring the imperative that each sex should dress to attract the other, Wilde is opting out of normal sexuality; but not, apparently, into another sexual domain. Effeminacy, here, correlates with degenerate leisure-class uselessness and its perverse ratification in aestheticism, but scarcely with same-sex passion. John Stokes is suitably circumspect when he remarks that 'morbid', a key term in the decadence debate, 'was also sometimes adopted as a provocative euphemism for homosexuality'; the instance he quotes is from 1905.[31]

Ellmann says that the English edition of *Degeneration* (1895) was 'exploiting the Wilde case', but the translation of this long work must have been in train well before the trials began. Opportunity to refer to Wilde's homosexuality occurred in the new German edition of 1896, but the only relevant addition is this note:

> My readers will surely know the shocking fate that befell this unfortunate man in 1895. I should have preferred to have avoided making any mention of Oscar Wilde, [rather than seem to] be placing my foot on a vanquished man who [already] lay bound on the floor. But although he was sentenced to hard labour [lit.: 'to severe gaol'], the English may have banned his plays from their theatres and his books from their bookshops, it is not so easy to erase his name from the social history of our time. Oscar Wilde remains the most informative embodiment of a mentality [*Denkweise*] which has played a part in modern spiritual life and which is still embraced by no small number of degenerates and their imitators. Consequently it seemed impossible to pass him by in silence and with averted gaze.[32]

Nordau does not appear surprised at Wilde's 'fate', but nor does he say 'I told you so' – what has happened to Wilde is 'shocking' and 'unfortunate'. He retains the chapter *despite* the revelation of homosexuality, because of the significance of Wilde's writings. Of course, we do not have to assume that Nordau is being altogether straightforward; nevertheless, it is plain that he does not consider homosexuality to be a central aspect of his theme, decadence.

Hostility to effeminate aestheticism and decadence was not ill founded. For a while, in certain circles, Wilde and others succeeded in establishing a dissident cultural formation around them. The manly purposefulness of industry and empire were challenged by an idleness and amorality that claimed the authority of art and class. Thus art was rendered politically effective, in the face of assumptions that it was frivolous or should be incorporated. The price was a link with a class whose influence was declining, and an aestheticism that despised explicit political responsibility.

Picturing Dorian Gray

Wilde's self-fashioning took two phases. In his dress he stressed aestheticism until his return from the USA in 1882; then he took up the dandy manner. This shift, from aesthete to dandy, enacts a change in class identification. The aesthete – it is apparent in *Patience* and *Candida* – is almost a bohemian. He lives on the edge of society, and the dragoons are annoyed partly by his upstart status. However, the (perceived) effeminacy of the aesthete offered another possibility: a conflation with the (perceived) effeminacy of the leisure class. For Huysmans, the connection could be presumed; to Nordau it was a matter for complaint. For Wilde, it was the dream ticket: a conjunction of art and the leisure class, in opposition to middle-class, philistine, masculine practicality. The ground of the association would be uselessness and amorality, and above all, the stance that linked them through the idea of leisured idleness: effeminacy. To the Reverend Richard A. Armstrong, it was a potent combination. He inveighed against 'writers of elegant and glittering literature, that lies on drawing-room tables, who gloss over evil, and make vice seem pretty and refined ... There are plays upon the boards, patronised by rank and fashion, which deal a deadly blow at maiden modesty and manly purity.'[33]

Leisured decadence was more promising as a base for the artist than bohemian exclusion, Wilde must have thought. 'The best work in literature is always done by those who do not depend upon it for their daily bread,' he wrote to an aspiring writer, 'and the highest form of literature, poetry, brings no wealth to the singer.' Regenia Gagnier sees this as the key to Wilde's manner: 'The late-Victorian dandy in Wilde's works and in his practice is the human equivalent of aestheticism in art; he is the man removed from life, a living protest against vulgarity and means-end living.'[34] Wilde worked hard (paradoxically) to establish it. 'The condition of perfection is idleness,' he declared; 'Dandyism is the assertion of the absolute modernity of Beauty.' The aesthetic critic, in his account, sounds like an idealized version of the leisured gentleman: 'Calm, and self-centred, and complete, the aesthetic critic contemplates life, and no arrow drawn at a venture can pierce between the joints of his harness. He at least is safe. He has discovered how to live.'[35] The defensive tone in this assertion indicates that Wilde is engaged in an ambitious venture.

Of course, most aristocrats were not interested in art, except perhaps as conspicuous consumption; they were busy ordering other people around (occupying positions of responsibility), hunting, shooting and fishing, and trying to maintain their estates (often by marrying new money or adopting modern business practices). The overlap between art and class was produced by Wilde, especially, through his theory and his representations of leisured idleness, sensibility, luxury, insouciance and natural superiority. This idea may be observed in the making in *The Picture of Dorian Gray* (1890).

The artist, Basil Hallward, is not presented as a dandy, or as effeminate (though he has an artist's long hands); he is, in fact, thoroughly in earnest about art and life. He instantiates a pre-Wildean idea of the artist as intense and sincere. He insists that to him Dorian is 'simply a motive in art', and laments his inability to influence him for the better.[36] This places Hallward entirely at odds with the dandy, Wotton; so one of them claims art and the other leisure-class insouciance. Neither of them combines the two, in the manner that Wilde was proposing. Such a new combination, it seems, is to be the contribution of Dorian. He, apparently, is the third term, merging art and leisured accomplishment. It is Dorian who says: 'For the canons of good society are, or should be, the same as the canons of art. Form is absolutely essential to it' (p. 142). 'Life has been your art. You have set yourself to music. Your days are your sonnets,' Wotton tells him (p. 217). Many young men 'saw, or fancied that they saw,' in Dorian 'a type that was to combine something of the real culture of the scholar with all the grace and distinction and perfect manner of a citizen of the world' (p. 129). 'Or fancied that they saw' is an important qualification: Dorian is not actually the effortlessly graceful person the other characters imagine – any more than the frantic Alfred Douglas was to be.

Camille Paglia says 'Dorian *becomes* Lord Henry'; she imagines a sinister power of 'homosexual generation'.[37] However, dandy manipulations of young men are almost never successful in Wilde's writing. Dorian is urged by Wotton to adopt 'a new Hedonism', but he becomes stupidly infatuated with Sybil Vane and guilt-ridden after abandoning her. His troubles arise from sentimental self-indulgence and want of intelligence and self-control, not from aestheticism and amorality. The painting registers his guilt, but does not control it; it merely prevents it from showing in his body. So although Dorian seems to reject Hallward, he retains his spiritual intensity; that is why he cannot tolerate Hallward remaining alive. This is not the insouciance that Wotton himself instantiates and had wanted combined with art in the person of Dorian. Murder, Wotton remarks, 'is always a mistake. One should never do anything that one cannot talk about after dinner' (p. 213). Dorian arrives at disaster not because he abjures conventional moral principles but because he remains under their sway. The alignment of art and leisure is broached, but not attained.

To accomplish this theme, it is not necessary for Wilde to make any of his characters homosexual; that is the burden of my argument so far. In the nexus of aestheticism, decadence and leisure, as Wilde received it, that is an optional extra. In *Dorian Gray* no one exactly meets the bill – though, as I will argue in a moment, the whole book is pervaded with queerness. Lord Wotton has the aristocratic decadence and exercises over Dorian the strange influence that sets the plot going, but his sexual involvements seem to be with women (pp. 101–2). Basil Hallward is in love with Dorian, but apparently not in a sensual way.

> The love that he bore him – for it was really love – had nothing in it that was not noble and intellectual. It was not that mere physical admiration of beauty that is born of the senses, and that dies when the senses tire. It was such love as Michael Angelo had known, and Montaigne, and Winckelmann, and Shakespeare himself.

We might be inclined to read this list simply as a coded allusion to queerness, but Dorian adds: 'Yes, Basil could have saved him' (p. 119). This is the theory Pater draws out of Winckelmann: the same-sex lover is precisely opposed to sensual excess – Dorian kills Hallward because he can't cope with his steady virtue. Careful commentators have seen this. 'That Dorian might have had sexual relations with Lord Henry, or even with his portraitist, Basil

Hallward,' Hans Mayer opines, 'seems excluded by the text.' Dorian's milieu, Dellamora observes, is homosocial rather than homosexual.[38]

Hallward comes closest to same-sex passion and is an artist, so we have one correlate in the Wildean queer image. But he is also idealistic and moralizing; other factors are disposed elsewhere – immoral debauchery (Dorian), and amoral, leisured insouciance (Wotton). The queer image refuses to cohere – refuses to meet our expectation that there will be a character in the twentieth-century Wildean image. This is an original move – more exciting than the more popular idea that Dorian, somehow, must be like gay men today.

Dorian is represented (in chapter 11) as repeating the debaucheries of Huysmans's protagonist in *Against Nature*, but there is no clear reference to anything that corresponds to the latter's same-sex experiences. He is accused of ruining the reputations of numerous women and of having corrupted young men, but the vice of one of these is specified as taking 'his wife from the streets', and of another as fraud. What Wilde had wanted, he said, was 'to surround Dorian Gray with an atmosphere of moral corruption. Otherwise the story would have had no meaning and the plot no issue. To keep this atmosphere vague and indeterminate and wonderful was the aim.'[39] Of course, that does not rule out same-sex passion, but neither does it make possible a secure labelling of Dorian's vice. Mayer thinks it has more to do with drugs than homosexuality; for Showalter, what happens to the picture suggests a venereal disease (she supposes that to be a special problem for homosexuals).[40]

A vice that would very well fit what happens to Dorian's picture is masturbation. His sins would 'mar its beauty, and eat away its grace. They would defile it, and make it shameful' (p. 119). Edward Thring said that as a consequence of masturbation 'the face loses its frank and manly expression'; Dean Farrar wrote, in 1862, of the masturbating boy: 'Within these two years he has lost – and his countenance betrays the fact in his ruined beauty – he has lost the true joys of youth, and known instead of them the troubles of the envious, the fears of the cowardly, the heaviness of the slothful, the shame of the unclean.'[42] Hallward can hardly believe the rumours about Dorian because such signs are absent: 'Sin is a thing that writes itself across a man's face. It cannot be concealed. People talk sometimes of secret vices. There are no such things. If a wretched man has a vice, it shows itself in the lines of his mouth, the droop of his eyelids, the moulding of his hands even' (pp. 149–50). The effects are of course shifted on to Dorian's picture. He is said to have been narcissistically drawn to it; now it will 'bear the burden of his shame' (p. 105); he recalls the erstwhile 'stainless purity of his boyish life' (p. 122). Henry Maudsley (generally a more advanced thinker) said 'these degenerate beings' – masturbators – become

> sullen, silent, and indisposed to converse at all; but if they do enter into conversation, they reveal delusions of a suspicious or obscure nature. They believe themselves subjected to strange influences, especially in the night, and sometimes that unnatural offences are practised upon them. Their minds seem to dwell much on such disgusting subjects ... the body is usually much emaciated, notwithstanding they eat well.[42]

Wotton's initial challenge to Dorian is framed in similar terms, though with a different evaluation: he accuses Dorian of 'self-denial' which

> broods in the mind, and poisons us. ... The only way to get rid of a temptation is to yield to it. Resist it, and your soul grows sick with longing for the things it has forbidden to itself, with desire for what its monstrous laws have made monstrous and unlawful. ... you have had passions that have made you afraid, thoughts that have filled you with terror, day-dreams and sleeping dreams whose mere memory might stain your cheek with shame – (p. 18)

Masturbation was not generally linked with same-sex passion. The danger was said to be physical exhaustion and psychological self-absorption. In fact, the solitary secrecy, the evasion of surveillance, was the principal objection, Ed Cohen suggests.[43]

My aim here is not to find a new clue to the hidden mystery of Wilde's novel but to indicate how tricky it is to get any fix on Dorian Gray's vices. The Victorians placed emphases that we do not place, saw vices where we see trivia, allowed confusions where we would expect clarity. The book should be viewed not as the cunning masking of an already-known queerness, but as reaching out towards formulations of same-sex experience that were, we keep observing, as yet nameless. Wotton is intrigued by Hallward's worship of Dorian: 'how strange it all was! He remembered something like it in history. Was it not Plato, that artist in thought, who had first analysed it? Was it not Buonarroti who had carved it in the coloured marbles of a sonnet-sequence? But in our own century it was strange' (p. 36). In part, no doubt, the questioning manner is a strategy to introduce the topic cautiously to a general public. But also, in 1890, it displays Wotton entertaining a new possibility, exploring a new kind of sensibility. It is not reasonable to assume that any idealistic stance was either hypocrisy or self-deception on Wilde's part, or on that of other same-sex apologists. *Dorian Gray* is helping to constitute just those terms in which we might wish, subsequently, to read it.

These possibilities are the more enticing because of the way Wilde managed, continually, to anticipate himself. As Bartlett remarks, 'Dorian Gray was imagined in 1890. Wilde first met Douglas in January or June 1891. ... He was a fiction, one that already existed in his books.' And 'Dorian's fatal punishment, lying dead, a wrinkled husk of a man,' Joseph Bristow suggests, 'anticipates Wilde's own in Reading Gaol'.[44] This is not uncanny; it is because Wilde's culture and his writing were propelling him, and all of us, towards the coherence that we observe in his life and writing; towards an image which as yet he could only intuit.

The Picture of Dorian Gray invokes the queer image, to some readers at least, *despite at no point representing it*. Wilde strews around the elements in the emerging bricolage, and some readers at least were able to tot up the sum. When you put down the book, that is what it appears to have been about. 'It is not irrelevant that in the popular imagination,' Claude Summers remarks, 'the name Dorian Gray conjures not an image of evil but of preternaturally extended youth and beauty bought at the trivial price of a disfigured portrait.'[45] It is not a matter of this or that coded reference, but of the entire text being a displaced vision of the danger of, and to, the desirable youth. Despite the moralism of Hallward and the insouciance of Wotton, Wilde's fable is ultimately complicit with Dorian's narcissism in this respect: the disfigurement of the picture depends on a correlation of corruption with loss of youth and beauty. The ageing process is made to represent moral degeneracy; then, as now, this is a proposition that seems unethical in mainstream culture but which answers to a fantasy in gay male subculture.

Same-sex passion seems always on the point of getting said in the novel; its omission, indeed, seems significant – since it is a likely element in the career of the debauched aristocrat. 'In the course of his evil career he is proved guilty of adultery, debauchery, luxury, greed, vanity, murder and opium addiction. Only one of his vices is hidden, only one sin cannot be named.'[46] Same-sex passion is the impossible point of presence, at which the text might spring into miraculous coherence. It was there, almost, for some readers at least.

As commentators have suggested, we may envisage Wilde as seeking to extend the range of sexual awareness, of purposefully writing for both a knowing and an unknowing readership.[47] Initial reviewers manifest varying degrees of knowingness. The *Daily Chronicle* called *Dorian Gray* 'a poisonous book, the atmosphere of which is heavy with the mephitic odours of moral and spiritual putrefaction – a gloating study of the mental and physical corruption of a fresh, fair and golden youth, which might be horrible and fascinating but for its effeminate frivolity, its studied insincerity, its theatrical cynicism, its tawdry mysticism ...'.[48] The *Chronicle*'s reviewer was more specific: he disliked Dorian's 'pretty face, rosy with the loveliness that endeared youth of his odious type to the paralytic patricians of the Lower Empire;' in similar vein, *Punch* said Dorian is 'Ganymede-like'. In these instances, reaching for a classical referent holds the concept at arm's length from contemporary society. The *Scots Observer*, however, averred that Wilde 'can write for none but outlawed noblemen and perverted telegraph-boys' – a pointed reference to the Cleveland Street scandal of 1889–90.[49]

The potential of the book became clear to Wilde's prosecutors when, in a precise act of bricolage, they put all the evidence together. Suddenly queerness seemed of the essence. *Dorian Gray*, Queensberry's plea of justification asserted, 'was designed and intended' by Wilde 'and was understood by the readers thereof to describe the relations, intimacies, and passions of certain persons of sodomitical and unnatural habits, tastes, and practices'.[50] Some readers did understand it like that; after the trials it is impossible not to do so. On the one hand, it was not unreasonable for Wilde's counsel to complain that 'hidden meanings have been most unjustly read into the poetical and prose works of my client'; the prosecution was unable to cite any sodomitical passages.[51] On the other hand, meaning is contextual, and once Wilde enters the dock and his relations with Alfred Douglas are invoked, the book is deafeningly queer.

Notes

1. J. E. Rivers, *Proust and the Art of Love* (New York: Columbia University Press, 1980), p. 182.

2. Michael Hurley, 'Homosexualities: fiction, reading and moral training', in Terry Threadgold and Anne Cranny-Francis, eds, *Feminine, Masculine and Representation* (Sydney: Allen & Unwin, 1990), pp. 162–3.

3. Frank Harris, *Oscar Wilde* (New York: Frank Harris, 1918), pp. 106–7.

4. Alfred Austin, 'The poetry of the period', in Joseph Bristow, ed., *The Victorian Poet: Poetics and Persona* (London: Croom Helm, 1987), pp. 120, 124. See Carol Christ, 'The feminine subject in Victorian poetry', *ELH*, 54 (1987), 385–401; Joseph Bristow, 'Nation, class, and gender: Tennyson's *Maud* and war', *Genders*, 9 (1990), 93–5, 104–9. This was of course another manipulation of gender ideology, not a way of paying respect to women; see Mary Poovey, *Uneven Developments* (London: Virago, 1989), pp. 122–3.

5. Ann Douglas, *The Feminization of American Culture* (New York: Avon Books, 1978), pp. 122, 314, *et passim*.

6. See Alan Sinfield, *Alfred Tennyson* (Oxford, Blackwell, 1986), pp. 11–21, 54–5; Alan Sinfield, *Literature, Politics and Culture in Postwar Britain* (Oxford: Blackwell and Berkeley: California University Press, 1989), pp. 26–30, 39–43, 199–201.

7. Matthew Arnold, *Selected Prose*, ed. P. J. Keating (Harmondsworth: Penguin, 1970), pp. 162, 252–3.

8. Charles Kingsley, *Literary and General Essays* (London: Macmillan, 1890), pp. 43–4, 47, 51. I am grateful to David Alderson for drawing my attention to this essay.

9. William Francis Barry, *The New Antigone*, 3 vols (London: Macmillan, 1897), I, 148.

10. Quoted in Sinfield, *Alfred Tennyson*, p. 138.

11. Browning, quoted in Richard Dellamora, *Masculine Desire* (Chapel Hill: North Carolina University Press, 1990), p. 70. See Rita Felski, 'The counterdiscourse of the feminine in three texts by Wilde, Huysmans and Sacher-Masoch', *PMLA*, 106 (1991), 1094–1105.

12. E. M. Forster, *Abinger Harvest* (London: Arnold, 1953), p. 13.

13. E. M. Forster, *Howards End* (Harmondsworth: Penguin, 1941),

p. 43. See Sinfield, *Literature, Politics and Culture*, pp. 39–47, 60–74.

14.   Richard Ellmann, *Oscar Wilde* (London: Hamish Hamilton, 1987), pp. 41, 80.

15.   Richard Jenkyns, *The Victorians and Ancient Greece* (Oxford: Blackwell, 1980), p. 150; see also pp. 148–53, 219–21, 225–6, 256–7.

16.   Walter Pater, *The Renaissance* (London: Macmillan, 1904), p. 220.

17.   Mary Renault, *The Charioteer* (London: New English Library, 1990), p. 114.

18.   Martin Fido, *Oscar Wilde* (London: Hamlyn, 1973), p. 31. See Leonée Ormond, *George du Maurier* (London: Routledge, 1969), ch. 7.

19.   Karl Beckson, ed., *Oscar Wilde: The Critical Heritage* (London: Routledge, 1970), p. 51. The review appeared in the *Woman's Journal*, a Boston publication. Cf. Patricia Flanagan Behrendt, who obscures Higginson's distinction between Wilde and Whitman, alleging that Higginson and Bierce are objecting to 'homoerotic sensuality' (*Oscar Wilde: Eros and Aesthetics* (London: Macmillan, 1991), pp. 31–2). Regenia Gagnier shows general sexual/gender confusion in English aestheticism (*Idylls* (Aldershot: Scolar Press, 1987), pp. 141–4).

20.   Jonathan Katz, *Gay American History* (New York: Avon Books, 1978), p. 673; Robert K. Martin, 'Knights errant and gothic seducers: the representation of male friendship in mid-nineteenth-century America', in Martin Duberman, Martha Vicinus and George Chauncey, Jr, *Hidden from History* (New York: Penguin, 1959), pp. 179–81.

21.   W. S. Gilbert, *Original Plays: Third Series* (London: Chatto, 1910), p. 93. Here I concur with Ed Cohen, *Talk on the Wilde Side* (New York: Routledge, 1993), p. 136.

22.   Gilbert, *Original Plays*, p. 103; cf. Brian Reade, *Sexual Heretics* (London: Routledge, 1970), p. 31.

23.   George Bernard Shaw, *Plays Pleasant* (Harmondsworth: Penguin, 1946), p. 120. I am grateful to my brother Mark for reminding me of *Candida*.

24.   Dellamora, *Masculine Desire*, p. 199.

25.   Labouchère is quoted by Ellmann, *Oscar Wilde*, pp. 149, 226.

26.   Oscar Wilde, *The Picture of Dorian Gray*, ed. Isobel Murray (Oxford University Press, World's Classics, 1981), p. 125. Cited hereafter by page numbers in the text.

27.   Joris-Karl Huysmans, *Against Nature*, trans. Robert Baldick (Harmondsworth: Penguin, 1959), pp. 214, 217.

28.   Max Nordau, *Degeneration*, 9th edn (London: Heinemann, 1896), p. 301. See Gagnier, *Idylls*, pp. 147–53.

29.   *The Spectator*, **62** (15 June 1889), 823–4.

30. Michael Rey, 'Parisian homosexuals create a lifestyle 1700–1850: the Police archives', in R. P. Maccubbin, ed., *'Tis Nature's Fault* (Cambridge University Press, 1988), p. 189.

31. John Stokes, *In the Nineties* (Hemel Hempstead: Harvester, 1989), p. 26.

32. Ellmann, *Oscar Wilde*, p. 471; Max Nordau, *Entartung*, 2 vols (Berlin NW: Berlag von Carl Dunder, 1896), 2, 131–3n. I am grateful to Russell Jackson for the translation. Cf. Cohen, *Talk*, pp. 15–18: Wilde may be alluded to in UK reviews of *Degeneration* – after the trials.

33. The Reverend Richard A. Armstrong, *Our Duty in the Matter of Social Purity* (London: Social Purity Alliance, 1885), p. 10.

34. Rupert Hart-Davis, ed., *The Letters of Oscar Wilde* (New York: Harcourt, Brace, 1962), p. 179; Gagnier, *Idylls*, p. 7.

35. Oscar Wilde, *Complete Works*, intr. Holland (London and Glasgow: Collins, 1966): 'Phrases and philosophies for the use of the young', p. 1206; 'A few maxims for the instruction of the over-educated', p. 1204; 'The critic as artist', p. 1042.

36. Wilde, *Dorian Gray*, p. 11. Hallward's declarations of devotion to Dorian were toned down slightly when Wilde adjusted the story from the initial magazine version for publication in book form (Neil Bartlett, *Who Was That Man?* (London: Serpent's Tail, 1988), p. 112).

37. Camille Paglia, *Sexual Personae* (New Haven: Yale University Press, 1990), p. 518.

38. Hans Mayer, *Outsiders*, trans. Denis M. Sweet (Cambridge, MA: MIT Press, 1984), p. 223; Dellamora, *Masculine Desire*, pp. 207–8.

39. *Dorian Gray*, pp. 142, 150–2, 163, 204–5, 210–11; Wilde, letter to the *Scots Observer*, 9 July 1890, quoted in H. Montgomery Hyde, *The Trials of Oscar Wilde* (London: William Hodge, 1948), p. 158.

40. Mayer, *Outsiders*, pp. 223–4; Elaine Showalter, *Sexual Anarchy* (London: Bloomsbury, 1991), p. 177.

41. J. R. de S. Honey, *Tom Brown's Universe* (London: Millington, 1977), pp. 170–1; Joseph Bristow, *Empire Boys* (London: Harper-Collins, 1991), pp. 133–6.

42. *Journal of Medical Science*, 14 (1868), p. 149, quoted by Alex Comfort, *The Anxiety Makers* (London: Panther, 1968), p. 116; see also p. 96.

43. Cohen, *Talk*, pp. 43–68, 89–90.

44. Bartlett, *Who Was That Man?*, pp. 195–6; J. Bristow, 'Wilde, *Dorian Gray*, and gross indecency', in Bristow, ed., *Sexual Sameness* (London: Routledge, 1992), p. 61.

45. Claude J. Summers, *Gay Fictions* (New York: Continuum, 1990), p. 44.

46. Bartlett, *Who Was That Man?*, pp. 93–4.

47. Gagnier, *Idylls*, pp. 61–2; Behrendt, *Oscar Wilde*, p. 181; William

A. Cohen, 'Willie and Wilde', *South Atlantic Quarterly*, 88 (1989), 219–45; Lawrence Dansen, 'Oscar Wilde, W. H. and the unspoken name of love', *ELH*, 58 (1991), 979–1000; Bristow, 'Wilde, *Dorian Gray*, and gross indecency'. I have tried to establish this kind of split reading for audiences of the plays of Noel Coward: see Alan Sinfield, 'Private lives/public theatre: Noel Coward and the politics of homosexual representation', *Representations*, 36 (fall 1991), 43–63.

48. Beckson, *Oscar Wilde*, p. 72; see Gagnier, *Idylls*, pp. 57–62.
49. Beckson, *Oscar Wilde*, pp. 73, 75, 76; also p. 69.
50. Hyde, *Trials*, p. 114; quoted from Cohen, *Talk*, p. 128.
51. Hyde, *Trials*, p. 229.

Chapter five

Speaking Its Name

The importance of being manly

'EFFEMINACY', I have been arguing, was a contested construct, and addressed a far wider range of concerns than sexual orientation. Manliness also was less specialized: it invoked diverse attributes and activities, not just being successful in cross-sex relations. This is not to say that same-sex practitioners were not regarded as effeminate; in the molly-house tradition, which persisted, they were. Mary McIntosh believes that the element of transvestism diminished in same-sex subculture during the nineteenth century. Male prostitutes were reported as of masculine build, and there was 'more stress upon sexual licence and less upon dressing up and play-acting'. However, the idea of effeminacy did not die out, by any means; two of Wilde's associates, Alfred Taylor and Arthur Marling, were described as cross-dressing.[1] Probably it depended still on the inserter/receptor distinction – which, I have argued, seemed either to license or efface one partner, inhibiting the emergence of the idea of 'the homosexual'. 'One of his hands which had been caressing my testicles slipped under my bum – a finger was slipped in the hole,' Des Grieux reports in *Teleny*, commenting, 'I seemed to be a man in front, a woman behind, for the pleasure I felt either way.'[2] The indeterminacy is germane: the sexual experience of the two men is failing to tidy itself into a masculine/feminine, active/passive, cross-sex model, despite Des Grieux's sense that it should. 'Why was not one of us born a woman?' Teleny laments (pp. 171–2). That might seem to sort it out; but which should it have been? – the reader may wonder – since their practice resists such categories. Social conformity would be at the price of erotic complexity.

'As far as we can tell,' Rictor Norton remarks, 'gay men did not think of themselves as women trapped in men's bodies until the sexologists began popularising this theory in the 1860s.'[3] Karl Heinrich Ulrichs framed the notion that the male homosexual might have 'a feminine soul enclosed in a male body'; this was further biologized by Richard von Krafft-Ebing, who proposed that the individual has masculine and feminine 'brain centres' in varying proportions. Havelock Ellis denied that male homosexuals were distinctively feminine, but he did not challenge the underlying, cross-sexual gender grid. 'It is sometimes supposed that in homosexual relationships one person is always active, physically and emotionally, the other passive', but this is often not so, Ellis writes: 'the invert cannot tell if he feels like a man or like a woman'.[4] This sounds as if all options are open, but it is still framed within the two general possibilities, as Ellis sees them: a man or a woman – active or passive. The invert is a confused amalgam of the two halves of a more fundamental, cross-sexual binary structure. Ellis goes on to quote several correspondents on the topic, revealing widely varying experiences and attitudes (pp. 284–6). Nevertheless, in the face of all this, he reasserts, 'there is a distinctly general, though not universal, tendency for [male] sexual inverts to approach the feminine type' (p. 287). And conversely with lesbians (pp. 244, 250, 255).

The sexologists were only one factor; concepts of same-sex passion were still up for grabs. Indeed, the most determined and prominent work on the idea of homosexuality was being conducted in opposition to the effeminacy model, on the programme that same-sex passion is quintessentially manly. Edwin Emmanuel Bradford's Eros allows little space for the feminine:

> Eros is up and away, away!
> Eros is up and away!
> The son of Urania born of the sea,
> The lover of lads and liberty.
> Strong, self-controlled, erect and free,
> He is marching along to-day.
>
> He is calling aloud to the men, the men!
> He is calling aloud to the men –

'Turn away from the wench, with her powder and paint,
And follow the Boy, who is fair as a saint':
And the heart of the lover, long fevered and faint
Beats bravely and boldly again.[5]

For Horatio Forbes Brown, effeminacy was what made the urban youth less than ideal:

> Dearer to me is the lad, village born, with sinewy members
> Than the fine face of a pale town-bred effeminate
>   youngling.

The distinction, though probably Brown does not want to elaborate it, may in fact be between urban knowingness and rural innocence. The poem celebrates grooms, horse-trainers, hunters and sailors:

> Dearest of all are soldiers, the young magnificent
>   swordsmen;
> Be it the stalwart form of a dark eyed insolent guardsman
> Or a light haired hussar with the down new fledged on his
>   smoothed lip
> Who with vigorous stride and clanking spurs, when they
>   meet me
> Know not how lovely they are, the sight of them how
>   overwhelming.[6]

'How lovely they are' (it is women who are supposed to be lovely) is made to coincide with the manly attraction of a 'vigorous stride' (though perhaps the spurs go a bit far).

In this model, neither partner has to be effeminate; in fact, the idea seems to be to eliminate everything to do with women.

As Sedgwick suggests, there was a class dimension here. Middle-class men were particularly likely to think of same-sex preference as making them more virile – because they were already disposed to distinguish themselves from the effete leisure class.[7] Bradford wasn't interested in the Greeks – they were effeminate southerners. Northern love could claim the virtues of middle-class work and purity:

Is Boy-Love Greek? Far off across the seas
  The warm desire of Southern men may be:
But passion freshened by a Northern breeze
  Gains in male vigour and in purity.[8]

This move was facilitated by a faultline in the prevailing middle-class ideology of manliness. The woman was supposed to maintain hearth and home, but this required at least some male commitment to domesticity. And that does not seem immediately heroic. The domestic ideal made life worth living for the suicidal speaker in Tennyson's 'The two voices' (1833):

One walked between his wife and child,
With measured footfall firm and mild,
And now and then he gravely smiled.

The prudent partner of his blood
Leaned on him, faithful, gentle, good,
Wearing the rose of womanhood.[9]

This is Tennyson's answer to those high-born maidens who, in other early poems, sit around in castles making things complicated for earnest, middle-class young men. But it doesn't sound very heroic.

Hence Tennyson's difficulty in *Idylls of the King* in presenting Arthur as head of the knightly round table, and, simultaneously, self-righteous husband; it is easy to hear a stronger emotional push when Sir Bedivere goes forth companionless. In the United States, in his book *The Young Man and the World* (1906), Indiana senator Albert Beveridge advised obedience to a mother's moral direction; this was her transcendent role in the properly constituted home. But, at the same time, a boy had to be a man: 'get out of the exclusive atmosphere of your perfumed surroundings'. For while a man 'strongly desires to meet the standards set for him by women, he also desires, almost all the time, and in almost every mood, to meet the standards set for him by men'. Working very hard for a political party – taking manly (Arthurian!) responsibility for the state – was Beveridge's recommended move.[10] Defensively male institutions, for men to escape to, were the counterpart of domesticity. 'For this was an age of bachelors, or of married men

who spent a large part of their lives as though they were bachelors.
... The existence of pubs, clubs and club-like institutions prevented
Victorian and Edwardian wives from occupying more than a seg-
ment of their husbands' time.'[11] England was run by this 'old-
school-tie' network – it was still being contested in the late twentieth century. In one aspect, a priority of male bonding in the west
in modern times has been to police itself against homosexuality; in
another aspect, as I have argued in relation to public school values,
the cross-over was all too enticing.

The embarrassment for writers of heroic, lad-love poetry
was the constitutional effeminacy of literary writing; they, above
all, needed poetry to be masculine. Walter Pater believed this was
established in a 'characteristic' passage from Johann Winckelmann:
'those who are observant of beauty only in women, and are moved
little or not at all by the beauty of men, seldom have an impartial,
vital, inborn instinct for beauty in art'.[12] However, Edward
Cracroft Lefroy was keenly aware of the disjunction between the
heroic boy football player and his own writing:

> If I could limn you, as you leap and fling
> Your weight against his passage, like a wall;
> Clutch him, and collar him, and rudely cling
> For one brief moment till he falls – you fall:
> My sketch would have what Art can never give –
> Sinew and breath and body; it would live.[13]

Poetry with the precise attack of the football player would be
marvellous, but the gap between the two yawned wide. In fact,
'manly' writing might be embarrassing – so complex was the deployment of masculine and feminine attributes. Whitman in *Leaves
of Grass* (1855) had invoked, all too well, the possibility of a manly
poetry of male intimacy. Gerard Manley Hopkins wrote, of his
'Harry Ploughman': 'when you read it let me know if there is
anything like it in Walt Whitman, as perhaps there may be, and I
should be sorry for that'; Hopkins thought Whitman a veritable
'scoundrel'.[14]

Edward Carpenter and John Addington Symonds specifically contested the effeminate model of same-sex love that Ulrichs
and Krafft-Ebing had proposed. Symonds repudiated 'the belief
that all subjects of inverted instinct carry their lusts written in their

faces; that they are pale, languid, scented, effeminate, painted, timid, oblique in expression'. While 'a certain class of such people are undoubtedly feminine', Symonds admits, the majority do not differ from 'normal men. They are athletic, masculine in habits, frank in manner'. These 'normal' homosexuals are 'passing through society year after year without arousing a suspicion of their inner temperament'.[15] Carpenter, in his account of men with same-sex preferences, grants that there are 'extreme specimens' — the 'distinctly effeminate type, sentimental, lackadaisical, mincing in gait and manners, something of a chatterbox, skilful at the needle and in woman's work, sometimes taking pleasure in dressing in woman's clothes'. But these are not 'the more normal and perfect types'. Carpenter quotes Dr Moll's opinion: 'a very large percentage, perhaps by far the majority of them, do *not* exhibit pronounced effeminacy.' Uranians of 'the more normal type', he says, possess 'thoroughly masculine powers of mind and body', and 'are often muscular and well-built'.[16]

Symonds's poem 'Paths of life' (1882) says marriage is for the hearth,

ordained
For lifelong fellow-service, high sustained
By hope of children and the world's great need.

Comradeship, however,

spreads
Tents on the open road, field, ocean, camp,
Where'er in brotherhood men lay their heads.
Soldier with soldier, tramp with casual tramp,
  Cross and recross, meet, part, share boards and beds.
    Where wayside Love still lights his beaconing lamp.[17]

This outlook was available in such prestigious pre-Christian instances as Nisus and Euryalus, Socrates and Alcibiades, Coriolanus and Aufidius, David and Jonathan. It is continuous with Plutarch's dialogue 'Of love', which Philemon Holland translated for the Elizabethans. There Protogenes prefers boy-love to 'the other delicate and effeminate love, that keepeth home and stirreth not out of doors, but keepeth continually in women's laps, under canopies or within curtains in women's beds and soft pallets, always seeking after dainty delights, and pampered up with unmanly pleasures, wherein there is no reciprocal amity'.[18] Charles Kains Jackson, in his essay 'The new chivalry' (1894), celebrated the male companionship 'of the river, of the hunt and the moor, the evening tent-pitching of campers out, and the exhilaration of the early morning swim' as ten times superior to the intimacy that men and women normally share.[19] As in Adrienne Rich's concept of the 'lesbian continuum', same-sex practices are proposed not as marginal to masculinity and femininity, respectively, but at their centres. Homosocial experiences are continuous with them, perhaps radiate out from them.[20]

Today, popular opinion is likely to regard as deluded and/or deluding the idea that homosexuality is quintessentially manly, though the gay scene has reasserted such a perspective (I discuss this in chapter 8). But in the second half of the nineteenth century, the idea of same-sex love as the *exclusion* of the feminine – in a direct continuation with earlier notions of effeminacy – was the ground upon which same-sex passion was most likely to be mooted. Hence the plausibility, then, of the boy scout movement and our tendency, now, to find scoutmasters funny.

Boy-love was often misogynist. Kains Jackson found it more virtuous because free from the demand for intercourse with women – which he called 'phallic filthiness' and attributed to 'Semitic influences'. He drew upon the class debate about manliness, purity and idleness by claiming that boy-love would be accompanied by a 'decrease of idleness', since both lovers will work whereas 'every girl of the least personal attractiveness nourishes the hope of being kept in idleness. Above a certain class the proviso "by a husband" is added'.[21] Carpenter was enthusiastic about the New Woman, and managed to avoid most of the misogyny – his critique of domesticity allows that there might be more fulfilling cross-sex relations.[22] Nevertheless, Carpenter was prepared to draw support from Richard Wagner, quoting his statement that 'beauteous naked man is the kernel of all Spartanhood; from genuine delight in the beauty of the most perfect human body – that of the male – arose that spirit of comradeship which pervades and shapes the whole economy of the Spartan State'.[23] John Addington Symonds professed this kind of sentiment; Walter Pater drew it from Winckelmann.

Misogyny arises in this model of same-sex passion because although Carpenter and his friends repudiate effeminacy and the hierarchy in the masculine/feminine binary that structures the sex-ologists' model – the model deriving from the molly-houses – they retain the binary structure. They merely turn it around. Carpenter was very ready to question the conventional manliness of the upper-class male. He described the typical public-school product as 'a picture of beefy self-satisfaction. Affection and tenderness of feeling, though latent in him, have never, owing to the unfortunate conditions of his life, been developed.' And hence the destinies of the world are in the hands of

> men so fatuous that it actually does not hurt them to see the streets crammed with prostitutes at night, or the parks by day with the semi-lifeless bodies of tramps; men to whom it seems quite natural that our marriage and social institutions should lumber over the bodies of women, as our commercial institutions grind over the bodies of the poor, and our 'im-perial' enterprise over the bodies of barbarian races.[24]

This seems powerful and true. Even so, Carpenter's case depends, still, on the idea of a true manliness which these men fail to attain. The empire builders, he says, are 'in the most important matters quite ungrown'; underneath you find 'no more than a public school-boy' (p. 30). The underlying ideal is a real man.

Once this chimerical figure is postulated, an element of the feminine may safely be acknowledged – though many boy-lovers prefer to appear wholly masculine. An even better ideal might be the real man with a judicious admixture of the feminine. 'Nature, it might appear, in mixing the elements which go to compose each individual, does not always keep her two groups of ingredients – which represent the two sexes – properly apart,' Carpenter says, such that in some character types there is 'a union or balance of the feminine and masculine qualities.' 'Like women they read charac-ters at a glance, and know, without knowing how, what is passing in the minds of others; for nursing and waiting on the needs of others they often have a particular gift; at the bottom lies the artist-nature, with the artist's sensibility and perception.'[25] So the homo-sexual man might have the best of all worlds; in fact, he might be the harbinger of a higher type. Women and men were moving closer together, Carpenter believed, since the arrival of the New Woman. But he was still playing variations on the binary structure of masculine and feminine attributes.

Manly homosexuality was celebrated also, Harry Oosterhuis has shown, by the group around the German journal *Der Eigene*, in the first quarter of the twentieth century. They abjured the notion that homosexuals were feminine in disposition, reasserting sexual friendship – 'chivalric love' and 'the love of friends'. Oosterhuis says they were constructionists, and repudiated the masculine/feminine binary structure:

> Homosexual and heterosexual behavior was predominantly determined culturally, they asserted, and the same was true of masculinity and femininity. Therefore, the association of homosexuality with effeminate men was also a consequence of social processes which reflected a self-fulfilling prophecy: the theories of Ulrichs, Krafft-Ebing, and Hirschfeld did not so much explain as model individual behavior.[26]

Actually, many of the writers Oosterhuis reprints are misogynist – tending, like Kains Jackson, to essentialize and derogate the female and the feminine. However, a clear constructionist case is made in a remarkable essay by Edwin Bab. The theory of a 'third sex', he points out, depends on the assumption that there are manly and womanly attributes which can be, aberrantly, located in the 'wrong' body. There is no basis for this: 'It is asserted that man is productive, woman reproductive and receptive. But only our customs, which make every productive activity highly difficult for the woman, are to blame for the fact that the number of productive women is relatively small.' This, I mean to argue, is the line gay men and lesbians should have maintained: we don't need masculinity and femininity. Indeed, Bab adds, 'One never loves women or men after all, but rather one quite distinct woman or one man. And the number of "grandes passions" in the life of an individual is never very great. Who is able to say that, when he has three times loved a woman, his inclination will not fall on a man the fourth time!'[27] Who indeed?

'Oscar Wilde'

The sexologists and the boy-love advocates made the masculine/feminine binary structure even more central and necessary while, at the same time, doing little to clarify its confusions. The Wilde trials exploded in the midst of all this urgent ideological work. As a consequence, the entire, vaguely disconcerting nexus of effeminacy, leisured idleness, immorality, luxury, insouciance, decadence and aestheticism, which Wilde was perceived as instantiating, was transformed into a brilliantly precise image. The parts were there already, and were being combined, diversely, by various people. But, at this point, a distinctive possibility cohered, far more clearly, and for far more people, than hitherto.

The elements of the queer bricolage were on the agenda: Fanny and Stella, but they were not upper-class or artistic; the rumoured aristocrat in the Cleveland Street scandal, but he was not artistic. Mark André Raffalovich came closer, but he denied that he was interested in carnal pleasure:

> Put on that languor which the world frowns on,
> That blamed misleading strangeness of attire,
> And let them see that see us we have done
> With their false worldliness and look up higher.[28]

The consolidation of a queer identity begins to take shape around Wilde in Robert Hichens's novel, *The Green Carnation* (the flower had been worn by Wilde and his circle).[29] Hichens moved in compatible circles with Douglas and Wilde, whom he met a number of times; his book, published in 1894, is a skit, though not an unfriendly one. The plot concerns whether the exquisite Lord Reggie Hastings will marry Lady Locke, the wealthy widow of an officer in the Malayan service; he is discouraged by his intimate older friend, the artistic Esmé Amarinth. Reggie regards marriage only as a convenience; he 'worshipped the abnormal'. Esmé, who has not allowed his own marriage to affect him, is fearful that he will lose Reggie. Esmé says: 'To sin beautifully, as you sin, Reggie, and as I have sinned for years, is one of the most complicated of the arts': the sins are less precisely specified than in *Dorian Gray*, but they seem not to involve relations with women.[30] Same-sex passion is on the agenda when Esmé pronounces on the Wildean theme of the natural:

> To me it means all that is middle-class, all that is of the essence of jingoism, all that is colourless, and without form, and void. ... Certain things are classed as natural, and certain things are classed as unnatural – for all the people born into the world. Individualism is not allowed to enter into the matter. A child is unnatural if it hates its mother. A mother is unnatural if she does not wish to have children. A man is unnatural if he never falls in love with a woman. A boy is unnatural if he prefers looking at pictures to playing cricket, or dreaming over the white naked beauty of a Greek statue to a game of football under Rugby rules. (p. 105)

Hichens does not use the word 'effeminate' – to the point where its absence is significant. Its antitype, manliness, is strongly present. Reggie 'tried to be manly' when he 'once spent a week with the commander of one of our armies of occupation', but 'never heard the same remarks so often in all my life'. He complains that soldiers 'are never original. They think it is unmanly' (p. 53).

Lady Locke, the prospective spouse, is initially baffled by Reggie and Esmé – she, for one, is unable to recognize signals of same-sex passion. But this is partly because of her contrasting experience; her 'husband had been a bluff and straightforward man of action, full of hard common-sense, and the sterling virtues that so often belong to the martinet' (p. 10). She is told that Reggie and Esmé wear the carnation to draw attention to themselves; 'By their dress? I thought that was the prerogative of women.' 'Men may have women's minds, just as women may have the minds of men,' her sophisticated cousin replies. Has Reggie a woman's mind then? 'My dear, he has a very beautiful mind. He is poetic, imaginative, and perfectly fearless' (pp. 15–16). Lady Locke gradually realizes how different Reggie is, and wonders:

> Was it the swing of Nature's pendulum? She had loved a hard, brusque man, and had found a certain satisfaction in his blunt and not too considerate affection. ... Perhaps it was really Lord Reggie's personal beauty or prettiness that attracted her, for, say what one will, a pretty boy steps easily

into the good graces of even a strong-natured woman. (p. 96)

This does not rule out Reggie as a husband; effeminacy still doesn't make him impossible for cross-sex passion. But Lady Locke does hope that Reggie might be not really like Esmé – merely copying him. Perhaps he is not really expressing himself by wearing the green carnation (p. 116). Her moment of truth, which leads her to abandon the match, is when she overhears Reggie promising a carnation to her delighted son – whom she wants to be 'like a soldier and obey the orders of his superior officer' (p. 128): 'Her mother's heart flushed with a heat of anger at the idea of Tommy, her dead soldier's son, developing into the sort of young man whom she chose to christen "Modern"' (p. 154).

Holbrook Jackson says 'countenance was lent' to rumours about Wilde's sexuality by Hichens's novel which, 'although making no direct charge, hinted at strange sins'.[31] However, while Willa Cather perceived in *The Green Carnation* an exaggeration of Wilde's 'drivelling effeminacy', she meant by this 'straining after the epigrammatics', not same-sex passion.[32] What is still missing in *The Green Carnation* is any sign of the network of lower-class boys that Wilde and Douglas were actually exploring, and for which Wilde was prosecuted. At one point Reggie expatiates on how he loves to satisfy every mental whim immediately:

> There are moments when I desire squalor, sinister, mean surroundings, dreariness and misery. The great unwashed mood is upon me. Then I go out from luxury. The mind has its West End and its Whitechapel. The thoughts sit in the Park sometimes, but sometimes they go slumming. ... they like the ruffians whom they meet there, and they hate the notion of policemen keeping order. (p. 9)

This obscures, if anything, the possibility of actual visits to East-End haunts of vice such as Dorian Gray had indulged; Reggie's expeditions are merely whimsical and imaginative. There is perhaps a stronger hint when Esmé wants to go at dawn to Covent Garden Market – 'I love the pale, tender green of the cabbage stalks, and the voices of the costermongers are musical in the dawning' (p. 20). 'Musical' may have signalled same-sex passion to some readers;

and could the cabbage stalks allude to the 'sentimental passion of a vegetable fashion' in *Patience*? But there the chapter ends, without affording the clinching ingredient in the queer image. Even so, *The Green Carnation* shows the potential queer identity getting constituted around Wilde and Douglas. It is a remarkable anticipation – to the point where Hichens withdrew the book as the trials proceeded, distressed by the extent to which he had helped to conceive the ground of Wilde's downfall.

The image of the queer cohered at the moment when the leisured, effeminate, aesthetic dandy was discovered in same-sex practices, underwritten by money, with lower-class boys. This was not at all what other idealistic, same-sex apologists had admitted, or perhaps meant – neither the public-school boy-lovers, nor the manly-comradely types. In the witness box Wilde tried initially to handle questions frivolously, in the tone he had perfected at the dinner table. This led him into major embarrassments, so he shifted his stance to one of sensitive, refined, high-minded idealism. He offered the earnest stance of Hallward in *Dorian Gray*, though still in the dandy manner of Wotton. His famous speech in defence of the love that dare not speak its name depends on such love rising above physical considerations: 'It is that deep, spiritual affection that is as pure as it is perfect. ... It is intellectual.'[33]

We do not need to assume that Wilde was hypocritical about this; he may well have hoped to find an ideal love among the boys he was addressing. But the prosecution made his assignations and financial transactions sound squalid, and represented the boys either as corrupted by Wilde, or as so corrupt already that no decent person would associate with them. It all seemed quite contrary to the leisure-class arrogance and aesthetic elegance that Wilde had been affecting. Prosecutor Edward Carson challenged:

Let us contrast the position which Mr Wilde took up in cross-examination as to his books, which are for the select and not for the ordinary individual, with the position he assumed as to the young men to whom he was introduced and those he picked up for himself. His books were written by an artist for artists; his words were not for Philistines or illiterates. Contrast that with the way in which Mr Wilde chose his companions! ... Then his excuse was no longer that he was dwelling in regions of art but that he had such a noble, such a democratic soul (Laughter.), that he drew no social distinctions, and that it was as much pleasure to have the sweeping boy from the streets to lunch or dine with him as the greatest *Littérateur* or artist.[34]

It was a transformation, Neil Bartlett remarks, as if Terence Rattigan suddenly turned into Jean Genet.[35]

At the Haymarket Theatre, Wilde's leisure-class characters might appear appropriately feminized, and his own, associated image might arouse no more than vague disquiet. But the trials constructed a different framework of interpretation: Wilde appeared, suddenly but ineluctably, as one who consorted with male prostitutes. Yet he was still the effeminate dandy. So the two figures coalesced. At this point, dandyism forfeited the protection from same-sex imputations that the image of general dissoluteness had afforded. The leisure-class man, not the insignificant molly, was the sodomite. Indeed, as the sexologists were saying, he was a more specific figure than the sodomite – the homosexual. The model was, therefore, quite different from that which produced the early-modern rake and the mollies. In those models, the 'active' male was exonerated (to a degree) or invisible, because he was still masculine. Effeminate leisure-class men might well be involved in same-sex practices as part of a general dissoluteness, but their effeminacy was mainly a function of their class and dissoluteness. All this had made it difficult to get a concept of 'the homosexual'. The Wildean model produced an image even more specific than that: the queer – dandified, aesthetic, effeminate. And, in the same move, the object of his attentions also came into view: the lower-class masculine youth. Now, it seemed, the masculine/feminine binary structure invoked a recognizable hierarchy – though in a confused and offensive (to orthodox notions) way. The queer is the leisure-class man, and in so far as he commissions the lower-class boy he is superior, in the masculine position. In so far as he is by definition effeminate, may invite unwelcome attentions from disreputable people, and may take the 'passive' sexual role, he is allowing himself to become inferior – in the feminine position. The queer was clearly in view, and clearly unacceptable.

In fact, of course, Wilde was not really the English aristocrat that he invokes. This permits a partial elision, which can always be disavowed when necessary. In one aspect, Wilde figures the leisure-class Englishman as queer; in another aspect, he was an imposter, insinuating his arriviste Irish degeneracy. The second aspect might have inhibited the influence of the Wildean image, but for one further factor. There was another person, a true aristocrat, at the trials: Lord Alfred Douglas. Of course, he was present only figuratively, because the idea of pillorying the real aristocrat was too awful for anyone to entertain (including Wilde). But although he wasn't called, Douglas was named; and hence contributed, I suggest, to a queer image which is, in fact, a composite: *Wilde + Douglas*. This pattern replicates that of the Bolton and Park and Cleveland Street trials, where rather dubious middle-class men featured, but the prospect of an unspecifiable member of the aristocracy lurked in the wings (and still intrigues commentators). For it was not just because of class deference that Douglas could not be called; also, he was dangerously plausible as a same-sex practitioner. As is often remarked, Douglas is anticipated in *Dorian Gray*; the culture was ready for such a figure. In *The Green Carnation* the Wilde character is represented as influencing the Douglas figure, but the latter is the principal mover of the action. In his person, traditional leisure-class debauchery converged upon contemporary anxieties about public schools and Oxford. The trials made Wilde all too apparent, and he had to be committed to a significant silence. But Douglas was already a silent presence, and hence totally available for the queer composite. In so far as the queer was Douglas, he embodied intrinsic leisure-class corruption; in so far as he was Wilde, the leisured gentleman could be imagined as the victim of perversion by an invasive other – an influence that might deepen and widen if not continuously repudiated. This ambiguity established precisely the model through which the twentieth-century queer simultaneously was and was not visible: in one aspect, any gentleman might be queer, in another, class hierarchy was only proper and the queer was an anomalous intrusion.

As I observed in chapter 1, following Ed Cohen, the queer image may be observed at its point of emergence in press reports of the trials: ' "Oscar Wilde posing as ＿＿＿" '. The immediate emphasis, often, was still to regard homosexuality as part of a general moral and intellectual corruption, rather than as the distinctive sexual nature of a certain kind of person. The *Daily Telegraph* declared:

> Young men at the universities, silly women who lend an ear
> to any chatter which is petulant and vivacious, novelists who
> have sought to imitate the style of paradox and unreality,
> poets who have lisped the language of nerveless and effemi-
> nate libertinage – these are the persons who should ponder
> with themselves the doctrine and career of the man who has
> now to undergo the righteous sentence of the law.[36]

'It was not only Wilde's homosexual behaviour which was being
tried,' R. K. R. Thornton comments, but 'a whole body of ideas,
moral, literary, and aesthetic'.[37] This is true; but the movement was
reciprocal. Even as the homosexual was embedded in that nexus of
attributes, that nexus fed into the idea of the queer, as the powerful
image of Wilde was assimilated and appropriated.

'Before he broke the law of his country and outraged human
decency', the *Evening News* asserted, Wilde

> was one of the high priests of a school which attacks all the
> wholesome, manly, simple ideals of English life, and sets up
> false gods of decadent culture and intellectual debauchery.
> . . . these abominable vices, which were the natural outcome
> of his diseased intellectual condition, will be a salutary
> warning to the unhealthy boys who posed as sharers of his
> culture.[38]

A before-and-after is posited here: Wilde's unhealthy ideas were
manifest in his dandified posturing, but *now* we can see what he
was really like – which is what we should have known all along
since it is 'the natural outcome'. So in future, it might be added, we
will be ready to recognize the homosexual. And this does not
include the 'unhealthy boys'; they only 'posed as sharers of his
culture': only Wilde is the true queer.

'The Wilde trial had done its work,' Carpenter wrote, 'and
silence must henceforth reign on sex-subjects.' However, it was a
Wilde-shaped silence. The *Echo* wrote: 'The best thing for every-
body now is to forget all about Oscar Wilde, his perpetual posings,
his aesthetical teachings and his theatrical productions. Let him go
into silence, and be heard no more.'[39] But, of course, this very
injunction is reproducing Wilde, circulating an image of him, the
image of the queer. The inhibiting of debate took a certain shape,

one determined by the notions that had accrued around Wilde. T. E. Lawrence's mother would not have Wilde's name mentioned by her undergraduate sons, especially in front of a girl.[40] 'Oscar Wilde' became, for many decades, the one form in which such speech might occur. Wilde observed this happening when he accepted, in 1898, that it might be a good idea to publish *The Ballad of Reading Gaol* anonymously. 'As regards America, I think it would be better now to publish there *without* my name. I see it is my *name* that terrifies.' Of course, the authorship would become known, but anonymity would allow readers not to notice it, and hence not to take the unacceptable risk of becoming involved with 'Oscar Wilde'. Even more strikingly, Wilde saw that this indirection would work positively; that it would constitute an attraction, as well as an alibi. 'The public like an open secret,' he wrote – intuiting, in precisely the theoretical terms of the 1990s, the prurient fascination that the oblique image of the queer was to produce.[41]

The notoriety of Wilde headed off the Victorian exploration of diverse models of same-sex relations and, in a twin move, afforded a simple stereotype as a peg for behaviour and feelings that were otherwise incoherent or unspeakable. It became much harder to maintain that same-sex practices might be an obvious way to intensify manly bonding; that model remained influential for some men, but it became a more precarious proposition. It became both important and difficult to distinguish artistic and queer tendencies. Colin Spencer's mother looked horrified when he wanted to study dance: 'Oh no, you'll become one of them' – 'It was not until my late teens that I realized what she had meant.' Another man recalls: 'My father held a very important position in the government service. He rather despised me for being interested in art. ... He was a literary person, very well read indeed, but he thought it was feminine or something to be interested in the arts. Which is quite extraordinary. We have nothing whatever in common.'[42] This man's father was well-read, even 'literary', but he certainly wasn't, like his son, 'artistic'. And it became harder still to envisage same-sex practices beyond a masculine/feminine matrix.

This effect worked for homosexuals, as well as for those who stigmatized them. Between 1900 and 1960, a dandified manner afforded by far the most plausible queer identity. As Ellis put it, 'the celebrity of Oscar Wilde and the universal publicity given to the facts of the case by the newspapers may have brought conviction of their perversion to many inverts who were before only vaguely conscious of their abnormality'. One correspondent reported that his erotic dreams had invariably involved women, 'with this one remembered exception: I dreamed that Oscar Wilde, one of my photographs of him incarnate, approached me with a buffoon languishment and perpetrated *fellatio*.' Gradually this man found himself to be homosexual: 'hypothesis merged into reality: I myself was inverted'. Maurice in Forster's novel refers to 'unspeakables of the Oscar Wilde sort'.[43]

To be sure, very many lesbians and gay men experience their sexualities as having always been there – since long before they met any homosexuals, or heard of the idea. When they did meet them, or come across the idea, they immediately recognized themselves. However, I believe this is because that first, baffling, bitter accusation – '*queer*' – is the last brick in the arch. The entire framework that supports it, in terms of appropriate and inappropriate gender behaviour, has been there since before we were born – as a set of social expectations. By the time most girls and boys sense themselves as lesbian and gay, most of the conditions for that recognition are already there; the others slide into place as the individual strives to make sense of herself or himself.

The convergence on the effeminate, leisure-class stereotype was experienced as a distinctive misfortune by Wilde's older son, Cyril. 'All these years my great incentive has been to wipe that stain away; to retrieve, if may be, by some action of mine, a name no longer honoured in the land,' he wrote to his brother. 'The more I thought of this, the more convinced I became that, first and foremost, I must be a *man*. There was to be no cry of decadent artist, of effeminate aesthete, of weak-kneed degenerate.' Cyril asked 'nothing better than to end in honourable battle for my King and Country'. That, the state could arrange: he joined the army on leaving school and was killed in action at the age of twenty-nine.[44]

Notes

1. Mary McIntosh, 'The homosexual role', in Kenneth Plummer, ed., *The Making of the Modern Homosexual* (London: Hutchinson, 1981), p. 38. On Wilde's associates Taylor and Marling, see H. Montgomery Hyde, *The Other Love* (London: Mayflower, 1972), p. 159.

2. Wilde and others, *Teleny*, ed. John McRae (London: Gay Men's Press, 1986), p. 118.

3. Rictor Norton, *Mother Clap's Molly House* (London: Gay Men's Press, 1972), p. 104.

4. Havelock Ellis, *Sexual Inversion, Studies in the Psychology of Sex*, vol. 2, part 2 (New York: Random House, 1936), p. 283. That the invert idea is fundamentally heterosexist is remarked by Eve Kosofsky Sedgwick, *Epistemology of the Closet* (Hemel Hempstead: Harvester Wheatsheaf, 1991), p. 87, referring to Christopher Craft, ' "Kiss me with those red lips": gender inversion in Bram Stoker's *Dracula*', *Representations*, 8 (1984), 107–34, p. 114. See Jeffrey Weeks, *Coming Out* (London: Quartet, 1977), pp. 23–32, 47–83; John Marshall, 'Pansies, perverts', in Plummer, ed., *The Making of the Modern Homosexual*, pp. 142–5; Frederic Silverstolpe, 'Benkert was not a doctor', in *Homosexuality, Which Homosexuality?* (Amsterdam: Free University and Schorer Foundation, 1987); Harry Oosterhuis, in Harry Oosterhuis and Hubert Kennedy, eds, *Homosexuality and Male Bonding in Pre-Nazi Germany* (New York: Harrington Park Press, 1991), pp. 12–15.

5. Edwin Emmanuel Bradford, *The New Chivalry* (London: Kegan Paul, 1918), p. 5; quoted in Timothy d'Arch Smith, *Love in Earnest* (London: Routledge, 1970), p. 88.

6. Published in 1900; Smith, *Love in Earnest*, p. 108.

7. Eve Kosofsky Sedgwick, *Between Men* (New York: Columbia University Press, 1985), pp. 207–13.

8. Quoted in Smith, *Love in Earnest*, p. 3.

9. *The Poems of Tennyson*, ed. Christopher Ricks (London: Longmans, 1969), p. 540.

10. Joe L. Dubbert, 'Progressivism and the masculinity crisis', *Psychoanalytic Review*, 61 (1974), 443–55, pp. 447–8.

11. Brian Harrison, *Separate Spheres* (London: Croom Helm, 1978), pp. 97, 102–4, and ch. 5 on 'Clubland'.

12. Quoted by Walter Pater, *The Renaissance* (London: Macmillan, 1904), p. 192.

13. Smith, *Love in Earnest*, pp. 72–3.

14. Quoted in Richard Dellamora, *Masculine Desire* (Chapel Hill: North Carolina University Press, 1990), p. 89; Joseph Bristow, ' "Churlsgrace": Gerard Manley Hopkins and the working-class male body', *ELH*, 59 (1992), 693–711, p. 704.

15. *A Problem in Modern Ethics* (1891), in Brian Reade, *Sexual Heretics* (London: Routledge, 1970), pp. 251–2. See Robert K. Martin, 'Knights errant and gothic seducers: the representation of male friendship in mid-nineteenth-century America', in Martin Duberman, Martha Vicinus and George Chauncey, Jr, eds, *Hidden from History* (New York: Penguin, 1989).

16. Edward Carpenter, *Love's Coming of Age* (London: Swan Sonnenschein, 1906), pp. 126–30.

17. Smith, *Love in Earnest*, p. 13.
18. Quoted in Bruce R. Smith, *Homosexual Desire in Shakespeare's England* (Chicago University Press, 1991), p. 38.
19. Reade, *Sexual Heretics*, p. 318.
20. Adrienne Rich, 'Compulsory heterosexuality and lesbian existence', in Ann Snitow, Christine Stansell and Sharon Thompson, eds, *Powers of Desire* (New York: Monthly Review Press, 1983).
21. Reade, *Sexual Heretics*, pp. 314, 317.
22. Carpenter, *Love's Coming of Age*, p. 87. Carpenter and Symonds readily acknowledged links between boy-lovers and themselves (Smith, *Love in Earnest*, p. 12).
23. Carpenter, 'Homogenic love' (1894), in Reade, *Sexual Heretics*, p. 341. Carpenter declared: 'Anything effeminate in a man, or anything of the cheap intellectual style, repels me very decisively': in Carpenter, *Selected Writings: 1: Sex*, ed. David Fernbach and Noel Greig (London: Gay Men's Press, 1984), p. 290; see John Fletcher, 'Forster's *Maurice* and the scapegoating of Clive', in Bristow, ed., *Sexual Sameness* (London: Routledge, 1992).
24. *Love's Coming of Age*, pp. 29, 31.
25. Carpenter, *Love's Coming of Age*, pp. 115, 117, 129.
26. Oosterhuis, in Oosterhuis and Kennedy, eds., *Homosexuality and Male Bonding*, p. 31.
27. Edwin Bab, 'Same-sex love, or *Lieblingminne*: a word on its essence and its significance', in Oosterhuis and Kennedy, eds, *Homosexuality and Male Bonding*, pp. 54–5.
28. Reade, *Sexual Heretics*, p. 226.
29. Hyde says the green carnation was an emblem of homosexuals in Paris (*Other Love*, p. 164), but Neil Bartlett has found no evidence for this (*Who Was That Man?* (London: Serpent's Tail, 1988), p. 53). Ellis believed homosexuals had a preference for green and says green cravats were worn as a badge in Paris; in New York, however, 'to wear a red necktie on the street is to invite remarks from newsboys and others' (*Sexual Inversion*, pp. 299–300).
30. Robert Hichens, *The Green Carnation* (1894; London: Unicorn Press, 1949), pp. 5, 23–7.
31. Karl Beckson, ed., *Oscar Wilde: The Critical Heritage* (London: Routledge, 1970), p. 331.
32. Bernice Slote, ed., *The Kingdom of Art: Willa Cather's First Principles and Critical Statements 1893–1896* (Lincoln: Nebraska University Press, 1966), pp. 135, 389–93. When in September 1895 Cather appreciated same-sex to be in view, she did not relate Wilde's artistic principles to his sexuality, but spoke more admiringly of his qualities. See Richard Dellamora, 'Traversing the feminine in Oscar Wilde's *Salomé*', in Thaïs E. Morgan, *Victorian Sages and Cultural Discourse* (New Brunswick: Rutgers University Press, 1990), p. 262.

33. H. Montgomery Hyde, *The Trials of Oscar Wilde* (London: William Hodge, 1948), p. 236.

34. Hyde, *Trials*, p. 166; see also pp. 252, 323–4.

35. Bartlett, *Who Was that Man?*, p. 31.

36. Hyde, *Trials*, pp. 11–12.

37. R. K. R. Thornton, '"Decadence" in later nineteenth-century England', in Ian Fletcher, ed., *Decadence and the 1890s* (London: Arnold, 1979), pp. 15–16. See Marshall, 'Pansies, perverts', p. 141; Jonathan Dollimore, *Sexual Dissidence* (Oxford: Clarendon, 1971), pp. 67, 240–1.

38. Hyde, *Trials*, p. 12.

39. Hyde, *Other Love*, p. 124; Regenia Gagnier, *Idylls of the Marketplace* (Aldershot: Scolar Press, 1987), p. 146.

40. John E. Mack, *A Prince of Our Disorder* (Oxford University Press, 1990), p. 10. See also Kevin Porter and Jeffrey Weeks, eds, *Between the Acts* (London: Routledge, 1991), p. 49. In 1898 none of the reviewers of *The Ballad of Reading Gaol* 'mentioned Wilde by name, although everyone knew he had written the poem' (Richard Ellmann, *Oscar Wilde* (London: Hamish Hamilton, 1987), p. 526).

41. Rupert Hart-Davis, ed., *The Letters of Oscar Wilde* (New York: Harcourt, Brace, 1962), p. 698. I am grateful to David Alderson for drawing this to my attention.

42. Colin Spencer, *Which of Us Two?* (London: Viking, 1990), p. 12; Porter and Weeks, eds, *Between the Acts*, p. 35.

43. Ellis, *Sexual Inversion*, pp. 63, 175–6 (this instance is discussed by Christopher Craft, 'Alias Bunbury: desire and termination in *The Importance of Being Earnest*', *Representations*, 31 (1990), 19–46); E. M. Forster, *Maurice* (Harmondsworth: Penguin, 1972), p. 136. See also Ellis, pp. 120, 352.

44. Vyvyan Holland, *Son of Oscar Wilde* (London: Hart-Davis, 1954), p. 140.

Chapter six

Class Relations

Suede shoes

THE emergence of the queer stereotype, as we should expect, was uneven. The author Beverley Nichols, as a boy in his teens during World War I, was taken up by an effeminate aesthete who lived nearby. Nichols's father (a businessman) evidently 'assumed that the sophisticated Mr Edwards, who had a baronet in his family, was introducing Beverley to the world of the gentry. He never budged from his belief that [Edwards] was a hell of a fellow with the ladies.' Edwards and Beverley had sexual relations, but Mr Nichols was able, still, to represent Edwards to himself as the pre-trials dandy. However, Edwards gave young Beverley a copy of *Dorian Gray*, and his father found him reading it. Instantly, Mr Nichols went frantic: he called Beverley a ' "pretty little boy", enunciating the word "pretty" in a shrill parody of a homosexual voice as he hit him across the face. Then he spat on the book and tore the pages with his teeth. "Oscar Wilde! To think that my son...." '[1]

The real-life Edwards could still be perceived as a leisure-class philanderer, but he was transformed into a homosexual when the name of Wilde was heard. Beverley did not understand what he had done, so next morning his father presented him with a piece of paper on which he had written (in Latin) 'The horrible crime which is not to be named'. The point is not just that the name of Wilde was the way to make the silence speak, but that the silence did not need to speak until Wilde's name was introduced. Here we catch the Wilde case in the process of constituting the queer image.

Beverley was to become the first man to wear suede shoes at Oxford.[2]

In school stories until about 1918, homosexual practice is certainly heard of among the boys, but is the kind of thing any of them might do. No distinct ethos accompanies it; in particular, it is not incompatible with games. 'The homosexual', still, is scarcely constituted as a figure. Caruthers, in Alec Waugh's novel *The Loom of Youth* (1917), is presented as committed to games and to the poetry of Byron and Swinburne. The latter is the ground for his 'romance' with young Morcombe: 'There was something in him so natural, so unaffected, so sensitive to beauty ... his face flushed with the glow of the leaping fire, talking of Keats and Shelley, himself a poem.' Caruthers's passion for Morcombe is not marked as damagingly homosexual; in fact the romantic affair keeps him from 'wild excesses', despite persistent temptation 'to plunge himself into the feverish waters of pleasure'.[3] In his book *Public School Life* (1922) Waugh denies that romances and same-sex practices need signify homosexuality:

> In this environment there is nothing unnatural about the attraction exercised by a small boy over an elder one. A small boy is the nearest approach possible to the feminine ideal. Indeed a small boy at a Public School has many of the characteristics that a man would hope and expect to find in a woman. He is small, weak, and stands in need of protection.[4]

Boys desire the feminine, Waugh says, and in the absence of girls they accept an approximation; 'it is in human nature to accept the second best' (p. 137). A special category of queers seems not to be required, or not for such as Caruthers and Waugh.

Robert Graves says he 'was unconscious of any sexual desire' in his love for a younger boy. His teachers were anxious, though – the secret was partly open. Graves justified himself by citing Plato, Shakespeare and Michelangelo. His rather defensive presentation of the topic, in *Goodbye to All That* (1929), indicates that by the time of writing he had become more aware. He interweaves the story of his romance with episodes in which he wins boxing matches against boys over his weight, knocks down boys who affront him, and is generally 'masculine' – at the same time as singing in the choir, editing a magazine and figuring in the poetry society.[5] This emphasis on Graves's stature as an all-rounder shows that, by the time of writing, he is keen to separate himself from the pattern that associates same-sex passion with aestheticism and a queer stereotype.

Graves left school just before war broke out in 1914, Alec Waugh a year later. Martin Green compares their attitude with the self-conscious aestheticism cultivated by Evelyn Waugh – the younger brother of Alec. The difference is because of their ages. The five years between them saw the development of a split, during the 1920s, between athletes and aesthetes – first at Oxford, then at Cambridge and public schools. Alec could be literary and love cricket, but Evelyn hated cricket and cultivated Diaghilev and the ballet. Of course, the split occurred unevenly; older attitudes persisted as well. But there was a new attention to Wildean dandyism in the 1920s. Green suggests that World War I legitimated a disillusionment with the 'Victorian' seriousness and responsibility that was seen as having produced the war, and, even more, the phoney attitudes that accompanied it: 'They refused to grow up into men of responsibility, fathers of families and of the state, soldiers.'[6] This disengagement from establishment values was expressed, in advanced circles, through a cult of 'Oscar Wilde' and the 1890s. Ronald Firbank and Harold Acton listened eagerly to Reggie Turner's stories of Wilde.[7]

The return of the aesthete seemed, once you were on the inside of it, to have been inevitable; 'the trial of Oscar Wilde was responsible for a flight from aestheticism which lasted twenty years,' Cyril Connolly wrote, as if aestheticism were a natural resource.[8] But the purposeful playing of the effeminate, artistic aesthete against the manly, athletic type is a fine instance of a reverse discourse (as proposed by Foucault – see pages 16–17 above). The despised sissy, the other of the Victorian boys' story, returned to challenge the system; hence what seems to us the excess of preciosity and exuberance. And so determined was this revolt that it embraced the queerness which, I have argued, had emerged so specifically in the figure of Wilde. 'To take a detached interest in the matter was a way of separating themselves from their parents' generation, to whom the whole topic had become taboo on account of Wilde,' Christopher Hollis recalls. 'It was *chic* to be queer, rather as it was *chic* to know something about the twelve-tone scale and about Duchamp's "Nude Descending a Staircase",' Alan Pryce-Jones says.[9] According to Goronwy Rees, homosexuality was 'among undergraduates and dons with pretensions to culture and a taste for the arts, at once a fashion, a doctrine and a way of life'.[10]

Auden saw in all this a price for the arts. The Wilde trials 'allowed the philistine man to identify himself with the decent man. Though the feeling that it is sissy for a boy to take an interest in the arts has probably always existed among the middle class and is not yet extinct, for many years after Wilde's trial it was enormously intensified.'[11] The price of the athletes/aesthetes split for homosexuals was a further closing down of options; it became the more implausible that they might be other than effeminate and generally Wildean.

In 1930, in his book *Degenerate Oxford?*, Terence Greenidge presents the split between athletes and aesthetes as a generally acknowledged fact. The latter, 'popular journalists' allege, are attracted to homosexuality: 'They do not employ such a crude word, but "effeminate" and "unmanly" become in reality synonyms.' In Greenidge's view this was overstated, and the aesthetes were, in the main, involved in naively romantic friendships, sometimes with athletes.[12] Even so, there were dangers, in particular 'the mass-production of effeminate men' whose 'feet will be shod with gay suede shoes. They will speak with artificial voices of a somewhat high timbre, also they will walk with a mincing gait' (p. 107). An element of the feminine was civilizing, Greenidge thought, but not too much.

The Oxford pattern fed back into public schools. Anthony Blunt says that at Marlborough already 'the generation before' himself – before 1924–25 – 'had started a sort of revolt against the toughs, against the absolute dominance of games. They had a pretty rough time of it.' Blunt started a magazine and wrote on the Wildean theme that all art is amoral; one parent threatened to remove his son from the school and the magazine was forbidden.[13] Louis MacNeice, who with John Betjeman was part of this revolt, suggests that it was of longer standing and quite local: 'Marlborough, unlike many public schools, had a strong highbrow tradition; there was always a group among the older boys that was openly against the government, that mocked the sacred code and opposed to it an aesthetic dilettantism.' For MacNeice, the association of aestheticism with same-sex practices occurred not at school but at Oxford, in 1926:

> At the first party I went to there was no drink but champagne, a young man played by himself with a spotted stuffed dog on a string and the air was full of the pansy phrase 'my dear'. I discovered that in Oxford homosexuality and 'intelligence', heterosexuality and brawn, were almost inexorably paired. This left me out in the cold and I took to drink.[14]

The variations in these accounts indicate that it is hard to say exactly when and where the athletes/aesthetes split became present, and when and where it became decisively linked to sexual preference. T. C. Worsley was well aware of the split, but still, as a schoolmaster in the 1930s, he knew 'no word for those who nowadays would be summarily described as "Queer" or "Bent". . . . The vice, if it is one, was hinted at in the wary disapproval with which any close association between boys and masters, or elder and younger boys was regarded. But without any nomenclature to describe it, it remained unspecified in everyday conversation.' But it was getting to be specified. At Harrow, where Terence Rattigan was a pupil, it became fashionable for boys in rebellion against school values 'to proclaim their genuine or affected homosexuality'.[15]

In 1905, in his novel *The Island Pharisees*, John Galsworthy's narrator observes two old Etonians among the audience at a play. One has 'a weather-tanned complexion' and 'a satirical and resolute expression'; the other has 'a chaffing smile; his thick, sleek hair, brushed with water and parted in the middle, his neat moustache and admirable waistcoat, suggested the sort of dandyism that despises women'.[16] These are Wildean figures; in effect, aspects of Lord Illingworth. The issue, still, is not queerness but general dissoluteness – the conclusions the narrator draws from the scene indicate this. He recalls his fiancée's remark, that she doesn't like unhealthy people, and says to himself: 'all *these* people, anyway, were healthy; they looked as if they had defied the elements to endow them with a spark of anything but health' (p. 37). This health is not invoked ironically; there is no suggestion of an underlying spiritual or psychological malaise. The old Etonians are specifically healthy. The narrator's project is to assert that these prosperous, healthy people have conventional attitudes to women's subordination in marriage. The episode is concerned with the status of women, not with queerness. Compare a similar scene, reported from the early 1920s by an old Etonian contemporary of Brian Howard and Harold Acton:

> One time I happened to be at the Alhambra when Brian and Harold walked into the stalls, in full evening dress, with long white gloves draped over one arm, and carrying silver-topped canes and top-hats, looking perhaps like a couple of Oscar Wildes. My step-mother was astonished at the sight of them, and thought they must be foreigners. I was much too nervous, at about fifteen, to say that they were two of my great friends from Eton. I was very relieved that we were safely installed out of sight in the dress circle![17]

This is 'Oscar Wilde' queerness.

During the 1920s, the stereotype was settled for two generations. It received wider circulation through Mordaunt Shairp's hostile play *The Green Bay Tree*, a hit in London and on Broadway in 1933. It is about a leisured and exquisitely cultured man, Dulcimer, and his adoptive son Julian: the latter is tempted away from marriage with the earnest Leonora by luxury and idleness. Finally the biological lower-class father shoots dead the aesthetic father-figure; but Julian remains trapped and ends up like Dulcimer at the start. An audience would not have to hear homosexuality in the play; in Richard Findlater's view it is so discreet that 'the audience might imagine that the moral corruption exercised by the central figure over the younger man was one only of cynical materialism and not sexual love'.[18] However, there are ample hints for those able and willing to hear. Dulcimer is called 'Dulcie', and has the affectation, amoral wit and concern with decor that mark the queer stereotype. When the play opens he is talking to his man-servant and decides to arrange the flowers – echoing the discussion about Lord Goring's buttonhole in *An Ideal Husband*.[19] However, there is an aesthetic problem: 'I'm terribly overdressed for doing flowers'; so Dulcimer considers allowing the servant to arrange them. But there are tulips – 'I don't think I could trust you with a tulip' (p. 56). Dulcimer puts on gloves and an apron, and does the flowers himself. When he has finished he demands: 'When on earth are you going to take all this [table of flowers] away? I look like a wayside shrine!' (p. 58).

If this camp insouciance seems charming, Dulcimer is soon revealed as cynically manipulative, attracting Leonora's accusations: 'Haven't you any conscience at all about keeping him from what is normal and healthy?' (p. 93). Hiding behind the positive terms in this question are the negative alternatives – immoral, abnormal, unhealthy. They add up, almost, to queerness, and only this might seem to justify an imputation of evil: 'You fascinate me,' says Leonora to Dulcie, 'like a snake fascinates' (p. 82).

The Green Bay Tree says almost nothing about homosexuality, but it strongly invites surmise. Jed Harris, its New York producer, observed: 'the suspicion had to be there. That's the only way you can explain what was going on.'[20] Leonora seems to know the score: 'I hope I shan't meet you one day in Piccadilly with a painted face, just because you must have linen sheets!' she says (p. 92). In fact most reviewers in New York and London discussed how far the play was about IT – 'Centuries back the Greeks had a word for it,' one wrote; 'it is somewhat difficult at times to discover what *is* at the bottom of Mr Mordaunt Shairp's garden,' said another, wishing he 'had not hesitated to call a spade a spade'. But they were generally appeased by the play's hostility towards whatever danger it was that Dulcimer seemed to represent – the *New English Weekly* complained of Dulcimer's 'exaggeratedly mincing deportment and his ugly caressing of chairs'.[21] T. C. Worsley didn't appreciate that his lack of interest in girls and passionate devotion to another boy, which persisted through undergraduate years, indicated a significant aberration. He was scarcely aware of the word 'homosexual': 'it implied, if anything, "cissiness". Cissy I certainly wasn't. Wasn't I on the contrary if not a tough, at least a masculine aesthete?'[22] He was enlightened by a young woman to whom he had been trying to make love, after they had been to see *The Green Bay Tree*. What such stories show, repeatedly, is that the potentially gay man had to find one or another milieu if he was fully to conceive his own sexuality, and the queer model was the most available.

When Wyndham Lewis wrote *Self Condemned* (1954) he knew what a queer looked like – he might be recognized even in wartime Canada: 'a figure swung past with swaying hips, and a violent arm sawing the air at his side, with little finger stiffly erect, having separated itself from the other figures. A *man*: a fairy-man'.[23] I have written elsewhere about a further fictional instance, Ambrose Silk in Evelyn Waugh's *Put Out More Flags* (1942); another is 'Pussy' Wilkinson in Jocelyn Brooke's *Orchid Trilogy* (1950). Pussy was cultured and leisured, and was 'a perfect period-piece – a man of the nineties who had managed to preserve the authentic aroma of that (to me) still fascinating decade. He had known Robbie Ross and Reggie Turner, and had even, on one memorable occasion, been introduced (at Dieppe) to none other than "Sebastian Melmoth" himself' (i.e. Wilde); he 'had never married'; when inebriated he would give 'his celebrated imitation of Sarah Bernhardt'.[24] Pussy takes into his house a rough diamond, Bert – 'half servant, half-*protégé* ' – whom he has bought out of the army. Dangerously, Bert is given to talking in pubs about what guardsmen will do for ten bob. These signals are the most explicit indication we get about the queerness of Pussy: his 'reminiscences remained always upon an impeccably polite level' (pp. 374–5), and so do the narrator's. Queerness would be plain enough, though, to anyone likely to read the book in 1950, when it was published; every detail speaks the Wildean unspeakable. The narrator, in effect, is a milder version of Pussy. This stalking-horse pattern, whereby a manifest queer exonerates a more central character, even while, for those with ears to hear, drawing attention to the likeli-hood of homosexuality, is common in mid-century writing (for instance in plays by Noel Coward).

Such representations consolidated the queer image, to the point where, unless there were really explicit signs, queers were generally assumed to be leisure-class. And conversely, leisure-class men might fall under suspicion, regardless of their actual prefer-ences. It may still be hard, today, to tell whether certain establish-ment mannerisms signal queerness, or not.

Ellis had thought in 1897 that the genuine invert was likely to belong to 'the professional and most cultured element of the middle class'. (The lower classes were supposed to have little anxiety about same-sex practices; as in so many things, Ellis believed, 'the uncultured man of civilisation is linked to the savage'.)[25] Even the middle-class gentleman, Sedgwick has sug-gested, though he might have attended the same school and univer-sity as the leisure-class man, 'seems not to have had easy access to the alternative subculture, the stylized discourse, or the sense of immunity of the aristocratic/bohemian sexual minority'.[26] This is precisely the case in *Teleny*, where Des Grieux, who is in trade, knows from his schooldays Briancourt, a general's son. The latter is dandified, Byronic, wealthy and accomplished; 'his manners were those of the French nobility, therefore perfect ... in fact, he possessed all those "small, sweet courtesies of life", which, as Sterne says, "beget inclinations to love at first sight"'. Briancourt has a house full of lascivious paintings and holds an orgy (which he calls a 'symposium'; his father, the general, is there too). Des Grieux is scarcely able to understand his own emotions, until introduced to this circle – 'a lot of pleasant fellows who'll be delighted to make your acquaintance'.[27]

The queer manner was immensely convenient for leisure-class men, who only had to inflect a mode to which they had been bred. If they wished, they might pass even *at the same time* as signalling the queer image to those they wished to reach. They could move conveniently into a 'dissolute' milieu which might include bohemians and prostitutes, and they had the resources to secure privacy. In the 1940s and 1950s, the most likely queer venues were 'some corner of a bar, usually in the "best" hotel', or in cities perhaps 'behind the façade of some "gentleman's club"'.[28] 'Of course, I didn't go to Oxford or Cambridge universities. Had I gone there I would have learnt far more about it,' a man from a professional background says. 'But I went to Durham.'[29]

Sorting out the men from the queers

To be sure, you could be homosexual without the queer model; the interviews in *Between the Acts* and *Walking After Midnight* offer many instances. Innumerable men continued in casual activity, as they had always done. Alan Bray asks himself how, given the intense hostility to same-sex passion in political and religious ideology in early-modern England, it nevertheless went scarcely checked, scarcely noticed, in diverse situations. The answer is that individuals simply did not associate what they were doing with the fearful image of the godless sodomite. They kept 'the contact between the myths and symbols of homosexuality and homosexuality itself to a minimum'.[30] So, I believe, with the twentieth-century image of the queer: only a proportion of the people who engaged in same-sex practices identified themselves with it. Some avoided thinking about what they were doing, or told themselves they weren't really doing it; others discovered Edward Carpenter and fortified themselves with his ideas of same-sex manliness.[31] In a self-fulfilling process, those who could identify as queer, such as Quentin Crisp, felt themselves drawn towards purposefully vivid manifestations, thus both consolidating the stereotype and making it appear more daunting to the faint-hearted.

Crisp was born in 1908. As a youngster, he found a group of effeminate lads, and they sat in a café making up and combing each other's hair. The conversation was full of 'stylised cattiness' – it 'was thought to be smart and so very feminine. It was better, I need hardly say, to seem like a truly appalling woman than not like a woman at all.' From time to time, when thrown out of the café, they 'waltzed round the neighbouring streets in search of love or money or both. If we didn't find either, we returned to the café and put on more lipstick.'[32] Crisp believes that homosexuals are excessively effeminate because, whereas women know they are feminine, homosexuals 'must, with every breath they draw, with every step they take, demonstrate that they are feminine' (p. 21). This is recognizably continuous with the old molly-house subculture. It converges with the Wildean image on the ground of dandified affectation and art (Crisp painted, wrote poetry, and worked as a commercial artist and as a model).

As is often remarked, the effeminate model of queerness was precisely self-defeating. Homosexuals, Crisp says, 'set out to win the love of a "real" man. If they succeed, they fail. A man who "goes with" other men is not what they would call a real man"' (p. 56). This is probably an inevitable outcome of the deployment of what I have called the cross-sex gender grid, but that grid was hard to avoid. 'I was over thirty,' Crisp declares, 'before, for the first time, I heard somebody say that he did not think of himself as masculine or feminine but merely as a person attracted to other persons with male sexual organs. ... They were all pseudo women in search of pseudo-men' (pp. 55–6). Jean Genet says the same: in Czechoslovakia in 1937 'I had the surprise of seeing for the first time a homosexual whose bearing was manly, even somewhat blunt', whose manner was 'graceful without being effeminate'. For many would-be queers, this was perplexing, distressing, and counter-productive. One man says: 'There was one particular guy who was the very first extremely effeminate gay I'd ever met – and he was my worst fear. I kept thinking, "I think I know I'm homosexual, but that's what homosexuals are – and I'm not like that".'[33]

It was hard to be queer without a model. Forster's novel *Maurice* (finished in 1914, published in 1971) is mainly about the difficulties experienced by the middle-class, suburban Maurice – not in coming to terms with his sexuality, but in finding out what it is. He blunders about, only obscurely aware of his own feelings: without relevant role models, he just doesn't know how to be queer. The serious-minded Clive, a student of leisured background, affords a bridge. He has been exploring Plato, but unfortunately gets from this mentor physical reticence as well as same-sex love, and refuses to allow himself to be 'carnal'. Plato is both enabling and restraining for Clive, as is his class privilege. He and Maurice do declare love, though, and caress and romp around physically. Homosexuality is evidently far enough from most people's thoughts for this to be possible – though the dons are aware of it. This relationship enables Maurice to postpone the realization of his yearning for a lower-class lover. The man who does know how to be queer – as we might anticipate – is the aristocratic Risley. He presents himself in Wildean manner – talking a great deal, in a 'wicked', teasing fashion, using 'strong yet unmanly superlatives' (p. 32); he likes Tchaikovsky and knows he was homosexual (Maurice likes waltzes), and terms the Pathétique symphony the 'Pathique' (p. 141).

Maurice first recognizes homosexuality in Risley and his 'set', while simultaneously refusing that image. Forster's particular project is to find a way past that leisure-class stereotype, but it is still necessary to get homosexuality on to the agenda in a form recognizable to Maurice and to readers. Maurice doesn't know about Plato till Clive tells him, and he doesn't know the word 'homosexual' (p. 158), but he knows about Oscar Wilde. When he has to pose the question to doctors, it comes out in terms of 'unspeakables of the Oscar Wilde sort' (pp. 136, 139). The novel is designed to show that Maurice doesn't have to be like Oscar Wilde. Indeed, he doesn't strike anyone as that type. He was 'a man who only liked women,' Clive thinks initially, 'One could tell that at a glance' (p. 69). However, Maurice despises the feminine as suburban and domestic; 'Home emasculated everything' (p. 51). In accepting that he loves men, he 'became a man' (p. 60); 'masculine love', he calls it (p. 207). At the end when Maurice and Alec, his lower-class lover, decide to challenge society and class together, Maurice believes 'He had brought out the man in Alec, and now it was Alec's turn to bring out the hero in him' (p. 208).

This idea of comradely masculinity draws specifically, according to Forster's terminal note, on Carpenter. As Sedgwick has observed, middle-class men were more likely to validate same-sex passion by repudiating aristocratic effeminacy (she suggests that the aristocratic type may be traced back to James VI and I – 'the King James Version?').[34] But by 1914 the Wildean, leisured image had made Carpenter's ideas more difficult to credit, and Clive – leisured, cultured, smaller and less robust – would seem the obvious homosexual. Cyril Connolly thought the book should have been written that way round: it is he 'who would seem the true homosexual, Maurice the temporary one, like many an easy-going athlete who falls in with the homosexual mores of a university before going on to marry his best friend's sister'.[35] Clive withdraws from that identity to be the Tory squire, surrendering it partly to Maurice, as I have argued, and partly to Risley, who was always the obvious candidate. This latter, Forster says, was based on Lytton Strachey (p. 220) – a central figure in the Bloomsbury milieu, and one who blatantly accepted the Wildean stereotype for himself.

None the less, Forster cannot envisage even Maurice's kind of homosexuality without the example of such as Risley and Clive; the latter's defection, both from homosexuality and from intellectual rigour, allows Maurice to subsume what he has learnt and push on to new understanding. 'Who taught you to talk like this?' Clive gasped. 'You, if anyone' (p. 214). Significantly, Maurice's search for a comrade finds its opportunity on Clive's country estate (while Clive pens his patronizing Tory address to the local electors). Though as a child Maurice was drawn to a suburban gardener, that image wouldn't quite match Forster's and Maurice's romantic aspirations. In fact, Forster contrives to have it both ways here: 'it was only by accident that [Alec] had appeared as an untamed son of the woods' – actually he came from 'a respectable family – publicans, small tradesmen' (p. 192). Thus Alec has the romance of the woods, and yet may be supposed to have adequate potential for comradely companionship. And Clive's estate contributes more than woods: it reinforces the class deference that both fuels the initial attraction of Maurice and Alec and enables them (in the British Museum episode) to overcome the ensuing mutual suspicion. The narrator and Maurice imply continually that the class difference between the two comrades is a misfortune, thereby eliding the extent to which it is, for both men, the attraction. All these ambivalences allow Forster to suggest that Maurice and Alec are not like Wilde and the boys he paid, while at the same time deriving a sufficient frissant and psychological validation from the Wildean model.

Forster acknowledged that the masculinization of Maurice is asserted in violation of his own experience. He says he created him to be 'completely unlike myself or what I supposed myself to be: someone handsome, healthy, bodily attractive, mentally torpid, not a bad businessman and rather a snob' (p. 218). In some ways this is a generous move: Forster trusts his cherished values to a man whom he does not altogether admire; also, he uses Maurice's common sense to suggest the decay of the leisure class. In other ways it is a more devious move, allowing Forster to squeeze out of the story what he perceived as his own, rather unfortunate, effeminacy. 'I want to love a strong, young man of the lower classes and be loved by him and even hurt by him. That is my ticket,' he said; today, we might regard that as one kind of comradely relationship, but Forster felt it involved some betrayal of manliness, and that the robust Maurice would make a preferable story. As John Fletcher argues, 'the formation of the masculine couple requires the exclusion of the unmanly intellectual'.[36] So the Wildean stereotype is still powerful in the novel, though by negation. Maurice and Alec make off to the woods, whereas Forster himself stayed in Cambridge, with the knowing dons and adventurous, leisure-class students. Forster thereby excludes from his happy ending not only himself but also men like Strachey – the most prominent and progressive homosexuals of the time; so determined is he to pursue the repudiation of effeminacy. The way to stop being an 'unspeakable of the Oscar Wilde sort', the novel suggests, is to stop appearing to be like Oscar Wilde.

Despite and because of all its awkwardnesses, Forster's project was of passionate concern to innumerable homosexuals who did not regard themselves as feminine. However, the suppression of *Maurice* until 1971 abandoned the field, again, to the

Wildean stereotype. When homosexuality came back into open discussion as a social problem, in Britain in the 1950s (this was the era of the social problem – juvenile delinquency, unmarried mothers, the colour bar, latch-key children ...),[37] Wilde became very visible. Hesketh Pearson's *Life* appeared in 1946; the transcript of the trials was written up by Montgomery Hyde in 1948; the current Marquess of Queensberry's account, *Oscar Wilde and the Black Douglas*, was published in 1949, Vyvyan Holland's *Son of Oscar Wilde* in 1954; Hyde added *Oscar Wilde: The Aftermath* in 1963. The *Complete Works* appeared (1948), and then an even more complete edition (1966). The full text of *De Profundis* was published (1949), a collection of essays (1950), the longer text of 'The portrait of Mr W. H.' (1958), the *Letters* (1962). *Dorian Gray* was filmed in 1945 and came out in Penguin in 1949. Hichens's *The Green Carnation* was republished in 1949; there were critical studies by Edouard Roditi (1947), George Woodcock (1949) and St John Ervine (1951). *Oscar Wilde*, by Leslie and Sewell Stokes, had been a stage success, despite uncertain notices, in London and New York in 1938–39; the film appeared in 1960 (with Robert Morley), and in the same year movie-goers could see *The Trials of Oscar Wilde* (with Peter Finch). 'God help us all and Oscar Wilde' is the camp catch-phrase in Charles Dyer's 1966 play about hairdressers, *Staircase*.

Queer manliness remained as aspiration none the less, but it was invariably in the context of an explicit repudiation of the stereotype. In Mary Renault's novel *The Charioteer* (1953) Laurie comes upon an effeminate milieu, but cannot locate himself there. 'They had identified themselves with their limitations; they were making a career of them. They had turned from all other reality, and curled up in them snugly, as in a womb.' The alternative, manly ideal is borrowed from Plato's *Phaedrus*: 'If a city or an army could be made up only of lovers and their beloved, it would excel all others. For they would refrain from everything shameful, rivalling one another in honour; and men like these, fighting at each other's side, might well conquer the world.'[38] In a novel set among airmen in World War II, such an ideal is not irrelevant. However, it is not easily to be achieved. Ralph comes close to it (he reminds Laurie of Jack in the nineteenth-century boys' story *Coral Island*; p. 332), but the sign of Ralph's manly decency is his repudiation of the very thought that most queers can reasonably claim heroic lineage: 'A

lot of bull is talked about Greece by people who'd just have been a
dirty laugh there' (p. 227). Like the charioteer in the *Phaedrus*, one
is always dragged off course by the horse of lower temper and
breed. Ralph and Laurie repudiate the effeminate scene, but they
have been physically damaged in the war, figuring their damaged,
queer condition. 'It's not what one is, it's what one does with it,'
Ralph says (p. 149). The manly task, as the novel projects it, is to
reject that part of oneself; a masculine homosexuality is the only
kind that can be admirable, but it is imagined as the heroic repudiation of the effete, effeminate norm.

A consequence is that same-sex relationships are good so
long as they are simply interpersonal. It is the same in *The Well of
Loneliness* (1928): contact with the scene is demeaning. This is the
sad failure of mid-century liberalism. Laurie objects to the very
word 'queer', as 'Shutting you away, somehow; roping you off with
a lot of people you don't feel much in common with, half of whom
hate each other anyway, and just keep together so that they can
lean up against each other for support'; Ralph strongly agrees (p.
172). However, some kind of scene was essential both for finding
partners and for the beginnings of a positive gay identity: the rescu-
ing of same-sex passion as personal integrity was well-meant, but it
stigmatized precisely those milieux that afforded some degree of
solidarity, and some way of signalling to likely partners. In *The
Charioteer*, despite the general drift of the fable, this is virtually
acknowledged. Ralph has drawn his partners from the scene, and it
is where he and Laurie recognize each other as potential lovers.
Indeed, it is suggested that knowledge of oneself as homosexual
requires some kind of interaction with a more knowledgeable
person. 'I know about myself,' Laurie says. Then 'presumably you
know about at least one other person', Ralph responds – and,
indeed, 'There was a man at Oxford ...' (p. 171). The question for
Laurie is whether he should enlighten Andrew – helping him to see
his own evident gay potential. Laurie sacrifices his love, allowing
Andrew to remain innocent and hence untainted. Queer heroism,
again, involves invalidating queerness.

The Charioteer, despite the premium it places upon manliness, cannot in fact imagine homosexuality without effeminacy.
Freudian scenarios are offered as explanations and partial justifi-
cations of the queerness of Ralph and Laurie, but not for the
effeminate queers. Probably Renault is applying the invert/pervert

schema (the former are innately homosexual, the latter have been got at), and probably it is supposed to explain why Ralph and Laurie may have a positive, manly future, whereas the others are pathetic even when they behave bravely in the face of enemy action. Nevertheless, the Freudian model does not evade effeminacy (I argue in chapter 7 that it uses the cross-sex grid), and Ralph and Laurie are not entirely distinct from the other queers. At school, Ralph had been 'trying to work up what I was into a kind of religion', but another boy whom he despised 'made me see it as just part of what *he* was' (p. 204). And even Laurie has things in common with the others. Like Risley in *Maurice*, Laurie uses knowledge about Tchaikovsky as a test of queer knowledge (p. 62). But it is not just a matter of art. His hypersensitive distaste is expressed through an immediate intuition for the nuances of the queer pick-up and a ready way with the smart, snobbish put-down. When Bunny says Ralph is at bottom 'an unfrocked scoutmaster', Laurie has no difficulty finding a bitchy response: ' "We didn't have a scout troop actually," he said. "But I think it's quite good. It keeps boys off the streets. Did you ever join one?" ' (p. 228). The very responses that show Laurie's refusal of effeminate bitchiness suggest his underlying complicity in it. This is because these are the marks of the queer, as Mary Renault was able to interpret him at that date. You only become an acceptable, masculine queer by repudiating yourself.

In the 1940s you didn't have sex with other queers, one man in *Walking After Midnight* observes, because of 'the stereotype that had been planted on us. We were queer, so we were much more like women than we were like men and so you had to go with men and not with your own kind. Of course, I realized years later that we were playing it all the wrong way round. We should only have gone for our own kind' (p. 45).

Rough trade and sugar daddies

The lower-class boy might have same-sex experiences with others of his own class, but need not regard them as involving a queer identity – because, after all, it was leisure-class men that had that. One of the respondents in *Between the Acts*, a man of lower-class origins, had a good deal of experience by the time he was in his late twenties, in about 1924. But, he says, he hadn't knowingly met any other homosexuals. Then he came across public-school types: 'I felt rather superior. Anybody can be a homosexual at a public school, I always said, I'm the real thing. With me I think I was born that way. It was very curious, the homosexuals I began to meet always seemed to me to be mummies boys.'[39] This comment is of course tangled, but it shows a triple appreciation of the relevance of the queer stereotype. First, lower-class men and boys seemed not to be homosexuals, because they didn't manifest a settled identity. Second, ex-public-school men are recognized as homosexuals – they have the effeminate ('mummies boys') identity. Third, their identity is dependent on the school subculture – to the point where, in a sense, they are not 'the real thing'.

From the working-class point of view, for the most part, queerness was identified with leisure-class privilege, and was respected and despised accordingly. John Shiers says:

> Working-class culture, the majority experience in society, had no space and no role for the homosexual, except as an object of hatred and ridicule. Hence the even greater invisibility of working-class homosexuals (but not working-class homosexual activity) than amongst the minority whose wealth could buy themselves privacy, or men who were able to 'de-class' themselves by working in 'effete' occupations

(meaning 'the theatre, hairdressing and catering').[40] This may be overstated, but the role for the explicit queer probably was no better than tolerated jester. The queer *bricolage* of effeminacy, aestheticism and class, in its whole derivation, stood at an opposite extreme from mainstream working-class values. Robert Roberts, who grew up in Salford in Edwardian times, recalls:

> In pub and workshop there was plenty of talk, *sub rosa*, about the unspeakable. The working class, always fascinated by the great criminal trials, had been stirred to its depths by the prosecution of Oscar Wilde in 1895. As late as the first world war the ribald cry heard in factories, 'Watch out for oscarwile!' mystified raw young apprentices. The proletariat knew and marked what they considered to be sure signs of homosexuality, though the term was unknown.

> Any evidence of dandyism in the young was severely
> frowned on. ... Among ignorant men any interests in music,
> books or the arts in general, learning or even courtesy and
> intelligence could make one suspect.[41]

Such people knew about the Wilde image, and one of the things
they knew was that such a man was not 'one of us'. In the nineteenth century, the middle class had defined itself against leisure-
class effeminacy; twentieth-century working-class culture defined
itself against the middle-class queer. In 1957 Richard Hoggart, who
himself had got culture and become middle-class, lamented the
'highbrow-hating' in the popular press: 'A case of homosexuality is
used as the jumping-off ground for an attack on the debased world
of Bohemia. ... The Arts Council is a "fiddle" by a lot of "cissies"
who despise the amusements of the plain Englishman.'[42] How can
working people be expected to enjoy good culture when it is so
persistently linked with queers?

   If a lower-class boy found a queer scene, as he well might if
he was in a compatible occupation, he could use it without having
to identify himself as queer. J. R. Ackerley's autobiographical novel
set in the immediate postwar period, *We Think the World of You*
(1960), shows this excellently. Frank's association with ex-sailor
Johnny leads him into complex jealousies and misunderstandings
with Johnny's working-class family. We see how the relationship is
tolerated yet excluded, despite Frank's money and authority as an
upper-middle-class man. Johnny is imprisoned (for housebreaking)
and Frank becomes devoted to his Alsatian, Evie. The dog is
situated like Johnny: she is imprisoned and kept away from Frank,
who wants to offer her a better life. But with the dog also, the
legitimacy, let alone desirability, of Frank's relationship is not acknowledged by the family. Frank is exasperated: 'And after all I'd
done for them! Stupid people, ignorant and obstinate, daring to
assert themselves against me!' He tries obsessionally to manoeuvre;
'Incomprehensible people!', 'inexplicable incidents', he thinks.[43]
But gradually he sees that the behaviour of Johnny's family is
'ordinary' enough; 'Their problems, in short, had been real problems', and he, on the whole, 'had been a tiresome and troublesome
fellow' (pp. 105–6; almost nothing of this gets into the 1988 film,
starring Alan Bates and directed by Colin Gregg). Frank even comes
to consider Johnny's eventual suggestion, 'What you've never 'ad

you never miss' (p. 116): perhaps little is gained by trying to give a dog or a person a 'better' lifestyle. The solution is that Frank should have the dog, for she affords an almost legitimate relationship – only almost, for she snaps at and harasses other people. Evie jealously excludes others, as Frank has been excluded, and manifests all the devotion, excitement and intensity that he has failed to find among lower-class men – implicated, as they are, in the 'ordinary' lower-class family world.

The lower-class man who was prepared to commit himself, as Crisp was, might affect the Wildean stereotype; for it had come to signal sexuality as much as class. But this would normally be at the price of family and neighbourhood hostility. Aestheticism was invaluable as a bridge because it was ambivalently situated. As an upward class aspiration it might appear specifically reputable – endorsed perhaps by school teachers. None the less, James Kirkup's parents were uneasy about his 'decadent aestheticism'. His father 'adamantly refused to allow me to attempt anything "artistic" or "cissy"' – ballet certainly, and even playing the piano. They couldn't stop Kirkup writing – that required no material support. Still his father was bothered: 'You're growing into a proper nancy-boy, with your long hair and all this book-reading.'[44] But observe even here the indeterminancy: Kirkup is not altogether pigeon-holed, he is only 'growing into' a nancy boy.

The implication of queerness with posh culture afforded, to all classes, institutional opportunities for meeting and ways of signalling to others. Many respondents in *Between the Acts* report that galleries and theatres were good pick-up places; 'One of the opening gambits would be, are you fond of music?'[45] Posh culture also afforded a sense of worth. 'For me, growing up gay and getting into this sort of culture felt like the same process, namely the process of establishing an identity,' Richard Dyer writes. 'Queerness brought with it artistic sensitivity – it gave you the capacity to appreciate and respond to culture. It was a compensation for having been born or made queer.' 'It also made you doubly "different" – queer and cultured. And how splendid to be different! Even if you were awful.' Dyer adds: 'Somehow to me cultural sensitivity was "feminine"; and being queer was not being a man – that was why the two went together.'[46]

The metropolitan subculture, in the 1930s, was dominated by economic factors. The scene was divided into boys – who were

on the game, amenable or kept – and 'the "steamers" or punters ...
[who] tended to be older and better off and, of course, in high
society'. The latter were the queers, whereas their lower-class
partners might well think of themselves as acting out of deference
or for money. Another observer remarks, of the boys, 'I don't think
they were all homosexual. I think they just obliged and probably
quite enjoyed it, and probably made a bit of money out of it';
probably they would marry.[47] Alec, in Forster's *Maurice*, sees himself in that light, until he falls in love with Maurice and is swept out
of his anticipated milieu.

The cross-class liaison, between the effete gent and the
'manly' lower-class boy, was the most significant consequence of
the queer stereotype. The bit of rough trade is that because he is
constructed in a binary structure with the posh queen.

> Even the ongoing relationships were based on money. The
> boys who went to live with these older people became
> dependent. A husband–wife relationship. Quite a lot of
> them went on forever you know. There were a lot of same-
> age friends, but they were non-sexual friends, you would
> just have them round to tea or something'.[48]

In 1960 Gordon Westwood reported that over a third of his sample
of 127 male homosexuals preferred relations with men of a different social status to themselves.[49]

The economic basis of the cross-class liaison was contrary,
of course, to the comradely ideal that Whitman, Carpenter and
Symonds had proposed. As Auden points out, it was the aristocratic
Douglas who introduced Wilde to rough trade and prostitution –
his affairs before that had been with young men of his own class.[50]
Actually, the classic comradely relationships also were mainly
cross-class. Carpenter's determined socialism probably helped him
to make this work, but Symonds's 'comrade' travelled with him as a
servant; there was perhaps an element of self-deception here. Be
that as it may, the Wildean stereotype may have installed economic
exploitation as a linchpin of queer relationships in a way that was
not quite inevitable; certainly it made it difficult to envisage a wider
range of possibilities. The queer stereotype subtends the bit of
rough as his necessary corollary.

Of course, sexual relations cannot be isolated from the

social hierarchies in which they are embedded, and there are innumerable ways to make something rewarding out of inequality. To a striking extent, the cross-class liaison replicated the wider class and gender patterns that prevailed. In one aspect, the social inferiority of the lower-class partner corresponded to the relative powerlessness of the heterosexual wife. In another aspect, the whole queer relationship was beyond the bounds of respectability, and hence very like illicit heterosexual relations – which consisted mainly of a man approaching female employees and prostitutes. The crucial opposition, therefore, was not between homosexuality and heterosexuality but between illegitimate and legitimate relations – between secrecy or scandal and marriage, family, domesticity and respectability.

In this second aspect, we should notice that it was all right for a man to go with prostitutes or have a mistress of a lower class, but he was not supposed to foul up his social stratum by forming extra-marital relationships with women of his own class. The queer cross-class liaison encoded just this assumption. Peter Burton grounds this in guilt and self-oppression. With *The Green Bay Tree* in mind, he perceives upper-class queers acting as 'father substitutes to a youth from the working class, often unworthy of their attentions'; if the relationship produced misery, that may indicate 'the level of guilt and self-loathing many gay men appear to have felt about themselves – thus, love equals suffering equals expiation of guilt'.[51] How intricate and contradictory the web of class feelings could become is illustrated in Denton Welch's *Journals*. He meets a ' "superior"-voiced soldier' and is perplexed:

> I thought, I like you, yet I hate you being almost educated. I cannot admire you as I would if you were a clod. This is a terribly muddled state to be in. It shows that I can never be true friends with anyone except distant women – far away. I wish for communion with the inarticulate and can only fray and fritter with the quick.[52]

Though Welch is 'muddled', he sees clearly how Bloomsbury notions of personal relationships fall into confusion when sexual desire crosses class boundaries.

Significantly, the Carpenter model was to reappear in the 1970s, especially in the writing of Jeffrey Weeks. Gay Liberation in

Britain was egalitarian, often socialist, and a return to Carpenter seemed to be one way of repudiating the leisure-class queer stereotype. In Noel Greig's Gay Sweatshop play *The Dear Love of Comrades* (1979 – titled from a Walt Whitman poem) everyone is manly and there is a good deal of tramping across the moors in the snow for Carpenter's lovers. He starts off idle, but takes on a punishing schedule of public lectures. The men have their petty jealousies, but there is not a whiff of camp. George Merril darns the socks, but it is explicitly denied that he is like a wife; he has made a free choice. Merril and Carpenter hang out the washing together, and anyway, we are told, working men used to do the washing until recently.[53]

If the cross-class liaison no longer seems the obvious choice for gay men, that too corresponds to a wider social change. The leading idea nowadays – that the most suitable kind of partner is someone whose outlook and interests are close to your own – matches closely the current heterosexual idea, especially in the middle classes, of companionate marriage. This, in turn, may be effecting a tyrannical confinement of the potential in gay relations. We need to sort it out.

In *Which of Us Two?* (1990) Colin Spencer prints love letters that passed between John Tasker and himself in the late 1950s, when they were both in their mid-twenties (I write 'Colin' for the young man of the letters, 'Spencer' for the older commentator). There were external obstacles to their intense sexual passion: John had two reasons for not staying in England – he wanted to avoid military service, and also to return to Australia, his country of origin. And both men needed to make money and wanted to establish careers – John as a theatre director, Colin as an artist and writer. There were personal insecurities as well: John wanted to dominate, according to Spencer, and Colin fought against that. Looking back, those are the principal difficulties that Spencer remarks.

But none of that was insuperable – as the letters keep saying. Bizarrely, it may seem to us today, the two men allowed the relationship to break up, and then spent years lamenting it as their great lost love. The further factors, we may discern, derived from the gay subculture, which led both men to cultivate significant alternatives to their relationship. Other attractive young men were the least surprising of these disruptive others. They were potentially direct rivals, but they figured mainly when Colin and John were apart, and could not match the intensity of the primary relationship. The young men coped with this disturbance by mutual lying; the pattern was very like that commonly experienced in heterosexual marriage.

Sugar daddies, which both Colin and John attracted, were more disruptive because they competed on a quite different terrain, that of high living and career opportunities. Edouard was 'middle-aged, highly cultured and intelligent and in the Diplomatic Corps'. Colin found himself becoming 'more and more fascinated by the elegance and style of his world, by the familiarity with which he spoke of screen and stage idols, of ballet and opera stars. His world, of course, was the one I wanted to belong to, yet I also knew that I was becoming swallowed up into John's life.' Edouard 'recounted everything he could do for me – the contracts, the galleries which would exhibit my paintings, the magazines which would publish my stories, the directors who would see my stage designs, all this and so much more.'[54] Colin's letters report his conquest of the English cultural scene as he moves from one prestigious and influential homosexual man to the next. Sex did not take place, Spencer tells us, but there is still an unavoidable sense of not-altogether-disinterested favours. Both John and Colin found this demeaning; thirty years later, Spencer is still ashamed to recount how he performed a striptease in order to get a flat – to the point where even in retrospect he can scarcely enjoy the humour of finding that Ravel's 'Bolero' is excessively long unless you happen to be wearing a great many clothes (pp. 84–5). However, Colin's success in the queer milieu produced opportunities to share its privileges, as for instance when Michael Davidson arranged 'the love of a Sicilian lad' as part of their holiday together. 'This certainly was not confessed to either John or Jill' (pp. 200–1).

Sugar daddies were disruptive because they ran counter to the high romantic terms in which Colin and John liked to frame their relationship. 'I am not, my dear, trying to coerce you back into the terrifying queer world,' John says; 'I just want you to remember those times when we gave each other more than our bodies, our hearts, our memories or our souls' (p. 217). At this point, the possibility of repudiating the cross-class liaison in favour of equality and mutuality comes fully into visibility. This corresponds to the decline in authority of the leisure class, and to the proclaiming of companionate marriage as the ideal within heterosexual relations (Colin and John sometimes say they are married; pp. 213, 216). That was the emergent dispute in gay culture: between the Wildean tradition, coming to be perceived as exploitative, and a mutual partnership. The latter may justify queerness – displacing the explicit concern, in *Maurice* and *The Charioteer*, with manliness. As Colin puts it, 'queers to be bearable had to be young lovers as we were, living together and faithful, otherwise it was waste, waste, waste' (p. 198). With mutuality as the criterion, rather than legal provenance, lesbians and gay men may assert the legitimacy of their relationships. 'There was nothing queer about us', John defiantly declares (p. 217). This dispute – the scene versus couples – continues.

However, even true love was not enough to overcome a tendency, in Colin and John, to privilege heterosexuality. Both men report relationships with women, presenting them in terms of disgust with the available queer milieu. Colin says: 'when you left, I couldn't endure it, as you couldn't, the one night stands, couldn't even endure the cheap glossy nauseating queer life' (p. 198). 'Darling, when I met Cynthia I wanted to marry her,' John responds – 'I too am very tempted because I too want to escape this useless wasteful camp world' (p. 209). However strong the heterosexual desire of these men, it is clear that the potential of their gay relationship is being undermined by a sense that queerness is inferior. Of course, the whole social system is telling them this. The most exalted moments of Colin and John are disturbed by the horrified gaze of outsiders – parents, landladies, policemen – who render them guilty and afraid. These incidents are reported but hardly elaborated upon. The distress they produce is, I believe, channelled into attacks upon despised features of the gay scene – the one-night stands and sugar daddies. As in *The Charioteer*, innocence tends to correlate with emotional authenticity.

Which of Us Two? records, ostensibly, the failure of the great love of Colin and John to prevail against the gay scene. It might be better to say that the dichotomy between inauthentic sex and the one great love is the problem that immobilizes Colin and John. Spencer notes the familiar heterosexual pattern whereby women are regarded as either mothers or whores (p. 232), but perhaps doesn't notice that this is being applied, in effect, to gay sexual potential: true love is with the madonna, scene contacts are with whores. For the grand passion is plausible only when they are separated; each time this happens, they are amazed by its intensity, but when they are together they can only intermittently sustain it. The opportunity for gay culture, still in the shadow of AIDS, is to develop ways of relating that are not confined by such heterosexual patterns.

John Tasker's Australian context seems not to affect the operations of the queer paradigm in *Which of Us Two?* I don't know how far Anglo-Saxon cultures outside England experienced a comparable development of the queer model (of course, there is no reason to expect it in non-Anglo-Saxon cultures). Michael Hurley shows similarities in Australia, and that they circulate particularly in the popular press and in literary writing: 'The appearance of the post-trial "Wilde" figure as demonic in the popular press, installed a new aspect in existing reading formations: the public was given a way of recognising male homosexuality.'[55] In the United States the Wilde trials, several correspondents told Havelock Ellis, had given 'definiteness and self-consciousness to the manifestations of homosexuality' – at least nine hundred sermons were preached on Wilde between 1895 and 1900.[56] At the same time, the molly-house model was thriving in cities at the turn of the century. In 1919–20 a navy investigation into homosexual practices still assumed this model, Martin Duberman shows – only the man playing the 'woman's part' was labelled as 'queer', and upper-class men and episcopal ministers were exempted from question despite effeminate manners. 'Many forms of behavior considered effeminate on the part of working-class men were regarded as appropriate to the status of upper-class men or to the ministerial duties of the clergy,' Duberman observes.[57] However, the queer image came into play as well: suspicion of queerness lighted eventually upon the upper-class men and ministers also. At this point, as I interpret Duberman's evidence, the older model jostled against the Wildean stereotype. In World War II, still, a sailor was able to assume that 'the stranger who performed fellatio' was 'homosexual', but not 'the man on whom it was performed'. 'The performer was a "fairy". The compliant sailor, not.'[58]

The balance of forces upon the queer stereotype seems to have been different in the United States. On the one hand, manliness is more vigorously required; on the other, the leisure class has had less authority, and has been regarded as 'unAmerican' in its orientation towards Europe. 'For American audiences,' John Clum

says, *The Green Bay Tree* 'established the stereotypical picture of
the homosexual as wealthy, effete – and British.'[59] This leads to the
dangerous situation where homophobia seems to be 'American'; in
England you may have to prove that you are not a disgusting
pervert, but you don't have to prove that you are English. 'A
mythological association has grown up,' Michael Bronski observes,
'about gay men, "high" culture, and the upper class.' Even today,
he adds, alongside the tough, virile image – 'the latest incarnation
of the American frontiersman' – there is a 'more European' image
of gay men, featuring 'a knowing, sophisticated glance' and 'a
precise poise and mannered grace. Like Oscar Wilde or Noel
Coward, they are decadent, effete although not obnoxious, decid-
edly upscale'.[60]

'In almost all American films, from comedies to romantic
dramas,' Vito Russo finds, 'working class American men are portrayed as much more valuable and certainly more virile than the
rich, effete dandies of Europe, who in spite of their success with
women are seen as essentially weak and helpless in a real man's
world.' This still may not mean same-sex passion – these dandies,
in the pre-trials mode, are successful with women. Until the 1930s,
Russo shows, there was plenty of effeminacy, but queerness had to
be in the eye of the beholder: 'The fact that most early movie sissies
were homosexual only if one chose to see them as being homosexual was simply a reflection of the fact that the existence of homosexuals in society was acknowledged only when society chose to do
so.'[61] Conversely, Russo does not find any homosexuals *not* in the
Wildean manner. In so far as there were any, that is how they were
expected to appear.

In 1959 Lawrence D. Mass and his friend Richard were
using an athletes/aesthetes split: they 'dated, excelled in sports and
were well regarded among our peers, so I knew we weren't
"homos" – the "queers" and "sissies" who were alternatively
ostracized, jeered, or otherwise victimized at school'.[62] In the early
1960s, a US man records, effeminacy was still central to queer
subculture: 'out' men were usually 'queens', 'effeminate'; 'Usually,
if you met somebody who was gay and butch, they were very
uptight, closety types and very, very neurotic.'[63] This is the initial
pattern in Harvey Fierstein's *Torch Song Trilogy* (1978–9). And,
conversely, gentrified manners might be taken as signalling queerness. Until recently, Donald Vining observes, 'Many a gay who

erred in assuming that a Southerner's gentle manner indicated probable receptivity to advances found himself thrown out of school, discharged from a job, beaten up, jailed, disgraced, or several of the above.'[64]

Camp and class

Jack Babuscio believes there is a 'gay sensibility'. It is camp, he says, and has four basic features: irony, aestheticism (defined by a Wildean aphorism), theatricality and humour.[65] These are virtually the ingredients of the dandified queer stereotype, except that Babuscio does not locate them in class terms. In my view camp, as used in gay male subculture, includes an allusion to leisure-class manners, deriving from the Wildean dandy. Hence, in part, the elements of theatricality and ironic disjunction: camp includes a 'sorry I spoke' acknowledgement of its inappropriateness in the mouth of the speaker. An appreciation of art – though that may be very much in earnest – fits well because posh culture is recognized, implicitly as being a leisured preserve, though perhaps impertinently invaded. Camp is not, therefore, as is usually imagined, grounded only, or even mainly, in an allusion to the femininity that is supposed to characterize women. That is there, but in compound with a lurking recollection of the impersonation (that is supposed to deceive no one) of the effeminate leisure-class dandy. Of course, younger users today need not be aware of all this. They are camp because other gay boys are camp.

Notes

1. Bryan Connon, *Beverley Nichols: A Life* (London: Constable, 1991), pp. 39–40. I am both pleased and annoyed to see that this episode has already been noticed by Eve Kosofsky Sedgwick, *Between Men* (New York: Columbia University Press, 1985), p. 95.
2. Martin Green, *Children of the Sun* (London: Constable, 1977), pp. 186–7. See Ed Cohen, *Talk on the Wilde Side* (New York: Routledge, 1993), pp. 100–1.
3. Alec Waugh, *The Loom of Youth* (London: Grant Richards, 1917), pp. 284–5. Waugh himself had experienced both romantic and sexual affairs, and had been asked to leave his school on account of

one of the latter (Alec Waugh, *The Early Years of Alec Waugh* (New York: Farrar, Strauss, 1963), pp. 50–1, 63).

4. Alec Waugh, *Public School Life* (London: Collins, 1922), pp. 137–8.

5. Robert Graves, *Goodbye to All That* (1929; Harmondsworth: Penguin, 1960), pp. 45–53.

6. Green, *Children of the Sun*, pp. 60, 152, 37–8.

7. Green, *Children of the Sun*, pp. 62–9, 107, 133–4, 195–6, 232; J. A. Mangan, *Athleticism in the Victorian and Edwardian Public School* (Cambridge University Press, 1981), ch. 6.

8. Cyril Connolly, *Enemies of Promise* (1938; London: Deutsch, 1973), p. 47.

9. Humphrey Carpenter, *The Brideshead Generation* (London: Weidenfeld, 1989), pp. 80–1.

10. H. Montgomery Hyde, *The Other Love* (London: Mayflower, 1972), p. 225.

11. W. H. Auden, 'An improbable life', in Richard Ellmann, ed., *Oscar Wilde*, Twentieth Century Views (Englewood Cliffs, NJ: Prentice-Hall, 1986), p. 136.

12. Terence Greenidge, *Degenerate Oxford?* (London: Chapman & Hall, 1930), pp. 82, 90–1, 98.

13. Anthony Blunt, 'From Bloomsbury to Marxism', *Studio International* (November 1973), 165–8, p. 164. 'There is no such thing as a moral or an immoral book. Books are well written, or badly written. That is all' (Oscar Wilde, *The Picture of Dorian Gray*, ed. Isobel Murray (Oxford University Press, World's Classics, 1981), p. xxiii).

14. Louis MacNeice, *The Strings Are False* (London: Faber, 1965), pp. 94, 103.

15. T. C. Worsley, *Flannelled Fool* (London: Alan Ross, 1967), pp. 40–1, 74; Michael Darlow and Gillian Hodson, *Terence Rattigan* (London: Quartet, 1979), p. 40. See also Hyde, *The Other Love*, pp. 222–5; Robert Graves and Alan Hodge, *The Long Week-end* (London: Faber, 1940), p. 124; Green, *Children of the Sun*, pp. 133–4, 203–4, 232, 346 *et passim*; Christopher Isherwood, *Down There on a Visit* (1962; London: Magnum, 1979), pp. 92–5.

16. John Galsworthy, *The Island Pharisees* (1904; London: Heinemann, 1933), p. 36.

17. Green, *Children of the Sun*, p. 115.

18. Richard Findlater, *Banned* (London: McGibbon & Kee, 1967), p. 142. See Kaier Curtin, *We Can Always Call Them Bulgarians* (Boston: Alyson Publications, 1987), pp. 176–88.

19. See Peter Burton, introduction to *The Green Bay Tree*, in Michael Wilcox, ed., *Gay Plays*, vol. 1 (London: Methuen, 1984), p. 53. The play is quoted from this edition.

20. Curtin, *We Can Always Call Them Bulgarians*, p. 183.

21. Curtin, *We Can Always Call Them Bulgarians*, pp. 183–7.

22. Worsley, *Flannelled Fool*, p. 26.

23. Wyndham Lewis, *Self Condemned* (Manchester: Carcanet, 1983), p. 214.

24. Jocelyn Brooke, *The Orchid Trilogy* (Harmondsworth: Penguin, 1981), pp. 371–3. On *Put Out More Flags*, see Alan Sinfield, *Literature, Politics and Culture in Postwar Britain* (Oxford: Blackwell and Berkeley: California University Press, 1989) pp. 60–2.

25. Havelock Ellis, *Sexual Inversion, Studies in the Psychology of Sex*, vol. 2, part 2 (New York: Random House, 1936), pp. 21, 64.

26. Sedgwick, *Between Men*, pp. 172–3. Sedgwick instances Carroll, Ruskin, T. E. Lawrence, Barrie and Ackerley as non-aristocrats. Her argument is disputed by Richard Dellamora as deterministic (*Masculine Desire* (Chapel Hill: North Carolina University Press, 1990), pp. 9–12). However, like Sedgwick, I am interested in the availability of milieux and discourses; certainly individuals will have discovered individual accommodations.

27. Wilde and others, *Teleny*, ed. John McRae (London: Gay Men's Press, 1986), pp. 141–2. On *Teleny* see Ed Cohen, 'Writing gone Wilde: homoerotic desire in the closet of representation', *PMLA*, **102** (1987), 801–13.

28. Bob Cant and Susan Hemmings, eds, *Radical Records* (London: Routledge, 1988), p. 15.

29. Kevin Porter and Jeffrey Weeks, eds, *Between the Acts* (London: Routledge, 1991), p. 52. I understand that Durham University is very lively now.

30. Alan Bray, *Homosexuality in Renaissance England* (London: Gay Men's Press, 1982), p. 79.

31. See Hall Carpenter Archives, Gay Men's Oral History Group, *Walking After Midnight* (London: Routledge, 1989), pp. 60, 133; Porter and Weeks, eds, *Between the Acts*, pp. 50, 110.

32. Quentin Crisp, *The Naked Civil Servant* (1968; New York: Plume, 1983), p. 26. See Marshall, 'Pansies, perverts', in Kenneth Plummer, ed., *The Making of the Modern Homosexual* (London: Hutchinson, 1981), pp. 146–7; Marjorie Garber, *Vested Interests* (London: Routledge, 1992), pp. 137–41.

33. Jean Genet, *The Thief's Journal*, trans. Bernard Frechtman (Harmondsworth: Penguin, 1967), p. 76; Hall Carpenter, *Walking After Midnight*, p. 133 (and see p. 60).

34. Sedgwick, *Between Men*, pp. 93–4, 172–7, 206–8.

35. Quoted by John Fletcher, 'Forster's self-erasure: *Maurice* and the scene of masculine love', in Bristow, ed., *Sexual Sameness* (London: Routledge, 1992), p. 83.

36. Fletcher, 'Forster's self-erasure', p. 90. Fletcher quotes Forster's remark about himself, from Francis King, *E. M. Forster* (London: Thames & Hudson, 1978), p. 80.

37. See Alan Sinfield, 'Closet dramas: homosexual representation and class in postwar British theater', *Genders*, **9** (1990), 112–31.

38. Mary Renault, *The Charioteer* (London: New English Library, 1990), pp. 150, 340.

39. Porter and Weeks, eds, *Between the Acts*, p. 29. See Jeffrey Weeks, 'Discourse, desire and sexual deviance', in Kenneth Plummer, ed., *The Making of the Modern Homosexual* (London: Hutchinson, 1981), p. 105; Jamie Gough, 'Theories of sexual identity and the masculinization of the gay man', in Simon Shepherd and Mick Wallis, eds, *Coming On Strong* (London: Allen & Unwin, 1989), pp. 126–8.

40. Cant and Hemmings, eds, *Radical Records*, p. 234.

41. Robert Roberts, *The Classic Slum* (Manchester University Press, 1971), pp. 36–7. I am indebted to John Banks for this reference.

42. Richard Hoggart, *The Uses of Literacy* (Harmondsworth: Penguin, 1958), p. 183.

43. J. R. Ackerley, *We Think the World of You* (1960; London: Four Square, 1963), pp. 73, 82–3.

44. James Kirkup, *I, of All People* (London: Weidenfeld, 1988), pp. 19, 54, 76.

45. Porter and Weeks, eds, *Between the Acts*, p. 62.

46. Derek Cohen and Richard Dyer, 'The politics of gay culture', in Gay Left Collective, eds, *Homosexuality: Power and Politics* (London: Allison & Busby, 1980), pp. 176–8.

47. Porter and Weeks, eds, *Between the Acts*, pp. 138, 113. See Marshall, 'Pansies, perverts', pp. 136, 148–9.

48. Porter and Weeks, eds, *Between the Acts*, p. 141; see Hyde, *Other Love*, pp. 221–2 and ch. 6; Jeffrey Weeks, *Coming Out* (London: Quartet, 1977), pp. 33–44; Sinfield, *Literature, Politics and Culture*, ch. 5.

49. Gordon Westwood, *A Minority* (London: Longmans, 1960), p. 118. Westwood was a pseudonym for the sociologist Michael Schofield.

50. Auden, 'Improbable life', in Ellmann, *Wilde*, Views, p. 124; so Richard Ellmann, *Oscar Wilde* (London: Hamish Hamilton, 1987), p. 366.

51. Peter Burton, introduction to *The Green Bay Tree*, in Wilcox, ed., *Gay Plays*, vol. 1, p. 54.

52. *The Denton Welch Journals*, ed. Jocelyn Brooke (London: Hamish Hamilton, 1952), p. 11; see pp. 40–2.

53. Noel Greig, *The Dear Love of Comrades*, in *Two Gay Sweatshop Plays* (London: Gay Men's Press, 1979), pp. 133, 137–8; 'Merrill' is the more usual spelling. See Weeks, *Coming Out*, ch. 6; Sheila Rowbotham and Jeffrey Weeks, *Socialism and the New Life* (London: Pluto, 1977).

54. Colin Spencer, *Which of Us Two?* (London: Viking, 1990), pp. 41–2, 44.

55. Michael Hurley, 'Homosexualities: fiction, reading and moral training', in Terry Threadgold and Anne Cranny-Francis, eds,

Feminine, Masculine and Representation (Sydney: Allen & Unwin, 1990), p. 164.

56. Ellis, *Sexual Inversion*, p. 352; Ellmann, *Oscar Wilde*, p. 515.

57. Martin Duberman, 'Christian brotherhood or sexual perversion', in Martin Duberman, Martha Vicinus and George Chauncey, Jr, *Hidden from History* (Harmondsworth: Penguin, 1991), pp. 295–7, 308. See Jonathan Katz, *Gay American History* (New York: Avon Books, 1978), pp. 68–81.

58. Quoted in Donald Webster Cory, *The Homosexual in America* (1951), with a retrospective foreword (New York: Arno Press, 1975), p. 188.

59. John M. Clum, *Acting Gay* (New York: Columbia University Press, 1992), p. 99.

60. Michael Bronski, *Culture Clash* (Boston: South End Press, 1984), pp. 140, 186.

61. Vito Russo, *The Celluloid Closet*, rev. edn (New York: Harper & Row, 1987), pp. 6, 32; see pp. 32–40. On effeminacy and the pioneer in the USA, see Alan Sinfield, *Faultlines: Cultural Materialism and the Politics of Dissident Reading* (Berkeley: California University Press and Oxford: Oxford University Press, 1992), ch. 10; Alan Sinfield, *Cultural Politics – Queer Reading* (Philadelphia: University of Pennsylvania Press and London: Routledge, 1994), ch. 3.

62. Lawrence D. Mass, Foreword, in James Kenneth Melson, *The Golden Boy* (New York: Harrington Park Press, 1992), p. viii.

63. Hall Carpenter Archives, *Walking After Midnight*, pp. 80, 87.

64. Quoted from the *Advocate*, 18 March 1982, p. 24, by James T. Sears, *Growing Up Gay in the South* (New York: Harrington Park, 1991), p. 407.

65. Jack Babuscio, 'Camp and the gay sensibility', in Richard Dyer, ed., *Gays and Film* (London: British Film Institute, 1977), p. 42. Cf. Andrew Ross, *No Respect* (London: Routledge, 1989), pp. 145–6; David T. Evans, *Sexual Citizenship* (London: Routledge, 1993), pp. 96–9.

Chapter seven

Freud and the Cross-sex Grid

FOR much of the twentieth century, the medical model of homosexuality seemed preferable to the good-and-evil model (though, as we have seen in other aspects, one did not tidily replace the other – AIDS has facilitated the revival of good-and-evil). Being sick entitles you to better treatment than being wicked. However, as Rictor Norton argues, it may have made matters worse.

> The oppression which the Georgian molly faced was largely external: fear of capture, conviction, and execution. But the oppression experienced by the Victorian margery and the modern poof and queer became internalised as shame and guilt – repression from which there is no escape. For many, especially for the puritan middle classes, fear was replaced by self-loathing, and executions were replaced by suicides.[1]

Norton's point, in part, is that looking back to earlier historical periods will help us to see that it doesn't have to be that way.

The medical model has come from all directions, but by the 1950s the Freudian version had become the most influential. In Britain Dr Eustace Chesser published *Odd Man Out: Homosexuality in Men and Women* (1959; it is a nice touch, I suppose, to include lesbians as odd men):

> Over-indulgence by the mother makes it difficult for a boy to break his infantile dependence on her. He remains tied to her apron-strings. She shields him from all those rough contacts

which would strengthen his masculinity. At a time when he is essentially bisexual (or more correctly, perhaps, ambisexual), the feminine side of him is dangerously encouraged.[2]

In the United States Donald Webster Cory, in his campaigning book *The Homosexual in America* (1951), attributes homosexuality to one or another malfunction in the Oedipal family romance – unbalanced love of a boy for his mother, effort of a boy to replace an absent or inadequate father, identification of a boy with his mother, lack of love for a boy from his mother. Cory particularly endorses Clifford Allen, who perhaps meant to help when he declared that the homosexual 'is ill in much the same way as a dwarf is ill – because he has never developed'.[3] Immaturity is not at odds with femininity, of course, since women are regarded as less than fully developed people. Gustav Bychowski considered the male practitioner of fellatio both feminine and immature: 'As a woman (identifying with his mother), the patient was submitting to men, letting himself be humiliated by them. Thus he was expecting to share their greatness and to become like one of them. On the other hand, however, he was the little child, still being suckled by the phallic mother.' Homosexuals, psychoanalysts asserted, 'seek out a male who pretends to be a female'; they 'impersonate a female', one analyst averred; 'passive homosexuals, therefore, dress, walk, talk and adorn themselves like women'.[4]

The cross-sex grid plainly informs these accounts. Masculine and feminine are the key attributes; normally they correlate with men and women respectively; when something goes wrong they dominate individuals of the 'wrong' gender. As Kenneth Lewes observes, 'Homosexuals were seen as deeply flawed and defective because they shared certain psychic characteristics with women.'[5] This chapter considers how far this outcome is a necessary corollary of Freud's theory.

'We may call them masculine and feminine'

David Halperin credits Havelock Ellis and Freud with a key stage in the development of the possibility of gay identity: separating sexual practices from gender. 'That sexual object-choice might be wholly independent of such "secondary" characteristics as masculinity or femininity never seems to have entered anyone's head' until Havelock Ellis's *Sexual Inversion* (1897) and Freud's *Three Essays*.[6] However, this move still does not displace the normative notions 'masculinity' and 'femininity'. In 'The psychogenesis of a case of homosexuality in a woman' (1920), Freud writes: 'A man in whose character feminine attributes obviously predominate, who may, indeed, behave in love like a woman, might be expected, from this feminine attitude, to choose a man for his love-object; but he may nevertheless be heterosexual, and show no more inversion in respect to his object than an average normal man.'[7] This does undermine the expectation of earlier sexologists that feminine men will be homosexual. Nevertheless, 'feminine attributes' are offered as a given; and they are assumed to have an underlying correlation with behaving 'like a woman' – another given. So although the idea of a feminine mind in a masculine body is reshuffled, the terms of its initial enunciation are not disturbed. Neither – and this is surely a consequence – is the assumption as to what 'an average normal man' is like.

What is surprising is that Freud is aware that he has adopted an unsatisfactory construct, but declines to pursue it further. He adds: 'psycho-analysis cannot elucidate the intrinsic nature of what in conventional or in biological phraseology is termed "masculine" and "feminine": *it simply takes over the two concepts and makes them the foundation of its work*' (p. 171; my italics). This pattern recurs – because, I believe, Freud is unwilling to relinquish masculine and feminine, however illogical he finds them to be.

In *Three Essays on the Theory of Sexuality* (1905), Freud dismisses the sexologists' theories of innate inversion as crude, and disputes the anatomical basis they had been claiming. Even a change-over of 'mental qualities, instincts and character traits' cannot be demonstrated, let alone a physiological cross-over. Nevertheless, the cross-sex grid is still there, in more complex psychological form. 'In men the most complete mental masculinity can be accompanied with inversion', Freud says; while some inverts feel themselves to be women in search of men, others look for what are 'in fact feminine mental traits'.[8] This is the point: the *fact* of 'feminine mental traits'; masculine and feminine attributes may be weirdly distributed in the case of homosexuals, but they are (1) known and (2) normatively attached to men and women respectively. Freud is still filtering all sexualities through a cross-sex grid.

It was the same, he continues, in ancient Greece: 'what excited a man's love was not the *masculine* character of a boy, but his physical resemblance to a woman as well as his feminine mental qualities – his shyness, his modesty and his need for instruction and assistance' (p. 10). This is what 'a woman' is supposed to be like – shy, modest and in need of instruction; those are her 'feminine mental qualities'. This cannot be accounted for as Freud addressing a contingent cultural arrangement, since he is purporting to explain same-sex practices in two very different cultures – among contemporary inverts and ancient Greeks. Nor can it be Freud's response to women of his time – innumerable Victorian women were not like that. The cross-sexual binary structure derives here from prior, unexamined notions about women and the feminine. Lesbians, Freud believes, are less troublesome to assess: 'the position in the case of women is less ambiguous; for among them the active inverts exhibit masculine characteristics, both physical and mental, with peculiar frequency and look for femininity in their sexual objects – though here again a closer knowledge of the facts might reveal a greater variety' (p. 11).

Freud's consequent suggestion, that the invert's sexual object is 'a compromise between an impulse that seeks for a man and one that seeks for a woman' (p. 10), maintains this emphasis. For bisexuality is still predicated on the masculine/feminine binary structure. It may threaten the discreteness of the categories masculine and feminine, but it retains them as a necessary framework of understanding. This is recognized by Juliet Mitchell when she emphasizes that, in Freud's view, 'human subjectivity cannot ultimately exist outside a division into one of two sexes', and therefore 'bisexuality is a movement across a line, it is *not* androgyny'.[9] Androgyny would unite the characteristics of both sexes, producing a new form (often termed hermaphrodite). Bisexuality is an indecision or alternation between two given and persisting forms; Freud attributes a primary bisexuality to the infant, but it is waiting to be resolved, through the Oedipus complex, into masculine or feminine.

In a series of footnotes to the passage about homosexuality in *Three Essays*, Freud sketches diverse caveats and elaborations, but he doesn't abandon the cross-sex grid. In 1915 the idea of the ambiguity of the 'sexual object' of the homosexual is tidied up with a further thought: that the object is thus 'a kind of reflection of the subject's own bisexual nature' (p. 10). In a note added in 1920 Freud grants the existence of two types of homosexuals, as Sandor Ferenczi had proposed: '"subject homoerotics", who feel and behave like women, and "object homoerotics", who are completely masculine and who have merely exchanged a female for a male object' (p. 13). Once more, these are re-combinations of the usual masculine and feminine attributes. Louise J. Kaplan has observed this: despite his statement that 'all human beings are capable of making a homosexual object choice', Freud often 'would think just like the sexologists he was rebelling against and write about male and female differences as though he had the prescriptions for normal femininity and masculinity'.[10]

In 'The claims of psycho-analysis to scientific interest' (1913) Freud comes to the point of recognizing that he has been using cultural categories as if they were biological categories.

> In spite of all our efforts to prevent biological terminology and considerations from dominating psycho-analytic work, we cannot avoid using them even in our descriptions of the phenomena that we study. We cannot help regarding the term 'instinct' as a concept on the frontier between the spheres of psychology and biology. We speak, too, of 'masculine' and 'feminine' attributes and impulses, although, strictly speaking, the differences between the sexes can lay claim to no special physical characterisation.[11]

This does seem to acknowledge that physical gender has no natural association with masculine and feminine attributes. Yet the connection creeps back as the paragraph continues:

> What we speak of in ordinary life as 'masculine' or 'feminine' reduces itself from the point of view of psychology to the qualities of 'activity' and 'passivity' – that is, to qualities determined not by the instincts themselves but by their aims. The regular association of these 'active' and 'passive' instincts in mental life reflects the bisexuality of individuals, which is among the clinical postulates of psycho-analysis.

'Active' and 'passive' are properly constituted concepts, the first sentence says, and it is for cultural convenience that we correlate them in ordinary life with sexual propensities. Even so, the second sentence says, this '*reflects the bisexuality of individuals*'. So there is after all a basis for the attribution of normative masculine and feminine characteristics: they are inscribed in human nature as the components of an *a priori* bisexuality. Active/passive is a front for masculine/feminine.

As Guy Hocquenghem notices, Ferenczi makes the same move in the essay on homosexuality that Freud admired. Ferenczi acknowledges at one point that what he has been calling 'maleness' and 'femaleness' should be understood as '*activity* (aggressivity) of the sexual hunger', and '*passivity* (tendency to repression), narcissism and intuitiveness'. Of course, this is the customary ideology of what men and women are supposed basically to be like, so the 'understanding' doesn't take us very far. Ferenczi adds: 'The physical attributes of sex are, of course, mingled in every individual – though in unequal proportion.' 'In other words,' Hocquenghem elucidates, 'it is all just a matter of the dosage – but the general characteristics are permanent.'[12] The 'physical attributes of sex' are given, and heterosexual men and women have them 'mingled' in a certain proportion – the one that manifests a positive resolution of the Oedipus complex and corresponds to prevailing ideological norms. Ferenczi, Hocquenghem concludes, produces 'a microcosmic homosexual world which luckily can be compared point by point with the heterosexual one, is metaphorically related to it as one entity parallel to another, and is cursed with being but a perverse caricature of normality' (p. 111).

Reading Freud is like reading Marx or the Bible: in such a massive and ambitious body of writing, almost any emphasis can be supported. I am not saying that Freud never questions the bases of masculinity and femininity; rather that, although he is aware of the questions that may be asked, the binary structure keeps finding its way back. As Jacqueline Rose argues, in respect of other concepts that are unacceptable today, the importance of this construct for Freud may lie in the indication it offers that something is being *forced*.[13] In *New Introductory Lectures in Psychoanalysis* (1933) Freud admits, totally, that his earlier resolution – making ' "active" coincide with "masculine" and "passive" with "feminine" ' – is either tautologous or trivial: it serves 'no useful purpose and adds nothing to our knowledge'.[14] Yet, a couple of pages later, he is asking himself 'how does a girl pass from her mother to an attachment to her father? or, in other words, how does she pass from her masculine phase to the feminine one to which she is biologically destined?' (p. 152). Freud more or less acknowledges that he is reverting to the kind of formulation that he has just repudiated: 'These wishes represent active as well as passive impulses; if we relate them to the differentiation of the sexes which is to appear later – though we should avoid doing so as far as possible – *we may call them masculine and feminine*' (p. 153; my emphasis). Freud needs to call them this because, despite his disclaimers, he does have a theory of femininity to offer in this lecture: penis envy. After an elaborate set of postulates – including a phallic period, a masculinity complex, a phallic mother, and passive instinctual impulses – he concludes that we should perhaps 'recognise this wish for a penis as being *par excellence* a feminine one' (p. 162).

A major idea is at stake in this particular instance of forcing. Freud doesn't want to let go of the cross-sex grid because the Oedipus theory depends upon it. According to that theory, infants identify with mothers and fathers – who are presumptively feminine and masculine. This may be observed in the 'Wolfman' analysis, where Freud records a breakthrough at the point where the boy 'discovered the vagina and the biological significance of masculine and feminine. He understood now that active was the same as masculine, while passive was the same as feminine'.[15] Negotiating this *discovery*, this *understanding*, is what the supposed Oedipus complex is all about; that is why the binary structure keeps creeping back, despite Freud's awareness that it involves an unacceptable biologism.

If you start from psychoanalysis, it is very hard to avoid coming back to this point. Kaja Silverman remarks at one moment, in her exciting book *Male Subjectivity at the Margins*, 'It should be evident by now that I am committed to a radically de-essentializing account both of femininity and of male homosexuality.'[16] Such an approach seems to be working when Silverman notes the 'anomaly' whereby Freud designates masochism 'feminine', in the face of evidence that it is manifested at least as frequently by males. Silverman offers two explanations for this blatantly ideological gender stereotyping. The first is that masochism is 'an accepted – indeed a requisite – element of "normal" female subjectivity, providing a crucial mechanism for eroticizing lack and subordination', and therefore only by women can it 'be safely acknowledged'. That is a social theory: masochism gets associated with women because they find it tactically useful and don't try to hide it. However, Silverman then elaborates that into the proposition that masochism is not pathological in women. From there, it is only a short slide into the Freudian assumption that there is a non-pathological, normative development, through interaction with the masculinity and femininity of father and mother respectively: while masochism 'can be effortlessly accommodated within the little girl's *positive* Oedipus complex, it can only be contained within the little boy's *negative* Oedipus complex' (pp. 189–90). When she gets to male homosexuality, Silverman finds 'we must be prepared to entertain the possibility' that a gay man might deploy signifiers of femininity not as a social strategy, but because 'an identification with "woman" constitutes the very basis of his identity, and/or the position from which he desires' (p. 344). After all the manoeuvring, we are still not far from the female soul in the male body.

The question, of course, if one hopes to derive the selection of homosexuality or heterosexuality from the Oedipus theory, is what determines the direction of the child's identification – with the father or with the mother. It is 'the relative strength of the masculine and feminine sexual dispositions', Freud declares in *The Ego and the Id* (1923).[17] Where can these dispositions come from? It must be biology: a homosexual or heterosexual resolution of the Oedipus complex depends on the subject's *prior disposition* towards the masculine or feminine. Freud postulates such a process in the 'Wolfman' analysis, where the boy's phantasies with regard to his mother and father are said to indicate a homosexual or heterosexual orientation 'according as the subject's attitude is feminine or masculine'.[18] Lewes summarizes:

> The sexual constitution of most male children contains a larger proportion of activity than passivity, and therefore inclines the child toward adopting an active stance with respect to the mother. In some children, however, the proportion of passivity is greater than that of activity, so the child is more inclined to adopt a passive sexual stance.[19]

Since in our society there appear to be more heterosexuals than homosexuals, the former would seem to be the 'natural' choice of most people. Thus the supposition of masculine and feminine dispositions builds in a heterosexual bias.

A psychology of guilt

Of course, constitutional, normative femininity is bad news for women. Elizabeth Cowie, a feminist trying to work within the Freudian tradition, observes: 'The equation active = masculine / passive = feminine is one of the most disputed but also resilient premisses within psychoanalytic theory. If it is simply true, then as feminine theorists we will have to pack up our books and go home.' Freud's views on femininity, Cowie says, 'contain a series of discontinuities, and even downright contradictions, so that he appears to give with the right hand what he takes away with the left.'[20] She sees a way round in the ideas of Jean Laplanche, who argues that the sexual drive arises in human interaction, rather than being determined by its source in the body.

The problem with Freud's notions of feminine sexuality, Laplanche says, is precisely that 'he has no proper conception of what activity and passivity are'. In this regard, Freud was 'completely taken in by ... ideology'. 'Is being masochistic more passive than active?' Laplanche asks. 'Is penetration more active than receiving the penis? Why? After all it is a very superficial point of view to think the male is active and the female passive in coitus.'[21] This is the crunch of the matter: there is no good reason to regard the active/passive binary structure as to do with men and women respectively, any more than the masculine/feminine binary for which it is sometimes the alibi.

Feminine and masculine are cultural constructs, obviously with the primary function of sustaining the current pattern of heterosexual relations. Very many heterosexuals are not respectively masculine and feminine, or not in certain respects, or not all of the time. That is why we observe heterosexuality plunged into inconsistency and anxiety; it is aggressive because insecure. For lesbians and gay men, the situation is indeed perverse: a model of how heterosexual men and women are supposed to be, which is tendentious, inadequate and oppressive in the first place, is twisted into bizarre contortions in order to purport to describe us. Who is active, who passive, in fellatio?

What we are actually struggling with is cultural prejudices that have been translated into laws of the psyche. Judith Butler comments: 'the dispositions that Freud assumes to be primary or constitutive facts of sexual life' are 'traces of a history of enforced sexual prohibitions'.[22] If a youngster is *disposed* not to develop a 'wrong' proportion of masculinity or femininity, it is because she or he discerns that it will attract stigma. According to Freud, the boy who chooses heterosexuality does so out of fear of castration by the father; but, as Butler observes, the inhibition must actually be 'the fear of "feminization" associated within heterosexual cultures with male homosexuality' (p. 59). A cultural taboo is naturalized.

And this, presumably, suits our social system; otherwise the two would not thrive together as they do. As Jeffrey Weeks says, expounding Gilles Deleuze and Félix Guattari's *Anti-Oedipus*,

> By concentrating on an oedipal triangulation of parents and child, [psychoanalysis] accepts the social, political and religious forms of domination in modern society, and is complicit with how capitalism has constructed social order ... it is both the discoverer of the mechanisms of desire and the organiser of its control.

For why should we corral the pressures and limits upon the individual into two batches labelled 'father' and 'mother'? 'The train is not necessarily daddy, nor is the train station necessarily mommy,' Deleuze and Guattari observe.[23] What they do not quite say, Guy Hocquenghem adds, 'is that the Oedipal system is not only a system of exclusive disjunction but also the system of oppression of one sexual mode, the heterosexual family mode, over all possible other modes'.[24]

For psychoanalytic notions, Hocquenghem says, constitute 'the most amazing system of guilt-inducement ever invented' (p. 59). They persuade whole categories of individuals to accept self-oppression as the price of difference. Asked by the manager of the Labour Exchange why he goes around looking as he does, Quentin Crisp replies, 'Because this is the way I am. I wouldn't like you or anyone else to think I was ashamed.' But Crisp was ashamed. He couldn't see that the 1967 UK act, legalizing many homosexual acts in private, would be much help: 'To rob blackmail of its potency, it would be necessary to remove the homosexual's feeling of shame. This no power on earth can do.'[25] Hocquenghem writes:

> Jailing homosexuals was sufficient at a time when sodomites were thought to be degenerates of the same type as the insane. Modern repression demands justifications, an interplay between legal guilt and the psychology of guilt. The judge's action is accompanied by the psychologist's understanding: the former stands for the positive institution of the judgement passed by normality, the latter implants guilt in the very heart of the individual. If repression is to be effective, the culprit must realise that it is necessary. The Law of the Father is vital to the fulfilment of the institutional laws. There is no real justice unless the accused has a guilty conscience. (p. 59)

The final twist is the reluctance of many gay men and some lesbians (there seems to be a difference) to repudiate psychoanalysis. First, such a repudiation seems to threaten a loss of explanatory resource. If you experience stigma to the extent that many lesbians and gay men do, any explanation may seem better than the sense that you are starkly intolerable, and the psychoanalytic strategy of noticing only confirmatory evidence allows people to believe that their family situation has indeed been formative in the way Freud proposed. Second, one should not appear to be flinching before the awful power of the law of the Freudian father; repudiating it is, by definition, a guilt-ridden project. So even if psychoanalysis does offer a limiting and demeaning picture of homosexuals, we should nevertheless, it is felt, entertain that picture. Psychoanalysis, like all successful systems, includes the conditions for its own reproduction.

It is not that I do not believe in psychic life, or that I would not like to have a theory of it. The trouble is, the plausible conceptual space for that exploration has been occupied, for our time, by Freudianism, which deploys fail-safe, double-bind, double-take and self-defence mechanisms of a subtlety undreamt of in Marxism or Christianity – the main alternative faiths of the century. So it is very difficult to envisage other terms with which to think our emotional processes. A substantially new framework, a paradigm shift, will be required to replace that, or even to challenge it effectively. And that will have to imply a major shift in social relations in the western world.

Today, the most likely therapeutic proposition is that we should get our so-called masculine and feminine attributes into due proportion. Richard Isay, attempting a gay-friendly version of psychoanalysis, observes that western culture devalues 'feminine' attributes, associates them with male gays, and thereby leads us to despise ourselves. He urges placing the same value 'upon sensitivity, compassion, nurturing, and loving as on aggressivity, competition, and productivity'.[26] Revaluing feminine attributes, he says, 'might enable heterosexual men to perceive that men who love other men may also be masculine' (p. 129). Does this mean that sensitivity is actually masculine, or that gay men are aggressive as well as sensitive, and hence masculine? Either way, we are invited to accept the priority of masculinity and the judgement of 'heterosexual men'. Isay is reshuffling the pack: the problem is the binary structure and its normative attribution to men and women, and he doesn't challenge that. He recycles another Freudian move when he says he has discerned 'the normal development of gay men' (p. 10; he is drawn to the idea of a genetic basis for homosexuality). Why do we need to decide what is normal? What about gay men whose 'development' hasn't been 'normal'? Will it be legitimate to 'cure'/discriminate against them?

Isay's warnings about heterosexist psychoanalysis are powerful, and his 'gay positive' or 'gay affirmative' therapy must be an improvement (p. 121). However, any therapeutic model is crucially limited. As Isay grants, 'it takes enormous effort for gay men to maintain their sense of dignity and self-worth in a society that remains inimical to them and their sexuality' (p. 133). Attempting to establish 'self-worth' in mainstream terms – the terms through which we are despised – must be futile. We cannot handle the oppression inscribed in the cross-sex grid by individual, personal, adaptation. Lesbians and gay men are not going to be accommodated in our societies without radical social change, and we are not going to feel significantly better about ourselves without an analysis that includes that perception. Adjusting to an oppressive system cannot be the answer; in the last analysis, it is not we who need the therapy.

Notes

1. Rictor Norton, *Mother Clap's Molly House* (London: Gay Men's Press, 1992), p. 261.

2. Dr Eustace Chesser, *Odd Man Out* (London: Gollancz, 1959), p. 54.

3. Donald Webster Cory, *The Homosexual in America* (1951), with a retrospective foreword (New York: Arno Press, 1975), pp. 67–75; Clifford Allen, quoted by Kenneth Lewes, *The Psychoanalytic Theory of Male Homosexuality* (London: Quartet, 1989), p. 149. See Henry Abelove, 'Freud, male homosexuality, and the Americans', *Dissent* (winter 1986), 59–69.

4. Gustav Bychowski, 'The ego of homosexuals', *International Journal of Psychoanalysis*, **26** (1945), p. 118; Sandor Rado (1949) and Edmund Bergler (1948, 1954), quoted by Lewes, *Psychoanalytic Theory*, pp. 135–6.

5. Lewes, *Psychoanalytic Theory*, p. 237.

6. David M. Halperin, *One Hundred Years of Homosexuality* (New York and London: Routledge, 1990), p. 16.

7. Sigmund Freud, *Standard Edition of the Complete Psychological Works*, ed. James Strachey, vol. 18 (London: Hogarth, 1955), p. 170. I am specially grateful to Rachel Bowlby for help with Freud.

8. Sigmund Freud, *Three Essays on the Theory of Sexuality*, ed. James Strachey (London: Hogarth, 1962), pp. 7–9. See George Chauncey, Jr, 'From sexual inversion to homosexuality: medicine and the changing conceptualization of female deviance', *Salmagundi*, **58–9** (1982–83), 114–46, pp. 117–28; Simon Watney, 'The banality of gender', *Oxford Literary Review*, 8 (1–2) (1986), special issue, *Sexual Difference*, 13–21; Carole-Anne Tyler, 'Boys will be girls: the politics of gay drag', in Diana Fuss, ed., *Inside/Out* (New York: Routledge, 1991), pp. 34–5; David F. Greenberg, *The Construction of Homosexuality* (Chicago University Press, 1988), pp. 383–96.

9. Juliet Mitchell, *Women: The Longest Revolution* (London: Virago, 1984), pp. 307–8; the whole book is relevant. See Judith Butler, *Gender Trouble* (New York and London: Routledge, 1990), pp. 54–65; Jonathan Dollimore, *Sexual Dissidence* (Oxford: Clarendon, 1991), pp. 253–67.

10. Louise J. Kaplan, *Female Perversions* (London: Pandora, 1991), p. 47. See also Valerie Traub, *Desire and Anxiety* (New York: Routledge, 1992), pp. 96–102.

11. Sigmund Freud, 'The claims of psycho-analysis to scientific interest' (1913), *Standard Edition of the Complete Psychological Works*, ed. James Strachey, vol. 13 (London: Hogarth, 1955), p. 182.

12. Guy Hocquenghem, *Homosexual Desire*, trans. Daniella Dangoor (London: Allison & Busby, 1978), pp. 109–10; all ch. 5 is highly pertinent.

13. Jacqueline Rose, *Sexuality in the Field of Vision* (London: Verso, 1986), pp. 92–3; and see Jeffrey Weeks, *Sexuality and Its Discontents* (London: Routledge, 1985), pp. 142–3.

14. Sigmund Freud, *New Introductory Lectures in Psychoanalysis*, trans. James Strachey, Penguin Freud Library, vol. 2 (Harmondsworth: Penguin, 1973), pp. 146–50. See further Mandy Merck, 'The train of thought in Freud's "Case of homosexuality in a woman" ', *m/f*, **11/12** (1986), 35–46; Rachel Bowlby, *Still Crazy After All These Years* (London: Routledge, 1992), ch. 8.

15. Sigmund Freud, 'From the history of an infantile neurosis', *Standard Edition of the Complete Psychological Works*, ed. James Strachey, vol. 17 (London: Hogarth, 1955), p. 47. See further Humberto Nagera, *Basic Psychoanalytic Concepts on the Libido Theory* (London: Maresfield Reprints, 1981), chs 19, 20; Stephen Heath, 'Joan Riviere and the masquerade', in Victor Burgin, James Donald and Cora Kaplan, eds, *Formations of Fantasy* (London: Methuen, 1986); John Fletcher, 'Freud and his uses: psychoanalysis and gay theory', in Simon Shepherd and Mick Wallis, eds, *Coming On Strong* (London: Allen & Unwin, 1989); Dollimore, *Sexual Dissidence*, pp. 195–204.

16. Kaja Silverman, *Male Subjectivity at the Margins* (New York: Routledge, 1992), p. 355.

17. Sigmund Freud, *Standard Edition of the Complete Psychological Works*, ed. James Strachey, vol. 19 (London: Hogarth, 1961), p. 33.

18. Freud, 'From the history of an infantile neurosis', pp. 101–2.

19. Lewes, *Psychoanalytic Theory*, p. 41; see pp. 35–47.

20. In John Fletcher and Martin Stanton, eds, *Jean Laplanche: Seduction, Translation, Drives* (London: Institute of Contemporary Arts, 1992), pp. 121, 129.

21. Fletcher and Stanton, eds, *Jean Laplanche*, pp. 79–80. I am grateful to John Fletcher for drawing my attention to Laplanche.

22. Butler, *Gender Trouble*, p. 64. See Kaplan, *Female Perversions*.

23. Weeks, *Sexuality and Its Discontents*, p. 174; Gilles Deleuze and Félix Guattari, *Anti-Oedipus*, trans. Robert Hurley, Mark Seem and Helen R. Lane (New York: Viking, 1977), p. 46; see pp. 117–20 *et passim*.

24. Guy Hocquenghem, *Homosexual Desire*, p. 124. See Dollimore, *Sexual Dissidence*, pp. 206–12.

25. Quentin Crisp, *The Naked Civil Servant* (1968; New York: Plume, 1983), pp. 51, 203.
26. Richard A. Isay, *Being Homosexual* (Harmondsworth: Penguin, 1993), pp. 128–9. See also Graham Jackson, *The Secret Lore of Gardening* (Toronto: Inner City Books, 1991).

Chapter eight

Subcultural Strategies

'WE' are, have to be, the outcome of our ongoing negotiations with the cultural repertoire that we perceive as available to us; there are no selves without culture. Those negotiations, I have shown, have been conducted in radically different terms through the centuries. 'Oscar Wilde' has been a shorthand notation for one way of apprehending and living our sexual and emotional potential. Indeed, far more than sexuality is implicated in that way: personal relationships, class, gender, race and ethnicity, our ideas of art and subculture.

Chapter 9 of Neil Bartlett's *Who Was That Man?*, 'Messages', comprises two letters to Oscar Wilde. The first breathes affection, respect and continuity, and incorporates our sense of Wilde into the scope for positive change today:

> Darling, it's all for you. We're doing all this for you. I wish you could be here to see us. The streets are not all that different – you wouldn't get lost – but we are very different these days. Can you imagine, tonight I walked down the Strand with my lover, and we talked about which pub we would go and drink in; we have a choice of places to go now, and the chances are that when we get there no one will know us. And then he put his arm round my shoulder.

The second letter begins: '*Oscar, you fat bitch*, Last night I dreamed your hand was on my face. You were there in the bed, big and fat like I've been told you were, lying in bed smoking and taking up all the room.'[1]

Cultural construction is both enabling and restricting. Of

course we should celebrate 'Oscar Wilde': he has authorized a good deal of gay culture as we know it. At the same time, he has been a means through which we have been held trapped in a particular set of assumptions – by a homophobic wider culture, and by ourselves. The ultimate project of this book is to promote a questioning of the constructions through which we have been living. This chapter assesses ways of handling the legacy of the Wildean model and the masculine/feminine binary structure today, and the further strategies that we might pursue.

Who are we?

The ultimate question is this: is homosexuality intolerable? One answer is that actually lesbians and gay men are pretty much like other people, in which case it just needs a few more of us to come out, so that the nervous among our compatriots can see we aren't really so dreadful, and then everyone will live and let live; sexuality will become unimportant. The other answer is that homosexuality in fact constitutes a profound challenge to the prevailing values and structures in our kinds of society – in which case the bigots have a point of view and are not acting unreasonably. We cannot expect to settle this question, but the hypothesis we adopt will affect decisively our strategic options.

The question whether we are intolerable begs the question of who 'we' are. A traditional way of coming at that is to consider whether everyone, or virtually everyone, has a potential for same-sex passion, or whether 'there is a distinct population of persons who "really are" gay'. The former model, Sedgwick suggests, is a *universalizing* one. Adrienne Rich deploys it when she writes of a 'lesbian continuum'; it enables her to call upon women generally to de-prioritize relations falling inside the oppressive pattern that currently informs heterosexuality, and to build powerful interactions with other women.[2] Sedgwick terms the second model *minoritizing*. This also is politically useful: it may help us to identify and consolidate our constituency. There is no consensus about which of these two models is correct; we tend to use them both, incoherently. However, deciding upon one of them would not resolve the question of whether we are intolerable. If everyone is potentially gay, the taboo about expressing that gayness and the consequent hostility might be the greater; if few of us really are, it might be more convenient to scapegoat us.

Another traditional take on who 'we' are is whether homosexuality is genetic or acquired. I considered in the previous chapter how Freudian theory seems to demonstrate acquisition but tends to fall back into biology. On 16 July 1993 the *Independent* newspaper headed its front page with a report of research at the US National Cancer Institute, claiming to have located 'a genetic factor' in homosexuality (the item was picked up from the journal *Science*).[3] It seems you should be on the look-out for gay uncles and cousins on your mother's side (work on lesbians, as you might expect, has not been so ardently pursued). Television and radio news carried the item through the day; the talk was all of whether this would make us more or less intolerable – in particular, whether people would wish to abort potentially gay offspring. Again, the question cuts both ways. On the one hand, many people might find it futile to harass people who are only manifesting a natural condition. On the other, genetic peculiarity would enable our enemies to regard us as an inferior species, an affront to an alleged evolutionary or religious demand that sex be in the service of procreation. Simon LeVay, a gay scientist who believes he has located a part of the brain that is distinctively formed in gay men, hopes to claim recognition in the United States for lesbians and gays as a minority having immutable characteristics, and hence civil rights protection from the Supreme Court (so we can be as well off as the American Indians). The drawback is illustrated in an exchange between LeVay and his father – who is entirely persuaded by his son's work. So how does LeVay senior see gay men now? He says he regards Simon as he would a child born with spina bifida, a hare lip, or some other developmental defect. LeVay junior finds this 'pretty humiliating' – though I don't see why he should, since it is a logical consequence of his theory. Indeed, the persistence of stigmatization is depressingly apparent; people with spina bifida may well feel they have a right not to be appropriated as the awful other by LeVay, senior and junior.[4]

These traditional debates – universalizing/minoritizing, genetic/acquired – are side-stepped by cultural constructionism, which regards gayness not, primarily or interestingly, as a property of individuals but as a mode of categorizing that circulates in societies like ours. It is a principal way that we use to demarcate the range of sexual potential. There may be an identifiable group of genes that contributes a propensity towards same-sex passion, but the forms through which it is expressed, if it is expressed at all, are culturally determined, and are only obliquely and residually linked to any originating stimulus. Trying to decide who the real homosexuals are, therefore, is to join the ideological circus, not to gain a vantage upon it. 'It is pointless to investigate the root causes of homosexuality,' Diana Fuss says, 'if we realize that homosexuality is not a transhistorical, transcultural, eternal category but a socially contingent and variant construction.'[5] The present study has been informed by constructionist theory; I have tried to show how same-sex passion takes diverse forms, how the Wildean model emerged out of less focused attitudes, and how individuals found themselves labelled with it, or accommodated themselves to it. Today still, not all people who engage in same-sex practices regard themselves as homosexual, or are so regarded by others; and not all people who regard themselves as homosexual, or are regarded as such by others, engage in same-sex practices. As Weeks remarks, someone we might regard as 'a homosexual prostitute' may not identify himself or herself either as a homosexual or as a prostitute.[6]

Constructionism shows the traditional questions to be unimportant and misleading – no wonder they can't be resolved. The case on whether homosexuality is genetic or acquired, or whether it is the property of a minority or of everyone, can be made either way – *because* it all depends on what is meant by homosexuality! The initial decision about the 'it' that is to be investigated shapes the outcome. If we say 'it' is the occurrence of any same-sex act, or of any intense same-sex bonding, then we will find hardly anyone to be immune and arrive at a universalizing model. If we require an acknowledged identity or engagement in a gay lifestyle before accepting that 'real' homosexuality is present, we will find fewer instances and hence arrive at a minoritizing model.

In the National Cancer Institute research, seventy-six homosexual men were investigated, and it was found that more of their brothers were gay than would be expected in the general population. The flaw here should be obvious: people who are ready to acknowledge their own gayness are vastly more likely (1) to realize, and (2) to admit, that they have gay siblings! It is all to do with identifications and perceptions. One advantage in this instance of genetic research, the reporter believes, is that it won't be subject to falling apart in the way that happened when genetic determination of manic depression was claimed: in the latter case, people from the 'wrong' side of the sample developed previously unsuspected symptoms. But, of course, there are very many men and women who move from gay into heterosexual relationships; whether they 'become straight' is a matter of cultural interpretation, not of genetics. No wonder seven of the forty pairs of gay brothers analysed directly disconfirmed the theory.

'Who are we?', properly understood, is a question about history, society and politics. We are partly who the dominant ideology says we are; partly who we, subculturally, say we are. The task, as Sedgwick puts it, is 'not so much to redefine "the homosexual", but to assume or resume some control over the uses and consequences of historically residual definitions'.[7] Our terms − 'gay', 'lesbian', 'lesbian and gay', 'lesbian, gay and bisexual', 'dyke', 'queer' − are markers of political allegiance, far more than ways of having or thinking about sex. We are encouraged to envisage these terms as identifying specific forms of desire and practice, but immensely diverse behaviours and fantasies find some place within them. They represent decisions about with whom we wish to be aligned, carved out in ongoing negotiations with the available repertoire. This can be complex. 'Sexually I am bisexual with a strong lesbian identity; politically I identify as gay/lesbian', one woman writes.[8]

Hence the intermittent and, I hope, careful place of lesbianism in the present study. I began with a question about Oscar Wilde and perceptions of male same-sex passion, so much of the argument does not apply, in any straightforward way, to lesbians. Their history is different − though Radclyffe Hall's *Well of Loneliness* (1928) has had much of the impact that the Wilde trials did. Nevertheless, I have written inclusively of lesbians and gay men wherever that has seemed plausible − but this signals a proposed political alignment, not an assertion that we are 'the same'. Some women, whom I respect, will regard such an alignment as inappropriate, or at least premature. That is for them to say − on some issues, plainly, we have different interests, and a gay man is still a man. In my view, all groups should be as separate as they want, and should talk to adjacent groups if, when, and as much as they want. Often it is better to sort yourself out first, then negotiate with the others.

In fact, 'gay men' is not a unitary category either. 'Given the injuries of race and class and nationalism, as well as the sheer diversity of homosexual desire and sexual behaviour,' Simon Watney remarks, a unified gay identity 'could never be more than, at best, a projective fantasy advanced for strategic purposes.' The problem with genetic research is its assumption of a unitary 'gay man' as the already-known object of analysis.[9] Actually, there are very many ways of experiencing same-sex passion – as there are cross-sex passion; many people manifest several of them, together and at different points in time. To display the range of experience, Sue George uses the Klein Sexual Orientation Grid, whereby you have to say on a scale of 1 to 7, in respect of past, present and ideal, whether you are more straight or gay in respect of seven aspects: sexual attraction, sexual behaviour, fantasies, emotional preference, social preference, self-identification, lifestyle. I believe this gives thousands of possible variants.[10] There are innumerable ways, some as yet undreamt, in which we might develop our sexualities.

The modern, western mode – the 'gay' mode – seems to depend on being able to move away from family and neighbourhood to an urban environment; consequently, it is primarily white, middle-class and metropolitan in orientation. That is perhaps not regrettable as such – as Mark Finch observes, some social base is necessary for the formation of a political grouping.[11] But we should not imagine it as even potentially universal. In many countries outside Western Europe and North America, the family is the prime economic unit and it is hard to live, even to envisage oneself, outside it. 'With only a sketchy identity as a person distinct from the identity as a member of a family, having a "sexual identity" and/or building an "alternative life-style" are literally inconceivable to many, even in urban centres,' Stephen O. Murray observes.[12] In Turkey, for instance, this produces an idea of homosexuality dominated by gender roles. According to Huseyin Tapinc, it is hard to envisage anything else: 'In such a polarized and fixed gender structure, which hinders the emergence of alternative models of identity for individuals, homosexuals are left with nothing but clearly defined gender roles. ... once you give up your culturally defined "manhood" the only place to find space is in the sphere of women.' At the same time, however, mutual male masturbation is regarded as *heterosexual* behaviour, and hence, Tapinc says, is free from stigma.[13] That attitude might have saved some grief for many individuals in twentieth-century Britain.

Of course, the western gay model, in which gendering is less clear-cut, is infiltrating countries such as Turkey – the word for it there is 'gay'. This produces a specific pattern of resentment and prestige. The resentment derives from the colonial heritage and continuing imperial exploitation, the prestige is evident in the use of such honorific terms as *moderno* in Peru, *internacional* in Mexico and Guatemala.[14] In these contexts, modern kinds of gayness may have more continuity with the Wildean, cross-class queer model (both the resentment and the prestige) than is comfortable for the westerner to contemplate: the disparities of wealth and the consequences for personal relations will often be similar. You can buy sexual attentions, like most things, in the Third World today, but may find yourself the object of a contempt that you wouldn't quite expect in London or New York.

Jonathan Dollimore takes the meeting of Wilde, André Gide and a young man called Mohammed in Algiers in 1895 as an epiphanic moment for modern western queer awareness. Wilde himself was a colonial and class intruder from Ireland, attracted to and exploited by the upper classes (including the Douglas family).[15] Such juxtapositions are still crucial in the mythologies of our sexualities. As Kobena Mercer and Isaac Julien observe, the emergence of the queer model in Europe coincided with the epoch of imperialism. 'The person of the savage was developed as the Other of civilisation and one of the first "proofs" of this otherness was the nakedness of the savage, the visibility of its sex.' And, of course, the masculine/feminine binary structure clicked into gear yet again: 'If the black, the savage, the nigger, is the absolute Other of civility then it must follow that he is endowed with the most monstrous and terrifying sexual proclivity. . . . But if this is too violent for you, there is always the Oriental', who is 'mute, passive, charming, inscrutable. Imperialism involved a hierarchy of races in the nineteenth century.'[16]

These ideas have returned to disturb and augment gay relations in North America and Western Europe. John L. Peterson remarks a distinction between 'black gays' and 'gay blacks', indicating an unavoidable prioritizing of identification.[17] Afro-Caribbean and Asian Britons particularly dislike the notion that coming out involves at least a partial or temporary rupture with family and community. As Sunil Gupta puts it, 'In a hostile white environment, for the first generation the community was their only hope of comfort and security. To turn your backs on it was to cut yourself off from both this security in real terms and from a sense of identity that was/is separate from the whites.' This is an experience not only for the first generation: in San Francisco, Kath Weston found, whites 'often described coming out as a transition from no community *into* community, whereas people of color were more likely to focus on conflicts *between* different identities instead of expressing a sense of relief and arrival'.[18] Gay liberation has learnt hugely from black Civil Rights and Pride movements, and white gays may learn from how other peoples handle family and neighbourhood allegiances. If we re-run all these arguments in respect of distinctive lesbian experience, many further possible modes of interaction may emerge. Gloria Wekker finds both continuities, disjunctions and specific inflections of age, class and explicitness in the sexualities of black women after slavery; 'the western categories of "homo", "bi", and "hetero" have insufficient justification in some black situations'. We have to acknowledge and celebrate difference, and look for dialogue.[19]

Some commentators have felt that without essential identities, deriving from an individual core of ultimate sexual preference, it will be difficult for lesbians and/or gay men to establish political engagement.[20] I believe this thought is misplaced, since individual self-consciousness is, anyway, an unpromising source of dissident identity and action. It is power structures that produce the system within which we live and think, and focusing upon the individual makes it hard to discern those structures; and if we discern them, hard to do much about them – since that would require collective action. Political awareness does not arise out of an essential, individual, self-consciousness of class, race, nation, gender or sexual orientation; but from involvement in a milieu, a subculture. 'In acquiring one's conception of the world one belongs to a particular grouping which is that of all the social elements which share the same mode of thinking and acting,' Antonio Gramsci observes.[21] It is through such sharing that we may learn to inhabit dissident preoccupations and forms – ways of relating to others – and hence develop a dissident selfhood. That is how successful movements have worked.

These issues have been most subtly considered by recent

theorists of lesbian identity. Judith Butler argues that identity develops in the process of signification: 'identity is always already signified, and yet continues to signify as it circulates within various interlocking discourses'; therefore 'the question of agency is not to be answered through recourse to an "I" that preexists signification'.[22] All gender is 'performative – that is, constituting the identity it is purporting to be'. We do not act out the gender that we are; we become gendered persons through actions. 'In this sense, gender is always a doing, though not a doing by a subject who might be said to preexist the deed' (p. 25). What we perceive as interior essence is a consequence of these processes, not their guarantor. These 'acts and gestures, articulated and enacted desires create the illusion of an interior and organizing gender core, an illusion discursively maintained for the purposes of the regulation of sexuality within the obligatory frame of reproductive heterosexuality' (p. 136). This means that heterosexuality has no epistemological priority: 'gay is to straight *not* as copy is to original, but, rather, as copy is to copy' (p. 31). So 'construction is not opposed to agency; it is the necessary scene of agency, the very terms in which agency is articulated and becomes culturally intelligible' (p. 147). Identity is not that which produces culture, nor indeed that which is produced as a static proposition by culture: rather, the two are the same process. Further, a static identity will obscure new political opportunities. A universalist identity, such as 'woman', effaces diversities of time and place and 'instates a definition that forecloses in advance the emergence of new identity concepts in and through politically engaged actions' (p. 15). We need the historical awareness to negotiate with last year's ideas of who we are, but we don't want to get trapped in them.

The dominant ideology tends to constitute subjectivities that will find 'natural' its view of the world (hence its dominance). Subcultures constitute consciousness, in principle, in the same way – but in partly dissident forms. In that bit of the world where the subculture runs you may feel confident, as we used to say, that black is beautiful, gay is good: there, those stories work, they build their own kinds of interactive plausibility. Subcultural milieux are where partly distinctive conditions of plausibility, alternative subject positions, are created. Validating the individual may seem attractive because it appears to empower him or her, but actually it undervalues potential resources of collective understanding and resistance. The task, therefore, is not the discovery of an ineluctable selfhood, but determined political allegiance.

Are 'we' intolerable?

In the question 'Are we intolerable?' then, 'we' is an unstable construction. In fact 'we' are, in part, a product of debates about intolerability. In some accounts 'we' purposely infect each other with the HIV virus; in other accounts 'we' produce great art. We are the focal point for a conflict of definitions.

The AIDS pandemic has produced some heartening and unexpected support for lesbians and gay men, and public attitudes are largely back where they were before the epidemic was widely known about.[23] But the way AIDS has been apprehended shows what is at stake. Homosexuality is laden with a huge ideological freight in our cultures, bearing mainly upon the masculine/feminine binary structure and related ideas about men, women and the family. In the early 1980s, it is easy to forget, gayness was becoming quite fashionable.[24] (This image may now be returning – some *pw* commentators are speaking of 'the gay nineties'.) This popularity was signalled by the vogue for Boy George (1982–83), and it lasted through Divine, Frankie Goes to Hollywood and Bronski Beat (1984) – then AIDS got into the tabloids. The idea was that we were doing better with the sex-and-love questions. Gay men had organized genial ways of meeting for casual sex, as well as loving couples that might manage, even, to evade gendered roles. We knew how to see other men without falling out with our partners; how to go to bed with friends, how to remain on close terms with former lovers, how to handle age and class differences. We were at ease experimenting with kinky games; we were getting the fun back into sex. So it seemed. In so far as all this had any substance, AIDS has not spoiled it. But for right-wingers AIDS was a godsend (so to speak). It countermanded, precisely, that alleged gay advantage. It had all been a fantasy, 'the family' should set the limits of important emotional experience, and gays have only 'pretended' families.

Now, these matters are (in my view) constituted culturally, and hence are in principle accessible to political intervention. But in practice, such a deeply embedded formation is hard to shift. Once we envisioned a relaxed sexual regime in which any of us might do almost anything. But sexual indeterminacy is truly distressing to very many people – because it acts, in Sedgwick's phrasing, as 'an unpredictably powerful solvent of stable identities'.[25] People have been socialized into sexualities and general attitudes that suit, or once suited, the maintenance of our kind of social system, and they don't want their identities dispersed. Like some animals reared in captivity, they don't want to be 'liberated'. Furthermore, progressive social attitudes seem to correlate, in our societies, with economic well-being. Under the current pressures of urban collapse, worldwide economic slump and ecological disaster, people want to hang on to what they think they've got.

There *are* people for whom hostility to homosexuals is phobic. They look out for opportunities to exercise phobic feelings; they can't let the topic alone. Critic and theatre-director Herbert Blau writes and publishes an article to tell us how he sympathized with his then wife when, performing in Genet's *The Balcony*, 'at one vertiginous moment [she] cried out fiercely against the imminence of becoming-otherness she felt imposing itself on her'. Blau continues: 'In a world of undecidability, that has to be reckoned with, *that* choice, refusing the slippage of ego, however, constrained by heterosexual categories, however illusory it might be.'[26] Blau's wife was entitled, as he sees it, to defend her ego against Genet's dispersal and threatened reconstitution of it; she didn't want her sexual identity undermined, even in the name of art. Whether this attribution of distress to Blau's wife is just, we cannot tell – she doesn't speak. What is clear is that he is distressed – despite his sensitivity to 'liberal principle'. Rather sadly, I think, he says: 'for myself, the really determining factor in what – allowing for all possible stress on self-accusation – you choose for yourself sexually is *disgust*' (p. 131). He says: 'thinking I would enjoy it, I walked up Christopher Street last summer at the fag end [yes, fag end] of the depleted [depleted by AIDS, I suppose] carnival of Gay Pride Day, with a disgust unexpected and almost uncontained by principle.' This feeling, Blau acknowledges, may be an 'embarrassing, arrogant, or reprehensible feeling', but it involves, none the less, 'a shadow of principle which warns that your perversion is going to make it impossible for me, at some warped upped ante of desire, to defend you' (p. 131). There is not going to be any arguing against that.

For very many others, 'homophobia' doesn't quite get to the

issue. Rather, the notion that queers are inferior and dangerous is structured into the language and social fabric. Almost everything in our societies, as one moves around from day to day, reinforces such notions; they seem to be common sense, to go without saying; they are in the structure of things. For many people, especially the young, prejudice is anxiously imitative of the group from which they wish not to be excluded; by whom they wish not to be humiliated. Getting called 'queer' threatens everything – whatever the actual desires of the individual. Such structural prejudice may be worked on and changed, up to a point (I suspect it is the same with misogyny and racism), because it may not be that important to the individual – not as important, perhaps, as being fair-minded. Adrienne Rich attributes to the black political scientist Gloria I. Joseph the thought 'that *homophobia* is an inaccurate term, implying a form of uncontrollable mental panic, and that *heterosexism* better describes what is really a deeply ingrained prejudice ... – a political indoctrination which must be recognized as such and which can be re-educated'.[27] This is the territory upon which most of our gains have been made. Nevertheless, ideological structures are not easily set aside – it is very hard to abandon an idea in defiance of not just opinion leaders but the entire articulation of the social order. All too often, I fear, liberal abrogation of structural prejudice is superficial, and will not survive a real challenge.

For while the non-phobic individual may benefit little by maintaining a prejudice, the system benefits a great deal. Lesbians and gay men, plainly, have a place in what Stanley Cohen terms 'the gallery of types that society erects to show its members which roles should be avoided and which should be emulated'. They are 'folk devils: visible reminders of what we should not be'.[28] The increased visibility of homosexuals over the last twenty-five years has transformed our opportunities; at the same time, it has made us more accessible to hostile appropriation. Before gay liberation, many people report having supposed themselves to be the only one. Now we are besieged with representations of ourselves, but very few are such as we would choose.

'As long as society is based on competitiveness and sexual repression,' Denis Altman observes, 'there will be a need to demarcate it into categories, to maintain socially induced repressions by stigmatizing heavily all those who fall outside the norm.'[29] In Hans Mayer's view, discrimination against outsiders is endemic to west-

ern societies; it manifests the historic failure of Enlightenment principles. The eighteenth-century ideal of equality was abandoned at
the point where the bourgeoisie gained control and founded its
order

> only on economic inequality, albeit within the framework of
> a universal equality so far as the letter of the law is con-
> cerned. This order transformed women into parasitic slaves
> since they did not earn money and were not supposed to. It
> fought Jewish emancipation via education and property. It
> was xenophobic from the start and became increasingly
> nationalistic. ... From now on there would be the normal
> and the degenerate, worthwhile and worthless human life.[30]

This was written in 1975; in the time of HIV and AIDS it screams
off the page. Our societies proclaim an ideology of equal opportunity, but they operate by producing and stigmatizing a whole
range of outsiders.

To be sure, there are continuous local changes – bad news in
Colorado, good news in Eire. We have to keep fighting for reforms;
they make a difference to people's lives, and if we don't fight they
won't happen. But changing structural intolerability is another
matter. In fact, the current positioning of sexual deviance, as a
spectrum extending from relatively 'good' types at one end (monog-
amous, same-age couples who keep their homes nice without drawing attention to themselves or aspiring to rear children) to 'bad '
types at the other (child-molesters etc.), seems to suit the prevailing
ideological conjuncture very well. It gives politicians, the media,
religious leaders, and the like, ample to chew on. The relative
invisibility of lesbians, for instance, allows the notion that women
are not 'like that' (they don't assert themselves and can't manage
without men) while leaving sufficient space for demonizing those
who insist on indicating otherwise.[31] Again, despite the official
embargo, innumerable people in the US military are, in fact,
reckoned by those around them to be gay – this is repeatedly
attested in a sequence of marvellously candid interviews, teased out
by Steven Zeeland. Allan Bérubé comments: 'While a few have been
targeted for discharge or were the victims of antigay violence, most
portray a social milieu of sexually-tense tolerance.' In particular, it

is assumed that certain jobs are typically done by homosexuals – signal corpsmen, cooks, medics and clerks.[32] So the military accommodates gay men up to a point, and in so doing exploits them to reinforce its dominant masculine ethos by cultivating a masculine/feminine split within its personnel.

It is not just that rights achieved so far by lesbians and gay men are contested; but that our societies seem well able to live with that contest. Numerous particular gains may be made, and many of us are so inured to our situation as to be almost pathetically grateful for them. But, overall, we have reached a structural situation from which it is going to be difficult to advance very far. The difficulty, I believe, is not incidental or circumstantial. The trick is to have us here *but* disgraceful.

In an important recent study, David T. Evans shows how our societies have positioned same-sex potential, holding it at a systematic distance from the rights of citizenship. Those rights have often been categorized as civil (individual liberty, freedom of speech and association, property, justice), political (opportunities to influence government) and social (the area addressed by welfare provision). Plainly lesbians and gay men are discriminated against in all these areas. This, Evans shows, is made to appear proper through a new distinction made in the Wolfenden Report (1957): between morality and legality.[33] Homosexual practices are located in a private realm where, though immoral, they may not require the attention of the law. So Wolfenden wanted to retain penalties for public soliciting, and it is in fact unlawful in the UK to propose to someone a sexual act that is, in itself, lawful. Despite the legalizing of many gay sexual practices in private, the alleged immorality of lesbians and gay men seems to justify the withholding of full citizenship in numerous, diverse respects – especially in familial and quasi-familial, contexts, from parenting and fostering to schools and entertainment in the home (television). Indeed, the positing of a private space has made it seem appropriate to police the public sphere with special rigour. At the same time, the private space is far from secure. To the contrary, the public/private boundary has become an obsessive focus for legal manoeuvring. In the 'Operation Spanner' case (1991–93) men were prosecuted for consensual sado-masochistic acts; the judges made case law, declaring that private immorality (as they regarded it) should after all fall under legal penalty. The courts have to 'draw the line between what is acceptable in civilised society and what is not,' one judge asserted.[34]

What gay men are left with, Evans points out, is the right to consume. According to the prevailing ideology of consumption, we are all 'unique individuals with needs, identities and lifestyles'; further, 'our sexual identities are our imperative, inescapable and deepest reality'. Hence 'the pursuit of the commodified self is the pursuit of the sexual self; individual, private, innermost, accomplished through the acquisition and conspicuous manifestations of style' (p. 45). Gay men fit well with these assumptions and are welcomed as ideal consumers, therefore (though, still, with restrictions on explicitness), but not as citizens in further senses.

Of course, consuming is something many gay men pride themselves upon. It is worrying to think that our concern with style, design, taste and fashion plays into the hands of John Major (UK Prime Minister at the time of writing), who with his 'Citizen's Charter' would reduce all citizenship to consumption and tax-paying. However, this is not the only field in which the achievements through which we hope to validate ourselves are being used to corral our culture and discount our claims. Ominously, we are being allowed achievements in music (men) and sport (women) — just those areas where blacks have been admitted to excel.

The campaign against Section 28 of the Local Government Act (1988), which prohibits the spending of money by municipalities on 'promoting homosexuality', drew upon the notion that gay men have produced a notable proportion of what is called art and literature. The campaign was courageous, well organized and much publicized, and arts celebrities came out. Astonishingly, at first sight, this carried precious little weight with the government and newspapers that support it; the votes in parliament were the same at the end of the campaign as at the beginning. The reason, I believe, is that people in our cultures *already know* that art is associated, stereotypically, with male homosexuals. As I have said, the association of art and effeminacy has, up to a point, been dissident; a way of repudiating masculine values of business, industry, empire and bureaucracy, and of calling into question the unquestioned dominance of patriarchal heterosexuality. For some purposes, our society credits this. However, art starts off as the subordinate term in the masculine/feminine binary structure, and from that position, always, it is very difficult to make much headway. The feminine is the basis both of dissidence and of stigma, and the latter is used to disqualify the former. As Genevieve Lloyd puts it, 'The affirmation of the value and importance of "the feminine" cannot of itself be expected to shake the underlying normative structures, for, ironically, it will occur in a space already prepared for it by the intellectual tradition it seeks to reject.'[35] It is hard to see a way out of this kind of trap. The system manages, all too well, to accommodate us without according us civil rights.

The pattern here is that our accomplishments are also the ground of our confinement. Hence the difficulty in knowing what, from the perspective of relations with those in authority over us, would be a 'good' move. Gay men are accused of being promiscuous, but if they form medium-term couples and keep house together, in the way that is approved for heterosexuals, they are warned against claiming even 'pretended families' (a phrase in the Section 28 legislation). Lesbians are accused of being unwomanly, but if they have children or seek to foster them, as women are supposed to do, that is wrong as well. If we make art and are stylish, that is taken as reason not to let us do or be anything else. There is a strategic principle here: when you are coming from the subordinate position, everything you attempt is recuperable. If you make a fuss, you are hysterical; if you keep quiet they roll over you. It suits the system if we are ultimately intolerable; it holds us at the point where we may seem to underwrite the normative ideology of manly men and feminine women. With these thoughts in mind, I return to questions of gay masculinity and femininity.

Gay styles today

The Wildean model of the queer is of course no longer simply dominant. It became increasingly unworkable as the class manner from which it derived lost authority and became more residual. Within the more suburban, egalitarian, competitive, consumerist ideological mix after World War II, the effete gentleman came to seem more peculiar; less worth imitating. And he offered less cover for the queer. Then the relative liberalization that followed the 1967 legal change in the UK and the 1969 Stonewall riots in the USA gave rise to the lesbian and gay political movements and to a burgeoning of commercial opportunities for gay recreative expression. These, in their different ways, augmented gay confidence, and this has taken the form, partly, of the cultivation of a diversity of styles, including (1) inconspicuous and (2) exaggerated manly styles.

Some of this masculinization is unselfconscious. For some men, gayness has become virtually unexceptional, except for occasional confrontational moments, so they feel little need for a distinctive mode of any kind. They look and act pretty much like other men of their respective class, age, ethnicity, neighbourhood and so on. There is no reason why this absorption into current mores should be inauthentic. The problem is that relatively few people are able to do it. Many men are avoiding effeminacy because they wish to pass as heterosexual. Despite initial liberationist optimism, a large proportion of gays are still subject to overwhelming pressure not to appear queer.

Often, present-day gay manliness involves a purposeful gesture: many relate their feeling of pride in gayness to the accomplishment of a manly style. Finding the Wildean model fatally implicated in self-oppression, stigma and snobbery, they prefer not to allude to it. As Bartlett remarks (without endorsing the thought), the achievement of gay subculture in the years before AIDS was to make us 'handsome, masculine, demanding and unafraid of our pleasures'. However, it may well be that the old model persists, in the sense that gay men, liberated to the point where they can envisage themselves as the desired as well as the desirer, now present themselves as the bit of rough formerly sought out by upper-class punters.[36] In fact, as I have shown, the idea of gay manliness does not derive only from post-1960s liberalization. In diverse social arrangements, from the ancient Greeks through the seventeenth-century rake to Carpenter and Symonds, same-sex passion has been legitimated through the claim that it is manly. Usually that has meant justifying the 'active' role and despising the 'passive' as inferior, i.e. womanly. In fact, matters may not be so clear-cut. In Mexico, men who engage in same-sex practices generally present themselves as *activos*, but 74 per cent of a sample acknowledged privately that they were insertive *and* receptive in intercourse.[37]

The current phase of gay manliness in present-day North America and Western Europe is different. Quite distinctively, a manly stance is not necessarily linked, within gay culture, with 'active' sexual practices. In gay self-presentation today, a masculine appearance may guarantee nothing about 'active' and 'passive'. This is only relatively true, and only for some men, but it has allowed a far fuller flourishing of gay manliness than otherwise could occur. A question, of course, is how far this presents a capitulation to the heterosexist priority inscribed in the masculine/feminine binary structure, and a restigmatization of gay men who want to be effeminate. As Weeks remarks, the notion that a gay man may be accepted so long as he is 'suitably "masculine" in appearance and manner' imposes 'new standards of behaviour for the supposed "deviant" which may be as restrictive, if more subtly so, as the old'.[38]

So far I have been considering unexceptional male appearance. We have also the exaggeratedly macho image – the short-haired, mustached 'clone' style, subsequent variations upon it, and the more vivid leather gear. Commentators have discussed whether macho-man should be regarded as aiming to legitimate himself, to capitalize on standard male hostility towards women, to compensate for powerlessness, to recreate the old illicit excitement through a pastiche outlaw style, or to undermine sexual stereotypes. Actually, there are diverse modes and diverse effects, and they cannot be comprised within a single thesis.

It seems clear, though, that macho-man is in reaction against effeminacy, and this means that the masculine/feminine binary structure has not gone away, only been redistributed. John Marshall remarks 'the extent to which definitions of male homosexuality continue to be pervaded by the tyranny of gender divisions'.[39] The work of the artist Tom of Finland is instructive. Before 1945, Tom explains,

> the gay men I met felt ashamed and guilty, like belonging to a lower human category because they had no right to enjoy their different sexuality. In my opinion it was very unfair, but even though I had to hide my own desires – or maybe because of it – I started drawing fantasies of free and happy gay men. Soon I began to exaggerate their maleness on purpose to point out that all gays don't necessarily need to be just 'those damned queers', that they could be as handsome and strong and masculine as any other men.[40]

Thus envisaged, acting like a man seems to be a recipe for

hating yourself while joining the mainstream of capitalism and patriarchy. One, of course, is likely to be the condition for the other. Evans relates masculine gay styles to commodification, which has 'required the modified incorporation of the male homosexual into the "active" sexual and economic "free" masculine world of sex needs'.[41] Macho-man may be reproducing attitudes of heterosexist male dominance in respect of language, interpersonal objectification and style, Gregg Blachford argues; 'the new styles are in many ways oppressive to women and to gay men themselves,' Jamie Gough says.[42] I don't think this can, or should, be gainsaid. There *is* a lot of male gay misogyny. The effeminate gay model inspires both admiration for women (or, rather, for an idea of them) and self-hating anxiety at losing the privileges of manhood. Today's masculine models may present in exacerbated form the prejudices of real (i.e. heterosexual) men. In any event, trying to be more like heterosexual men is not likely to help.

To be sure, we are talking about fantasy and signification, not the real world, and exaggerated male gay styles draw attention to their constructedness. Tom of Finland's creations are sheer fantasy. 'Gay masculinity is not, in any simple way, "real" masculinity, any more than camp is "real" femininity. It is more self-conscious than the real thing, more theatrical, and often ironic', Gough observes.[43] In other words, manliness may be as camp as effeminacy, and hence in no straightforward collusion with heterosexism. This kind of argument is elaborated by Sue-Ellen Case in respect of butch/femme roles: in traditional lesbian bar culture, there was much talk of who was which, but this was 'play on the phallic economy rather than to it. ... these penis-related posturings were always acknowledged as roles, not biological birthrights, nor any other essentialist poses'. Case is arguing, against essentialist feminists, that queer modes relate only residually to heterosexual models; indeed, as Monique Wittig holds, they are uniquely outside the conventional sex–gender system. They 'evade the notion of "the female body" as it predominates in feminist theory, dragging along its Freudian baggage and scopophilic transubstantiation. These roles are played in signs themselves and not in ontologies. ... Therefore, the female body, the male gaze, and the structures of realism are only sex toys for the butch–femme couple.'[44] Some lesbian commentators do not grant this kind of dispensation to male homosexuals, but the doubling of the penis would seem as disconcerting to the sex–gender system as its absence. And, as Cora Kaplan once put it, the gay penis is not pointing at women.

I return shortly to the further implications of such arguments. Here it must be said that there is no decisive line between fantasy and actuality. Real-world oppression is legitimated through signification, and rapists act out their violent fantasies. Some gay men batter each other, and some lesbians. Despite familiarity with conventional sado-masochistic imagery of caps, straps and boots, one may gasp when Tom of Finland's biographer tells cheerfully how during the Nazi occupation of Helsinki Tom 'began to have the sex he had dreamed of with the uniformed men he lusted after, especially once the German soldiers had arrived in their irresistible jackboots'.[45] This comment shows how, in the moment of endorsing male aggression, macho-man may be reconstituting himself as the victim that the effeminate man was previously. This too is, of course, disturbing to conventional assumptions, but not all disturbances are progressive.

Such considerations should promote, once more, a question about how far we want to become tolerable within a heterosexist structure that has such an intolerable history of oppression and mystification. I suppose lesbians and gay men should have the same rights as other people to administer unfair classroom tests, make bogus claims in advertisements, sell drugs that don't work, tell lies about people in newspapers, have their relationships approved by the state, fit up suspected terrorists, fire missiles at cities. But are 'real men' the people with whom we want to associate ourselves? On the other hand, the problem, once more, is not lesbians and gay men, who struggle to make sense of themselves in such unpropitious conditions, but the prevailing sex and gender arrangements. 'If gender is socially constituted,' Dollimore observes, '*so too is desire*. Desire is informed by the same oppressive constructions of gender that we would willingly dispense with.'[46] The prevailing patterns of sexual expression are not to be wished away; we are living them. They are subjecting heterosexuals, as much as homosexuals, to thwarted and petty lives. Gay men since the time of Wilde have been casting around for identity and status in a system that sets out to disqualify anything they attempt; no one is entitled to pass easy judgement upon the strategies they have deployed. We must have these arguments among ourselves; for the time being, gay men are entitled to present a manly stance if they want.

Yet, it must be said, dumping effeminacy because it has been stigmatized hardly seems heroic. In fact, macho-man has a good deal in common with the effeminate, Wildean tradition – not surprisingly, since he is premised on a comparable acceptance of the masculine/feminine binary structure. Both modes afford group solidarity and ready signalling to other men; both risk collusion with the oppressive system they may aspire to evade or undermine, but may be defended as distinctive features of gay subculture. I turn now to the cultivation of a 'feminine' mode.

Finch says camp is out of date – a feature of 'pre-gay movement culture. [It] becomes important when it speaks to that historical experience', for example in the 1950s poetry of Frank O'Hara.[47] This, I believe is premature. Present-day gay styles retain large residues of earlier formations, often jumbled together incoherently in the one instance. When asked whether drag can really be important in the 1990s, Bartlett replied No; but 'almost all the things that are now traditionally gay are very important for that fact alone, and they represent gay space'. The point is 'seeing a gay entertainer in a room full of gay people, speaking a language that no one else could understand'.[48] From this base, some instances may take off into new articulations of the history upon which they draw.

Effeminacy has over manliness the advantage of being a central gay cultural tradition which we may proudly assert. They told Jean Genet he was an effeminate queen, so he decided to be one. At sixteen, he found himself in a brutal reformatory: 'I felt the cruel shame of having my head shaved, of being dressed in unspeakable clothes, of being confined in that vile place.' His strategy was that 'to every charge brought against me, unjust though it be, from the bottom of my heart I shall answer yes'. So he 'owned to being the coward, traitor, thief and fairy they saw in me', and thus, by embracing the conditions of repression, discovered strength through abjection. This amounts to a personal reverse discourse such as Foucault posits: homosexuality learns 'to speak in its own behalf ... in the same vocabulary, using the same categories by which it was ... disqualified' (Foucault's theory often seems like an elaboration on Genet's life).[49] The difference is that Foucault does not envisage throwing the system into reverse all by oneself; today many of us find positive support in gay subculture, and the situation is less desperate than it was for Genet. One way to preserve those gains is to keep faith with the struggles of earlier generations, and one way of doing that is to reassert stigmatized gay traditions.

Because we have inhabited the Wildean model, then, its residues are significant. This is not a very strong claim; I am not endorsing an intrinsic 'gay sensibility'. I agree with Michael Bronksi: 'If gay men, as a group, decided to attend baseball games *as* gay men, to socialize during them *as* gay men, and to center a large part of their cultural interest around baseball gossip, a whole new set of stereotypes would grow up around baseball as the national gay sport.'[50]

The case for a gay sensibility is presented by Jack Babuscio. He believes that the marginal situation of gay men may produce 'a creative energy' (OK, but marginality may also prompt nervous conformity), and hence may produce 'art'. Unfortunately this feeds us straight back into conventional gender constructs – Babuscio proposes 'a gay sensibility that is not so completely identified with its "masculine" persona roles that it cannot give expression to its "feminine" component'.[51] The case against this move is put by Richard Dyer. As a young man, Dyer used the idea of gay sensibility to cheer himself up for being queer, but sees now that 'the equation of artistic queerness with femininity downgraded both femininity and me. I negate myself by identifying with women (hence refusing my biological sex), and then put myself down by internalizing the definition of female qualities as inferior'.[52] Art, like drag, is one of the places where gay men have invested, but that idea is not, by itself, progressive. It is Camille Paglia, a right-winger, who likes to proclaim that 'only the drag queens, my heroes, have preserved the old gay aesthetic, which elevates eternal beauty and imagination over politics'.[53] In art you suffer, I reply; in politics you try to do something about suffering.

Bronski fears that art has been only 'a means of attaining a certain degree of acceptance', and prefers the explicitly lesbian and gay post-Stonewall subcultures. Bartlett makes a similar point by citing against Larry Kramer's conventional celebrities – Proust, Henry James, Tchaikovsky, Cole Porter, Plato and so on – an alternative list, including such transgressive figures as Carpenter, Genet, Simeon Solomon and William Burroughs, or featuring disco music, leathers, 'hundreds of anonymous pornographes and drag artists, all my friends and lovers, and all the gay politicians in London'.[54] Of course, the idea that gay men are distinctively artistic is part of the package that got installed through the Wilde trials, and it has been swathed in nervous discretion. Even writers, painters and choreographers whom we have reason to think of as gay have very often adopted a heterosexual point of view in their work. It is because they would not have been published, shown or performed otherwise; and/or were persuaded to believe that their work should be 'universal' – that is, heterosexual.

In so far as art is one of the things gay men have done, it is worth going on doing. However, we are far too prone to assume that gay-oriented work is all very well, but getting into the mainstream is what counts. This is self-oppressed. Mainstream recognition is by mainstream criteria; the centre takes what it wants, and under pressure will abuse and abandon the subcultures it has plundered. We are accepted as purveyors of artistic culture on condition that we be discreet, thereby acknowledging our own unspeakableness. Decoding the work of closeted homosexual artists discovers not a ground for congratulation but a record of oppression and humiliation. What we celebrated in the Section 28 campaign was not our culture but our contribution to their culture.

Mind you, art could be useful. Quentin Crisp found it afforded some protection against street assaults: one 'member of the gang would whisper, "But he's an artist. I seen him in Chelsea".' Immediately the grip on my person would loosen and, in a shaken voice, my aggressor would say, "I didn't know".' One respondent in *Between the Acts* was told, in bed, 'I let you do this, because you are an artist.'[55]

Gender-bending

Art is a space where femininity is permitted, and that permission limits its dissidence. The case may be different in camp, drag and lesbian butch/femme role-playing, where categories of gender and sexuality are more provocatively juxtaposed. This broaches a whole further dimension to lesbian and gay cultural modes: by definition, almost, they gender-bend. If a man displays feminine traits he disconcerts by confusing supposed gender properties; if a gay man appears manly, he disconcerts by refusing the stereotype our cultures associate with his sexuality. Similarly with butch/femme roles. Question: 'When does a lesbian boy become a man?' Answer: 'She doesn't' — Della Grace.[56]

If it is evident that an imitation is taking place (a totally successful impersonation would be another matter), role-playing may effect an unwonted conjunction of alleged masculine and feminine traits, such that the perceiver is unable to hold to one or the other. Thus regarded, a radical potential may be claimed for various lesbian and gay styles. Esther Newton presented this case back in 1972.

> The effect of the drag system is to wrench the sex roles loose from that which supposedly determines them, that is, genital sex. Gay people know that sex-typed behavior can be achieved, contrary to what is popularly believed. They know that the possession of one type of genital equipment by no means guarantees the 'naturally appropriate' behavior.[57]

This may disturb any idea of fixity, and hence any notion that there are, or should be, natural or preferred positions. The argument has been developed by Butler, who holds that it is the false notion of 'an original or primary gender identity' that is parodied in gender-bending. 'In imitating gender, drag implicitly reveals the imitative structure of gender itself — as well as its contingency.'[58] The mechanism is like that Homi Bhabha proposes in respect of imperialism. Mimicking of colonial manners by subordinate peoples accomplishes 'at once resemblance and menace': the resemblance is inappropriate, and therefore menaces, through 'its *double* vision which in disclosing the ambivalence of Colonial discourse, also disrupts its authority'.[59] This effect does not depend on the intentions of the mimic. He or she may be sincerely imitating an imperial or heterosexist manner, but the effect is impertinent, half-mocking — tending to expose imperial or heterosexist superiority as an ideological construction. Butler is looking 'to articulate the convergence of multiple sexual discourses at the site of "identity" in order to render that category, in whatever form, permanently problematic' (p. 128).

There are perhaps two dangers here. The first, less obvious, is that gender-bending may be becoming suspiciously fashionable — drawing us into a depoliticizing postmodernism. 'Contemporary theory seems to open the closet door to invite the queer to come

out, transformed as a new postmodern subject, or to invite straights
to come into the closet, out of the roar of the dominant discourse,'
Case observes. Thus we may slide away from the erotics and the
politics of queer cultures (Andy Medhurst remarks that some postmodernism looks like straights catching up with camp).[60]

Second, if most people in our societies were ready to be
persuaded that all gender is imitative and contingent, gender-
bending would help us all to recognize genders and sexualities as
provisional, of equal priority, and entailing their own auto-critique.
And we might leave the matter there. As it is, we know that very
many people, when challenged, throw up barriers of reaction, and
that these may be both subtle and determined. They are assisted, in
respect of sexualities, by a dominant ideology which still tells us
that gender correlates with biology, that one kind of sexuality is
superior, and that this system is essential, natural, Darwin- and
God-given. This ideology tends to override even the most artfully
subversive performance. I fear the dominant copes all too conveniently with the colonial mimic: simply, he or she can't be the
genuine article because of an intrinsic inferiority. After all, lesbians
and gay men have long been perceived as disturbing conventional
categories – masculine souls in feminine bodies and so on – and it
hasn't got us very far. Gay pastiche and its excesses may be pigeon-
holed as illustrating only too well that lesbians and gay men can
only play at heterosexual roles. As Newton suggests, drag may
reinforce a notion that gender and sexuality – as opposed to their
superficial trappings – are deep, essential, ineluctable. 'Ultimately,
all drag symbolism opposes the "inner" or "real" self (subjective
self) to the "outer" self (social self).' It is difficult to prevent the
perceiver from using prior assumptions about the naturalness of the
sex–gender system to control his or her experience. Such objections
to drag are put forcefully by Carole-Anne Tyler in a recent essay.[61]

Nevertheless, some kind of disconcertion must sometimes be
possible, depending on the nature of the audience. The mistake is to
expect a single stylistic manoeuvre to have a reliable effect – either
dissident or conformist. It is like expecting the letter *i* always to
correlate with littleness – with tiddly titbits: 'big' breaks the pattern. It depends on the instance and the context in which it occurs.
Camp and drag have to be addressed not in the abstract but as
social practices. Dollimore observes, 'Nothing can be intrinsically
or essentially subversive in the sense that prior to the event subver-

siveness can be more than potential; in other words it cannot be guaranteed *a priori*, independent of articulation, context and reception.'[62] Suppose I wear *this* T-shirt with *those* trainers, we think – that will get the straights running for their *Daily Telegraph*. However, the task is not to specify the one, true strategy, but to be flexible and cunning – as the dominant is.

The diverse implications of cross-dressed role-playing in lesbian theatre are displayed by Kate Davy (rather surprisingly, Davy denies a comparable range to male drag). At the WOW (Women's One World) Café, a lesbian theatre space, the Split Britches troupe presented butch and femme roles in *Paradykes Lost* (1988) in the way I was discussing in the previous section, as having 'meanings for lesbians in a same-sex, lesbian culture'. The idea was not to undermine heterosexist stereotypes but to draw upon and elaborate lesbian subculture. Consequently, the performance was misinterpreted by reviewers using other perspectives – one thought the women were playing men, rather than alluding to butch lesbian styles.[63] On another occasion, the strategy was different – for an anticipated heterosexual, though avant-garde, audience. 'Outside of lesbian venues, butch/femme can too easily be read as male/female', so for these circumstances Split Britches contrived, in *Dress Suits to Hire* (1987), a performance that 'scrambles the signals, the processes of identification' (p. 162). This is the unsettling and unfixing effect of gender-bending, and apparently it worked. However, when *Dress Suits* was presented 'in a conventional theatre setting, in the legitimate (and legitimizing) institutional setting of a major university, the work's potential to subvert dominant ideology was seriously undermined' (p. 166). The dissident effect depended on the audience having some knowledge or intuition of how it was intended to work. This kind of range occurred with the Cheek by Jowl production of Shakespeare's *As You Like It* (1991). I found myself uncertain, from moment to moment, whether I was watching a boy, a girl, a girl playing a boy, or a boy playing a girl playing a boy. ... However, some of my friends were initially disappointed because they'd been expecting to whoop it up in a gay version; once they got the idea, they were delighted.

To set the failures of camp and drag down to the perfidy of gay men, or indeed of Butler, Garber or Bhabha, is unproductive. The ambivalence of gender-bending was acknowledged at the start of gay liberation. Dennis Altman quotes Mike Silverstein, writing in

Gay Sunshine in 1970: 'To the extent that Camp accepts the conception of the male homosexual as womanly and therefore inferior to real men it is self-hate. But much of Camp is something far more positive, a guerilla attack on the whole system of male–female roles our society uses to oppress its women and repress its men.'[64] This contradiction is not to be resolved; drag is popular in both reactionary and radical milieux.

Indeed, it is hard to know what lesbian and gay imagery – or for that matter feminist imagery – would not be recuperable in dominant terms. Genet claims to distinguish two programmes:

> When a pederast dyes his hair blue, he is able to launch a revolutionary programme by himself; but when, after dyeing his hair blue, he beefs up his breasts with hormones and goes to live with a man, he is merely parodying the system. He is keeping up appearances and not challenging anything at all. Society is amused. He becomes a kind of curiosity, which the system is quick to digest.[65]

Actually, neither of these programmes is reliably subversive or conformist. The fact is, the prevailing order is hostile to same-sex passion, and will dirty up any image that we produce. The strategies available to lesbian and gay people, and other subordinated groups, are always double-edged. Genet later realized this, in respect of the black person writing literature: (she or) he 'must use the very language, the words, the syntax of his enemy, whereas he craves a separate language belonging only to his people. ... He has then only one recourse: to accept this language but to corrupt it so skilfully that the white men are caught in his trap.' But the dominant is not so easily subverted, so intricately is it installed in the conceptual structures that we inhabit: 'Finally, every young American black who writes is trying to find himself and test himself and sometimes, at the very centre of his being in his own heart, discovers a white man he must annihilate.'[66]

The difficulty in deciding how best to handle effeminacy is systemic: we have been constructed – variously but ineluctably – through the masculine/feminine binary structure. So have heterosexuals. This fundamentally misogynist and class-ridden construct, deriving from a powerfully constitutive moment in nineteenth-century culture, has hampered and perplexed gay men, and has hindered the making of common cause with other oppressed groups, especially working people and women.[67] Lesbians and gay men can play with its boundaries, perhaps displaying its incoherence in ways that may undermine its power. In her article 'Sexual indifference and lesbian representation', Teresa de Lauretis assesses diverse modes through which 'lesbian writers and artists have sought variously to escape gender, to deny it, transcend it, or perform it in excess, and to inscribe the erotic in cryptic, allegorical, realistic, camp, or other modes of representation'.[68] All of this is worth trying; there is no magical way out.

Dissident potential

I have proposed a strategic principle: when you are coming from the subordinate position, everything you attempt is recuperable. It has to be remembered that it is not we who make lesbians and gay men so controversial. We do not try to prevent girls and boys finding out about the range of sexualities; we do not ask to be unmentionable, to have our opportunities for meeting policed, our subculture subject to regulation, our jobs at risk. Because we are thus harassed, our lives and our politics take their present forms; it is hard to imagine what lesbian and gay cultures would be like without mainstream wariness and hostility. Homosexuality and heterosexuality are mutually defining concepts; the one is stigmatized because it is not the other. That is why our strategies are bound, almost, to be reactive. OutRage holds a kiss-in because the law says we can't kiss in the street. We have to invoke dominant structures to oppose them, and our dissidence, therefore, can always be discovered reinscribing that which it aspires to critique.

So if I am not concluding with a straightforward endorsement of ACT UP, Queer Nation and OutRage, it is not because I think we shouldn't upset people, but because I fear we cannot upset them enough. 'OutRage activists are not interested in seeking acceptance within an unchanged social system, but are setting out to "fuck up the mainstream" as visibly as possible,' Cherry Smyth declares.[69] The problem is, how to do it. An anonymous pamphlet 'Queer Power Now!' (London, 1991) exhorts: 'It's time to take it into the streets. Get out there! Take them on! Be yourself! And if you don't like this [pamphlet], get out and make some NOISE yourself. Write books. Be safe. Burn buildings. Shoot closets. Screw in the streets.' Of that list of projects, only the attack on property would seriously trouble the system, and when other groups try that the main outcome is an increase in state surveillance and control.

At the same time, the very contradictions and conflicts that facilitate manipulation of deviant groups by the dominant are also the points at which subordinated cultures find space to assert themselves. The very structures that make it hard for dissidence to escape the dominant also make it hard for the dominant to contain dissidence. A dominant discourse cannot prevent 'abuse' of its resources. Even an attempt to stigmatize gayness must first bring it into visibility; even to misrepresent, one must present. And once that has happened, there can be no guarantee that the subordinate will stay safely in its prescribed place.

For the prevailing structures produce us, as well as the bigots. (This is literally true – unlike ethnic groups, lesbians and gay men are born of the straight community that despises them.) The nuclear family and the stigmatization of same-sex passion emerge out of the urban anomie that accompanies capitalism; but so do the weakening of the family and gay liberation. Despite his suspicion of commodification, Evans sees in the 'fragmentation of the boundaries of immorality and legitimacy ... immense possibilities for battles over further citizenship gains and losses'.[70] Within these bounding faultlines, innumerable local contradictions flourish. Section 28 forbade local authorities to spend money in ways that might promote homosexuality; it was designed to inhibit the circulation of lesbian and gay culture and, by making councils nervous about certain projects, it has done that. However, it also brought out on to the streets a generation that had become satisfied with its discos and decor. And lesbians and gay men recognized a common cause virtually for the first time; this was a precise response to parliament, for the first time, legislating against women and men together.[71] Even the US military, despite its anti-gay policy, functions as an opportunity for young men, and I dare say women, to 'find themselves' homosexually – enabling them to escape their small-town and family environment and experience a foreign city such as Frankfurt. 'I didn't even know gay clubs existed until I got over here', says John; now he is ready to turn out for a Pride march. Russ joined up to satisfy his father, who wanted the army to make him a man. And did it? 'Please. I came out when I was here. If anything, it made me a queen.'[72] However, most of Zeeland's soldier interviewees, it must be admitted, are conservative.

The readoption of 'queer' is a case in point. I have used the word historically, as the one in currency during the heyday of the Wildean model. In the 1970s, 'gay' was established as a way of moving on from all that. However, a key difficulty for any oppressed group is that you don't control your own language. Unless, like the original Puritans, you can find a new England to go to, you are in continuous negotiation with the dominant language group. And by definition – being dominant – they set most of the terms. Lately 'gay' has been used continually in the UK gutter press alongside their words ('poof' and so on), and thereby is contaminated with many of their resonances. We can't prevent that happening; we just don't have the economic, political or cultural power. We can attempt a new manoeuvre, though – one that draws attention to the influence of the dominant, even over our self-definitions, and turns that process back upon itself. The idea, of course, is not to identify and cleave to the one true word that will speak our essential name and nature, but to select an appropriate strategy. The aggression and ambition in the readoption of 'queer' are directly proportionate to the degree to which its use proposes to overturn the historic, hostile meaning. It plays for much higher stakes than if we tried to reinstate, say, 'the third sex'. There would be less disturbance if we did that, and, correspondingly, we would have less to gain. 'Queer' says, defiantly, that we don't care what they call us. Also, it keeps faith with generations of people, before us, who lived their oppression and resistance in its initial terms.

The trouble is, for many gay men and lesbians, 'queer' still features in a daily anguish. Schoolteachers may have to take it from pupils and colleagues because to dispute it might be to invite dismissal. If you are struggling to be gay, the last thing you want is someone living in other circumstances telling you that you don't measure up because you can't think of yourself as queer. In a rural context, just to keep going may require more courage than getting arrested on a demo in the city. Many contact ads still promise or require discretion, and those people need more, not less, consideration from activists. Some of the older people interviewed for the OurStory project – an oral history of lesbian and gay life in Brighton in the 1950s and 1960s – were terrified of being recognized.[73] Plainly they have not shared the exhilaration and reassurance of coming out; and, looking back, I don't think the rest of us did much to include them in. Unlike ethnic groups, we don't have built-in generational interactions – we don't, for the most part, have gay grannies. If we want a subculture that is good for older people and enables us to learn from and with them, then we have to work for it – as OurStory was doing.

We need our activists, and, I believe, our intellectuals, and we need them to keep in touch with other people. Our best resources are numbers and commitment. To maximize these, we have to build a stronger subculture – more vigorous, intelligent and various – one in which many more of us can feel that we have both support and opportunity to contribute. We are entitled to the resources of central and local government, like other people, but we know we can't depend on that. While AIDS was thought to affect only gay men governments did almost nothing about it; but for gay subculture, thousands more would be dying now. We have to work harder at our own agendas – not so as to withdraw from mainstream society but to establish the terms on which we want to handle it. We have to combat our self-destructive features (misogyny, racism, ageism), while fighting for diverse kinds of sexual expression, diverse kinds of relationships. We have to cope with HIV and AIDS, and warn people of the danger.

Of course, we don't all agree. That is hardly surprising; in our various situations, we experience all the faultlines of the dominant culture, some of them in exacerbated form, and suffer the massive difficulty of any subordinated group: self-oppression – tending to believe what they say about us. All this doesn't make people feel more comradely. However, subculture does not mean establishing a party line, but working questions out – I prefer 'subculture' to 'community' partly because it doesn't have cosy, togetherness connotations. We don't, we now realize, have to be clones – though we can if we want. De Lauretis critiques 'the presumption of a unified lesbian viewer/reader, gifted with undivided and non-contradictory subjectivity'.[74] As a matter of fact, no one knows what the medium-term outcome of different strategies might be. We are taking various routes; we have to recognize, dispute, negotiate each other's needs, elaborating ourselves across a range of discourses, some of them special to us, many in overlap and ongoing dialectic with other cultures. We need to be heterogeneous, contentious – without falling into blaming each other for the situation in which we find ourselves. Thus, by the intensity of our engagements, though in conditions not of our own choosing, we can decide who we are.

The change in our opportunities since the hey-day of the Wildean model has been large; to record and illuminate that is one goal of this book. In my view some lesbian and gay apologists are wrong when they suggest that people cannot become gay.[75] There is every reason to suppose that numbers of lesbians and gay men are increasing as legal and social oppression is reduced. Lives of shameful fantasy or obscure frustration are opening out onto new opportunities, though also into new realms of distress and difficulty. Despite and because of our successes, we are still, in the structure of western societies, intolerable. For some of us this is not unwelcome. 'If you've got a black list, I want to be on it' (Billy Bragg, 'Waiting for the great leap forwards'). But it depends how you are situated; romantic defiance may be insufficient compensation if you are prosecuted for soliciting or your child is taken away. We are in a continuing struggle and, as hitherto, some of us will lose. Apart from suicide and mental illness, we still have the routine distress of family hostility, being passed over for employment and promotion, never feeling altogether at ease with neighbours. Watching the huge numbers of young people on Pride marches, I am sometimes gripped with anxiety, at how vulnerable they are making themselves to an unknown future. If we accept continuing contest as a necessary politics, it must not be with any complacency.

Notes

1. Neil Bartlett, *Who Was That Man?* (London: Serpent's Tail, 1988), pp. 211–12. For Michael Hurley '"Wilde" is part of a social mobilisation of a viciously negative system of sexual regulation': Michael Hurley, 'Homosexualities: fiction, reading and moral training', in Terry Threadgold and Anne Cranny-Francis, eds, *Feminine, Masculine and Representation* (Sydney: Allen & Unwin, 1990), p. 164.

2. Eve Kosofsky Sedgwick, *Epistemology of the Closet* (Hemel Hempstead: Harvester Wheatsheaf, 1991), p. 85; see pp. 84–90; Adrienne Rich, 'Compulsory heterosexuality and lesbian existence', in Anne Snitow, Christine Stansell and Sharon Thompson, eds, *Powers of Desire* (New York: Monthly Review Press, 1983).

3. Robert Pool, 'Evidence for homosexuality gene', *Science*, 261 (16 July 1993), 265–396, pp. 291–2.

4. LeVay interviews his father in 'Born that way?' (London: Windfall Films for Channel Four, 1992). See Simon LeVay, *The Sexual Brain* (Cambridge, MA: MIT, 1993); David Fernbach, 'Hyping the hypothalamus', *Gay Times*, July 1993, pp. 60–1.

5. Diana Fuss, *Essentially Speaking* (New York: Routledge, 1989), pp. 107–8.

6. Jeffrey Weeks, *Against Nature* (London: Rivers Oram Press, 1991), pp. 65–6.

7. Eve Kosofsky Sedgwick, *Between Men* (New York: Columbia University Press, 1985), p. 90. See Joseph Bristow, 'Being gay: politics, identity, pleasure', *New Formations*, 9 (1989), 61–81, pp. 61–8. Dean Hamer is quoted from the *Independent*, 16 July 1993, p. 1.

8. Sue George, *Women and Bisexuality* (London: Scarlet Press, 1993), p. 164.

9. Simon Watney, *Policing Desire* (London: Comedia, 1987), p. 20.

10. George, *Women and Bisexuality*, pp. 169–81.

11. See Mark Finch, 'Sex and address in "Dynasty"', *Screen*, 27(6) (1986), 24–42, p. 24.

12. Stephen O. Murray, ' "Underdevelopment" ', in Ken Plummer, ed., *Modern Homosexualities* (London: Routledge, 1992), p. 34.

13. Huseyin Tapinc, 'Masculinity, femininity and Turkish male homosexuality', in Plummer, *Modern Homosexualities*, pp. 45, 40.

14. See Tapinc, 'Masculinity, femininity', p. 46; Murray, ' "Underdevelopment" ', p. 29; Rhonda Cobham, 'Misgendering the nation: African nationalist fictions and Nuruddin Farah's *Maps*', and Cindy Patton, 'From nation to family: containing "African AIDS" ', both in Andrew Parker, Mary Russo, Doris Sommer and Patricia Yaeger, eds, *Nationalisms and Sexualities* (New York: Routledge, 1992), pp. 47–8, 226. See Joseph Carrier, 'Miguel: sexual life history of a gay Mexican American', in Gilbert Herdt, ed., *Gay Culture in America* (Boston: Beacon, 1992).

15. Jonathan Dollimore, *Sexual Dissidence* (Oxford: Clarendon, 1991), chs 1, 21. See Eve Kosofsky Sedgwick, 'Nationalisms and sexualities in the age of Wilde', in Parker *et al.*, eds, *Nationalisms and Sexualities*, pp. 242–3.

16. Kobena Mercer and Isaac Julien, 'Race, sexual politics and black masculinity', in Rowena Chapman and Jonathan Rutherford, eds, *Male Order* (London: Lawrence & Wishart, 1988), pp. 106–8.

17. John L. Peterson, 'Black men and their same-sex desires and behaviors', in Herdt, ed., *Gay Culture in America*, pp. 153–7.

18. Sunil Gupta, 'Black, *brown* and white', in Simon Shepherd and Mick Wallis, eds, *Coming On Strong* (London: Allen & Unwin, 1989), p. 176; Kath Weston, *Families We Choose* (New York: Columbia University Press, 1993), p. 134.

19. Gloria Wekker, 'Mati-ism and black lesbianism: two ideal typical expressions of female homosexuality in black communities of the

diaspora', in John P. DeCecco and John P. Elia, eds, *If You Seduce a Straight Person, Can You Make Them Gay?* (New York: Harrington Park, 1993), p. 152. On dialogue, see Mercer and Julien, 'Race, sexual politics', pp. 100–3.

20. See, for instance, Andy Medhurst, 'That special thrill: *Brief Encounter*, homosexuality and authorship', *Screen*, 32 (Summer 1991), 197–208.

21. Antonio Gramsci, *Selections from the Prison Notebooks*, ed. and trans. Quintin Hoare and Geoffrey Nowell-Smith (London: Lawrence & Wishart, 1971), p. 324. See Michael Bronski, *Culture Clash* (Boston: South End Press, 1984), pp. 3–13.

22. Judith Butler, *Gender Trouble* (New York and London: Routledge, 1990), p. 142. See Fuss, *Essentially Speaking*, ch. 6; Celia Kitzinger, *The Social Construction of Lesbianism* (London: Sage, 1987).

23. See Jason Annetts and Bill Thompson, 'Dangerous activism?', in Plummer, ed., *Modern Homosexualities*.

24. See Watney, *Policing Desire*, p. 80.

25. Sedgwick, *Epistemology*, p. 85.

26. Herbert Blau, *The Eye of Prey* (Bloomington and Indianapolis: Indiana University Press, 1987), p. 130.

27. See Adrienne Rich, *Blood, Bread and Poetry* (New York: Norton, 1986), p. 200. See Dollimore, *Sexual Dissidence*, pp. 245–6; Fuss, *Essentially Speaking*, pp. 109–10; Alan Sinfield, *Literature, Politics and Culture* (Oxford: Blackwell and Berkeley: California University Press, 1989), pp. 121–2.

28. Stanley Cohen, *Folk Devils and Moral Panics* (St Albans: Paladin, 1973), pp. 10, 18. See Dollimore, *Sexual Dissidence*, chs 14, 16.

29. Dennis Altman, *Homosexual: Oppression and Liberation* (Sidney and London: Angus & Robertson, 1972), p. 219.

30. Hans Mayer, *Outsiders*, trans. Denis M. Sweet (Cambridge, MA: MIT Press, 1984), p. 18.

31. See Anna Marie Smith, 'Resisting the erasure of lesbian sexuality', in Plummer, ed., *Modern Homosexualities*; Cherry Smyth, *Lesbians Talk Queer Notions* (London: Scarlet Press, 1992), pp. 22–4, 26–7.

32. Allan Bérubé, foreword to Steven Zeeland, *Barrack Buddies and Soldier Lovers* (New York: Harrington Park, 1993), p. x.

33. David T. Evans, *Sexual Citizenship* (London: Routledge, 1993), pp. 50–4.

34. Smith, 'Resisting the erasure of lesbian sexuality', in Plummer, ed., *Modern Homosexualities*, p. 212.

35. Genevieve Lloyd, *The Man of Reason* (London: Methuen, 1984), p. 105.

36. Bartlett, *Who Was That Man?*, p. 219. See Murray Healy, 'Skinheads, masculinity and queer appropriation', unpublished MA dissertation (University of Sussex, 1993), pp. 26–31.

37. Murray, ' "Underdevelopment" ', in Plummer, *Modern Homosexualities*, p. 30.
38. Jeffrey Weeks, *Coming Out* (London: Quartet, 1977), pp. 63–4.
39. John Marshall, 'Pansies, perverts', in Kenneth Plummer, ed., *The Making of the Modern Homosexual* (London: Hutchinson, 1981), p. 154.
40. *Tom of Finland Retrospective* (Los Angeles: Tom of Finland Foundation, 1988), preface.
41. Evans, *Sexual Citizenship*, p. 101; see pp. 94–104.
42. Gregg Blachford, 'Male dominance and the gay world', in Plummer, ed., *Making*, p. 204; Jamie Gough, 'Theories of sexual identity and the masculinization of the gay man', in Shepherd and Wallis, eds, *Coming On Strong*, p. 121. See Martin P. Levine, 'The life and death of gay clones', in Herdt, ed., *Gay Culture in America*.
43. Gough, 'Theories of sexual identity', p. 121.
44. Sue-Ellen Case, 'Towards a butch–femme aesthetic', *Discourse*, 11 (1988–89), 55–73, pp. 65, 70. See Monique Wittig, *The Straight Mind* (Hemel Hempstead: Harvester Wheatsheaf, 1992); Elizabeth A. Meese, *(Sem)erotics* (New York University Press, 1993), pp. 72–8, 103–25.
45. Valentine Hooven III, introduction, *Tom of Finland* (Köln: Benedikt Taschen Verlag GmbH, 1992), p. 6. See David Island and Patrick Letellier, *Men Who Beat the Men Who Love Them* (New York: Harrington Park, 1991).
46. Dollimore, *Sexual Dissidence*, p. 325.
47. Finch, 'Sex and address', pp. 36–7.
48. Neil Bartlett, 'Visions of love', *Rouge*, 8 (Oct.–Dec. 1991), 20–2, p. 21.
49. Jean Genet, *The Thief's Journal*, trans. Bernard Frechtman (Harmondsworth: Penguin, 1967), p. 145; Michel Foucault, *History of Sexuality*, vol. 1, trans. Robert Hurley (New York: Vintage Books, 1978), p. 101; see pp. 16–17 above. Cf. Colin Spencer, *Which of Us Two?* (London: Viking, 1990), p. 85; Evans, *Sexual Citizenship*, p. 97.
50. Bronski, *Culture Clash*, p. 142.
51. Jack Babuscio, 'Camp and the gay sensibility', in Richard Dyer, ed., *Gays and Film* (London: British Film Institute, 1977), pp. 40, 55. See Medhurst, 'That special thrill'.
52. Derek Cohen and Richard Dyer, 'The politics of gay culture', in Gay Left Collective, eds, *Homosexuality: Power and Politics* (London: Allison & Busby, 1980), pp. 178–9.
53. Camille Paglia, 'Junk bonds and corporate raiders: academe in the hour of the wolf', *Arion*, 3rd series, 1 (1991), 139–212, p. 198.
54. Bronski, *Culture Clash*, pp. 12–13; Bartlett, *Who Was That Man?*, pp. 253–4. Cf. Larry Kramer, *The Normal Heart* (London: Methuen, 1987), pp. 76–7.

55. Quentin Crisp, *The Naked Civil Servant* (1968; New York: Plume, 1983), p. 54; Kevin Porter and Jeffrey Weeks, eds, *Between the Acts* (London: Routledge, 1991), p. 29.
56. Smyth, *Lesbians Talk*, p. 36, and pp. 36–46.
57. Esther Newton, *Mother Camp: Female Impersonators in America* (Englewood Cliffs, NJ: Prentice-Hall, 1972), p. 103.
58. Butler, *Gender Trouble*, p. 137. See also Leo Bersani, 'Is the rectum a grave?', *October*, **43** (1987), 197–222; Andrew Ross, *No Respect* (London: Routledge, 1989), pp. 145–65; Dollimore, *Sexual Dissidence*, ch. 20; Marjorie Garber, *Vested Interests* (London: Routledge, 1992).
59. Homi Bhabha, 'Of mimicry and men: the ambivalence of colonial discourse', in James Donald and Stuart Hall, eds, *Politics and Sociology* (Milton Keynes: Open University, 1986), pp. 199, 201.
60. Case, 'Towards a butch–femme aesthetic', p. 63; Andy Medhurst, 'Pitching camp', *City Limits*, 3–10 May 1990.
61. Newton, *Mother Camp*, p. 100; Carole-Anne Tyler, 'Boys will be girls: the politics of gay drag', in Fuss, ed., *Inside/Out* (New York: Routledge, 1991).
62. Jonathan Dollimore and Alan Sinfield, eds, *Political Shakespeare* (Manchester University Press, 1985), p. 13.
63. Kate Davy, 'Reading past the heterosexual imperative', *TDR: The Drama Review*, **33** (1989), 153–70, pp. 155–6. See Kate Davy, 'Constructing the spectator: reception, context and address in lesbian performance', *Performing Arts Journal*, **10**(2) (1986), 43–52; Case, 'Towards a butch–femme aesthetic'; Jill Dolan, 'Breaking the code: musings on lesbian sexuality and the performer', *Modern Drama*, **32** (1989), 146–58; Lynda Hart, 'Identity and seduction: lesbians in the mainstream', in Lynda Hart and Peggy Phelan, eds, *Acting Out* (Ann Arbor: Michigan University Press, 1993).
64. Altman, *Homosexual*, p. 127. See Blachford, 'Male dominance', p. 204; Evans, *Sexual Citizenship*, pp. 174–86.
65. Edmund White, *Jean Genet* (London: Chatto, 1993), p. 610.
66. Jean Genet, introduction to George Jackson, *Soledad Brother* (Harmondsworth: Penguin, 1971), pp. 22–3.
67. See Sedgwick, *Between Men*, p. 217.
68. Teresa de Lauretis, 'Sexual indifference and lesbian representation', *Theatre Journal*, **40** (1988), 155–77, p. 159. See Alan Sinfield, *Cultural Politics – Queer Reading* (Philadelphia: University of Pennsylvania Press and London: Routledge, 1994), ch. 4.
69. Smyth, *Lesbians Talk*, p. 20.
70. Evans, *Sexual Citizenship*, p. 54. See John D'Emilio, *Making Trouble* (New York: Routledge, 1992), pp. 7–13.
71. See Smith, 'Resisting the erasure' and Vicki Carter, 'Abseil makes the heart grow fonder: lesbian and gay campaigning tactics and Section 28', both in Plummer, ed., *Modern Homosexualities*.

72. Zeeland, *Barrack Buddies and Soldier Lovers*, pp. 79, 77, 252–3, and the foreword by Allan Bérubé, p. xi.
73. Brighton OurStory Project, *Daring Hearts* (Brighton: QueenSpark Books, 1992), p. 10. On attitudes to community, see Weston, *Families We Choose*, ch. 5.
74. De Lauretis, 'Sexual indifference and lesbian representation', p. 170.
75. So Evans, *Sexual Citizenship*, pp. 143–5; D'Emilio, *Making Trouble*, p. 12.

Index